THE OTHER GOVERNMENT

THE
OTHER
GOVERNMENT

Power
& the
Washington
Media

William L. Rivers

UNIVERSE BOOKS
New York

Published in the United States of America in 1982
by Universe Books
381 Park Avenue South, New York, N.Y. 10016

82 83 84 85 86/10 9 8 7 6 5 4 3 2 1

Printed in the United States of America

Library of Congress Cataloging in Publication Data

Rivers, William L.
   The other government.

   Includes index.
   1. Government and the press—United States.
2. United States—Politics and government—1945—
I. Title.
PN4738.R53   071'.53   81-40694
ISBN 0-87663-365-3   AACR2

Contents

Acknowledgments

*T*his book is the product of four years of work. It began with my first trade book in 1965, *The Opinionmakers,* and my second trade book in 1970, *The Adversaries: Politics and the Press.* Then, as the news media were becoming a more vital force each year, I decided, in 1977, to write a book about the growing power of the Washington correspondents.

Let me thank especially Rusty Todd, who is now the city editor of a daily newspaper, the *Columbia Missourian.* Because he is an excellent researcher and writer—one who is an observer with a careful eye for what he sees—he interviewed several Washington correspondents and reported perceptively about their work. I know that when he publishes his book about the various public relations people in Washington, D.C., it will be thoroughly researched and well written.

James Arntz and Jeffrey Perl, who are also excellent editors and writers, have guided me during the last stages of writing this book. From time to time they steered me back on course—until I thought they should be co-authors. I also thank Deborah Styles, an editor who put the last touches on the manuscript so expertly that I bow in deference.

Leonard Sellers deserves gratitude for his excellent writing on the many varieties of investigations, some of them diabolical, undertaken by correspondents. I am also grateful to Ronald Shafer of the *Wall Street Journal,* who wrote a fascinating article about the way television makes a story out of elections, and to Philip Hilts's assessment of Walter Cronkite, in the *Washington Post*'s magazine.

Let me also thank the Markle Foundation for awarding me a small grant to do some of the research for the book.

Instead of listing all those who helped me, let me refer you to the pages of this book, where I mention everyone who guided me through the many labyrinths of Washington, D.C.

William L. Rivers

1

Why the Press Is the Other Government

The Press has become the greatest power within Western
countries, more powerful than the legislature, the executive,
and the judiciary. One would then like to ask: By what law has
it been elected and to whom is it responsible?

—Aleksandr Solzhenitsyn

*T*he capital city of the United States of America, like the federal
government it houses, was constructed according to plan. The
original city, most of which still stands, is the physical equivalent of
Jefferson's Declaration of Independence, of Madison's Constitution,
and, in general, of the whole assortment of utopian notions that Carl
Becker has called "the heavenly city of the 18th-century philoso-
phers." As London's Crystal Palace symbolized, for all the world,
the progressivism, utilitarianism, and scientism of the 19th century,
so the Washington of L'Enfant, at least in certain kinds of weather,
is an artwork of the Enlightenment—a perfect emblem of the 18th
century's spacious, optimistic, slightly naive view of man.

As with any good work of art, every feature of official Washington
has a meaning. The various presidential monuments, the Supreme
Court building, and the Capitol itself reflect, massively, the founding
fathers' dream of resurrecting the Roman Republic (there even are
fasci beside the speaker's platform in the House of Representatives).
A tall, cigar-store Indian perched atop the Capitol's great dome can
render the general effect, for the finicky observer, less classical than
kitschy. But this touch of the frontier serves to remind us that

7

Washington was designed to be the set piece of a continental empire.

By contrast, the executive mansion, at 1600 Pennsylvania Avenue, is a structure so austere and virginal that posterity has named it, simply, the White House. Beside the White House, and housing its senior functionaries, is the EOB, the old Executive Office Building—a Victorian ostentation of *nouveau riche* power in which Walt Disney might have felt more at home than Queen Victoria.

Official Washington is majestic and orderly, erratic and tasteless. Its architecture represents the impossible simplicity and systematic character of the U.S. Constitution. It also reflects the labyrinthine complications and overelaboration that were the inevitable products of the Industrial Revolution, of Manifest Destiny, of one civil and two world wars, of bread-and-circus electioneering—the inevitable products, in other words, of two centuries of human foible.

But there is another side to Washington—another government. In a high-rise building on Pennsylvania Avenue, near the old Executive Office Building, is a floor of small offices whose windows overlook governmental Washington—the White House, the Capitol, the great monuments and museums along the mall, and the gargoyled mug of the old EOB.

"Here. Look. This is the best view of Washington," says Mel Elfin, capital bureau chief of *Newsweek* magazine. If you can appreciate the incongruous, Elfin is doubly right. These windowed cubicles of one significant organ of that Other Government reflect not only a different organization from that of official Washington, but also a distinct view of man.

Just outside Elfin's office window is a little balcony with a few chairs and a low-slung rail to keep one (barely) from becoming hamburger on the pavement below. The balcony is covered with screaming green Astroturf, which provides a startling emphasis in the foreground to the classical travertine and brownstone edifices beyond. Some old potted petunias and a couple of tomato plants struggle to cope with what appears to be constant neglect.

Somehow, the bedraggled pots fit the scene. Everywhere in the *Newsweek* offices are similar images of an eccentricity that is born of hard-nosed realism. Everywhere, there is also awesome disorder; for although the *Newsweek* offices are fairly plush by press standards, this week they are being renovated—new carpets, some rearranged partitions, and the addition of a kitchen and conference room.

Also being renovated is the National Press Building, some three blocks from the old EOB and *Newsweek* offices, and fourteen blocks from the Capitol. Since 1908, this venerable structure has been the focal point for most Washington news operations. It was definitely showing its age. Its brickwork was crumbling, its hallways were yellowed and dingy. In the ornately plastered lobby, elevators chugged up and down like old mules about to give up the ghost, while reporters and editors muttered disagreeably about how long it took them to get up to their offices.

The National Press Building was in an advanced state of decay. It is certain that the Washington press headquarters is getting a face lift. The Other Government—the Washington news corps—has come to consciousness of its power and is gradually moving into larger, more official, less eccentric structures.

Richard Rovere once suggested that our attitudes toward national politics—and, indeed, our national politics—might have been profoundly different if the founding fathers, instead of creating the nation's capital on the mud flats of the Potomac, had set it down in the center of 18th-century Manhattan. Our federal politicians and public servants would not now be jousting in the limiting and incestuous environment of a municipality given over entirely to government. With the national government as but one sector of a complex city, federal officials could not have avoided rubbing elbows and shaking hands with the nation's literati and its social critics. The condition that resulted might have rendered American politics less peripheral and vague in the national literature, and American social criticism less divorced from the political realities.

Rovere made this point most authoritatively. In order to write about national affairs for *The New Yorker*, Rovere himself commuted to Washington from his work in New York City. He often lamented that "very few reflective, literary intelligences deal with public affairs in this country," and he attributed this problem to the singularity of concerns and the cultural remoteness of Washington, D.C. For political man, no city is more exciting, more electric, than Washington. But for those with other or broader passions, no city is so stultifying. Among the intellectual and creative elite who have been honored in Washington, few have been willing to linger longer than it took them to finish their dinners at the White House.

The result of Washington's cultural estrangement from the nation has been the elevation of Washington's journalists to a kind of academy of national sages and prognosticators. In most other world capitals—which, usually, are also highly cosmopolitan cities—the journalist must vie with the novelist, with the playwright, with the artist, and with the critic in reporting, in analyzing, and in interpreting national public affairs. In Washington, news correspondents win by default. As a result, they have acquired the authority and sometimes even the power of a shadow government.

The Washington press corps has certainly acquired the trappings of power. Privileged as no other citizens are, the correspondents are listed in the *Congressional Directory;* they receive advance copies of governmental speeches and announcements; they are frequently shown documents forbidden even to high officials; and they meet and work in special quarters set aside for them in all major government buildings, including the White House. Fantastic quantities of government time and money are devoted to their needs, their desires, and their whims. Some White House correspondents talk with the president more often than his own party leaders in the House and in the Senate, and there are correspondents who see more of the congressional leaders than do most other congressmen.

No wonder, then, that Washington correspondents feel what one presidential assistant has termed "an acute sense of involvement in the churning process that is government in America." A close view of this involvement so impressed Patrick O'Donovan, a former Washington correspondent for the London *Observer,* that he said, "The American press fulfills almost a constitutional function."

Indeed, in Washington today, correspondents who report for the news media possess a power beyond even their own dreams and fears. They are only beginning to become aware that their work now shapes and colors the beliefs of nearly everyone, not only in the United States but throughout most of the world.

For the American public, full acceptance of the media's new authority and responsibility came at the end of the Watergate crisis, when the president of the United States posed his word against that of the press and lost. But Watergate was less coup d'état than it was climax. It was the end of a long evolution that was first observed by a newsman nearly fifty years ago, during the trial of the Lindbergh baby's kidnapper and killer. At that time, Walter Lippmann commented that in our democracy "there are two processes of justice, the one official, the other popular. They are carried on side by side, the one in the courts of law, the other in the press, over the radio, on the screen, at public meetings."

Lippmann's observation remains true today, yet those who would end this discussion on the question of the court verdict versus the popular verdict are missing a much greater issue. For the basic question is not just whether we have two parallel systems of justice in this country, but whether we have two governments. Do we have a second, adversarial government that acts as a check on the first and controls public access to it? Indeed we do—and this Other Government is made up primarily of the more than two thousand news correspondents stationed in Washington.

In our daily lives, we trace a path from home to work and back. Without the news media, we would know almost nothing beyond our own sphere of activity. The public's knowledge of national government depends not on direct experience and observation, but on the news media; and it is the media that set the agenda for public discussion and decision.

To a large degree, the employees of the government—including the president himself—must also depend on the reports of the news media for information about some of their most important concerns. In government, as elsewhere, each worker is circumscribed, and his sphere is small. A congressional assistant may spend much or all of one day absorbing details about the religious leaders of Iran and learning much more than is published or broadcast about the imminence of all-out war in the Middle East. But he hasn't the time to inform all of his colleagues about his new knowledge, and he is likely to know less about House debate that day than any tired tourist from North Carolina who wandered into the public gallery to give his feet a rest. Both the tired tourist and the congressional assistant must depend on the newspapers to find out what happened that day in the Senate.

In an article for a journal of political science, former Senator H. Alexander Smith of New Jersey made it clear that members of Congress are not Olympians who learn what they know in closed-door hearings and secret communiqués. They, too, must depend on the media. Senator Smith listed thirteen different sources of information for congressmen; but the news media, he wrote, "are basic and form the general groundwork upon which the congressman builds his knowledge of current events. The other sources . . . are all supplements to these media."

Even presidents, with their vast and powerful apparatus of information, often end up relying as much on the press as on their own informational systems. John Kennedy admitted that he acquired new information from *The New York Times* about his own secret sponsorship of the Bay of Pigs invasion. Eleven days before the invasion that the CIA had been shepherding so carefully, the editors of the *Times* informed Kennedy that their correspondent, Tad Szulc, had discovered the secret and that a detailed news report was imminent. Kennedy persuaded the publisher to postpone publication until after the landing in Cuba. But, during the discussions with the *Times* editors, the president picked up new information about the mounting of the invasion.

Afterward, in regret at the fiasco, Kennedy said to Turner Catledge, the executive editor of the *Times,* "If you had printed more about the operation, you would have saved us from a colossal mistake." Again, a year later, Kennedy told the publisher of the *Times,* "I wish you had run everything on Cuba. . . . I am just sorry you didn't tell it at the time." The president thus recognized the power and value of the news media: Reporting the coming invasion would undoubtedly have resulted in its being vetoed.

Even the strongest and most capable president requires such reporting; for he is *always* insulated from the realities of his administration by the fears and ambitions of his subordinates. He cannot possibly sort and absorb all of the vital information that is produced by governmental agencies and activities. Many believe that the fall of Richard Nixon was foreordained by his hatred of and isolation from the media.

The influence of the Washington press corps is also recognized in the third branch of the federal government. Justice Potter Stewart said in 1975, with something like wonder: "Only in the two short years that culminated last summer in the resignation of the president did we fully realize the enormous power that an investigative and adversary press can exert."

The courts have long been suspicious of that power, and over the years, they have waged a largely silent battle with trial reporters over the reporters' access to and publication of courtroom proceedings. Moving ponderously, the courts have attempted to close off much of the access of the news media. Moving quickly and sometimes deviously, the media have anticipated and occasionally forestalled these efforts, very often using one courtroom and one judge against another.

The Other Government wins some, loses some. During the fifty years since Walter Lippmann's observation about public and private trials, legal maneuvers between the federal government and its courts and the national news media have resembled a very intricate and symmetrical minuet. The courts move to gag orders and to secret trials. The media, stalemated, take the issues to higher courts and begin to employ attorneys as reporters.

But the dance does not always include willing partners, and the Other Government is usually less effective than official Washington at some of the more subtle steps. Often the official government will make the news media an unwitting participant in the never-ceasing warfare among its various branches and agencies.

Twenty years ago, a young reporter was writing an article about the powerful Brooklyn congressman, John J. Rooney, who headed the House of Representatives subcommittee that controlled the State Department budget. Every year, Congressman Rooney savaged the State Department budget request by speaking against "booze money for those striped-pants cookie-pushers." He alarmed the young reporter by exclaiming angrily, "I want to keep an open mind and be fair, but if you people in the press keep harping on it, I'm afraid you'll make me whack the budget too much."

The reporter then interviewed the assistant secretary of state, who had the task of arguing in Congress for whatever budget the department thought reasonable. The reporter asked him how badly Rooney's attacks crippled the budget request. "Why, not at all," the assistant secretary answered. In fact, he explained, Congressman Rooney was "the best friend the Department of State had." By berating Old Foggy Bottom on the floor of the House, even as he was pushing a generous budget, Rooney persuaded the representatives who abhorred striped pants that he had the State Department's number. Rooney's strong words were a facade that enabled the congressman to sneak more money into the budget than Congress would otherwise have granted.

That sounded to the reporter like double-talk, but no matter how many people the reporter interviewed, they were almost evenly split on the question. In the end, the reporter decided that Congressman Rooney was not a friend of the State Department; that he was, in fact, an irresponsible budget slasher. But even as the reporter was typing his article, he worried: It *could be* that Rooney is a clever ally of the State Department. Any Washington reporter can be convinced at times that Machiavelli is alive and advising congressmen.

A few months later, in 1961, the same young reporter was feeling the impact of the new Kennedy administration. Like other Washington correspondents, he was invited for the first time in history to share with a president both the crushing responsibility and the glittering aura of the greatest center of leadership in the Western world. Before 1961, the White House had been a closed preserve. Information was channeled through the president's press secretary, and some news correspondents never so much as met the White House advisers and chief assistants. A reporter who had arranged an interview with an Eisenhower assistant without going through Jim Hagerty, the president's press secretary, was so elated that he telephoned his editor in New York to say, "I broke around behind Hagerty!" The important news was not the substance of the interview but the fact that he got one.

When Kennedy took over, correspondents wandered through the White House offices in such numbers that they created a traffic problem. President Kennedy was his own most effective promoter. He practiced personal salesmanship with the élan of one accustomed to establishing the rules of the game. Kennedy made such a fetish of giving exclusive interviews that his press secretary, Pierre Salinger, once observed that he had to go to the Oval Office to find the White House correspondents.

The heady effect of this unaccustomed presidential attention is demonstrated by the behavior of our young reporter on the morning he received a call from the White House that the president wanted to talk to him. It was a snowy, miserable day. With a studied show of nonchalance, the reporter announced his coup to his colleagues, drew on his topcoat and one of his galoshes, and clumped out the door toward the elevator, leaving the other galosh on his desk.

I was the reporter who wrote the article about Congressman Rooney and who interviewed President Kennedy. I was then working for the now-defunct magazine *The Reporter*. Although I quit being a Washington correspondent near the end of 1961, I remained fascinated by the profession and by the sharpening power struggle between the Washington press corps and the federal government. Through secrecy, through the courts, through its press representatives, the government has awesome control over the public image of itself. Only the news media can exert an effective counterbalancing influence on the public's perception of government. Surely, if the government closes off freedom of access in any area, a balanced picture of government will give way to government propaganda.

Yet, there is another side to this issue. In 1978, philosopher-novelist Aleksandr Solzhenitsyn—an outsider, a Russian—observed, with considerable disapproval, that "The press has become the greatest power within Western countries, more powerful than the legislature, the executive, and the judiciary." How could he believe that? What of the effective machinations of a shrewd congressman or of a suspicious judge? What of the overwhelming power of an attractive and canny president? What of the sheer size of the federal bureaucracy and its countless daily actions and decisions, which can vitally affect the course of society? Is it possible, despite the odds, that Solzhenitsyn is on to something?

We must remind ourselves periodically that the American republic's founders granted to the press, alone among private business institutions, the task of protecting the U.S. Constitution. Contemporary Washington correspondents are well aware of this responsibility and are proud of their independence from the official government and from the biases of their editors and publishers and station owners back home.

This independence marks the sharpest difference between Washington correspondents and their local brethren and between the Washington press corps today and that of previous generations. In 1936, Leo Rosten made this statement to a group of newspaper correspondents and asked whether it was true in their experience: "My orders are to be objective, but I *know* how my paper wants stories played." Slightly more than 60% of the correspondents replied yes, indicating that they felt at least subtle pressure from their editors and publishers. In 1960, the mark came down dramatically; only 9.5% replied yes to the same question.

That difference is so dramatic that one may think that there was a misunderstanding or a mistake. Another statement, which also tested freedom from home-office pressure, drew a similar response, however. Rosten asked the correspondents in 1936 whether this could be said of their work: "In my experience I've had stories played down, cut, or killed for 'policy' reasons." Slightly more than 55% of the correspondents answered yes. In 1960, only 7.3% affirmed the same statement. During the twenty years since 1960, that downward trend has continued.

Yet, as my own experiences with President Kennedy and Congressman Rooney indicate, the independence of the contemporary Washington correspondents may be something of a mirage. In any event, what truly counts is not so much the independence of the reporters as their service of the public interest. How well do the news media serve our interests? How much do they show us of official Washington?

Learning about the national government from the news media is like watching a tightly directed play. The director features the president at some length, the leading congressmen as secondary players, and the cabinet and justices of the Supreme Court as cameos and walk-ons. There are seldom any other entries in the dramatis personae, although there are *three million* employees of the national government. Any effort to move beyond the stage to see the undirected reality is useless. We must understand this: that the *image* of government appears to us primarily through the news media, and that the *reality* of government is often quite different from that reported by the two thousand news correspondents who help to create that image.

The public and the government are awash in a torrent of media reports. Yet, inquiring into how the news media actually serve the public yields a different perspective. Radio and television are mainly useful in signaling news events, providing the immediate—and sketchy—reports that announce happenings. More and more, we depend on television, despite the fact that our understanding is distorted by the brevity of the news reports. Broadcast journalists skim the top of the news, working with headlines, leads, and the bulletins that alert the public. Only occasionally does a documentary flesh out the news. Av Westin, a news executive of the American Broadcasting Company, has said: "I think television news is an illustrated service that can function best when it is regarded as an important yet fast adjunct to the newspapers. I know what we have to leave out; and if people do not read newspapers, news magazines, and books, they are desperately misinformed."

Newspapers cannot compete with radio and television for rapid transmission, and they cannot compete with television for the sheer impact of seeing and hearing news in the making. But a newspaper is available at any time, and it can provide a vast range of information on many subjects. The importance of the newspaper has been described best by a man who was interviewed during a newspaper strike: "I don't have the details now; I just have the result. It's almost like reading the headlines of the newspaper without following up the story. I miss the detail and the explanation of events leading up to the news."

Most magazines can treat their subjects in greater depth than newspapers, but they generally cannot cover as many *different* subjects. Even the news magazines, which attempt to cover a wide range of subjects in some depth, do not publish as much information in their weekly issues as can be found in a single issue of a large daily newspaper. Like people who write books, those who write for magazines can seek out the unreported, flesh out the information that has been presented only in silhouette in broadcasts and newspapers, and report matters that the faster media have missed in the rush to meet deadlines.

It would seem that such a division of labor would help us to learn about *everything* that goes on in the government: radio and television rapidly reporting the action; newspapers putting most of the stories into context; and the magazine writers and book authors reporting the major stories more fully, and with more grace and flavor. But this range of public affairs reports, however carefully some may be fashioned, often seems the reflection of a faulty mirror. The mirror is first held this way, then that way, but how narrowly it is focused! The presidency, the congressional leaders, the State Department, and the Department of Defense are in view. Only occasionally is mention made of such bureaus as the Departments of Energy, of Transportation, of Agriculture, or of such agencies as the Federal Communications Commission, the Food and Drug Administration, the Interstate Commerce Commission, and the many other agencies that figure so importantly in our everyday lives. Only a few such agencies ever make it to the front page, to the television screen, to the radio interview.

Protesting the narrow focus of the Washington press corps, Derick Daniels, former executive editor of one of the Knight-Ridder newspapers, argued that journalists must recognize the reader's needs and desires:

> Yes, yes, we understand that the poor slob in the kitchen is interested in the price of soap when she *ought* to be interested in Congress. But I mean recognizing squarely, as a matter of intellectual honesty, that the kitchen is really, *in fact,* just as important. . . . the amount of knowledge and information collected, and the studies available through the U.S. govern-

ment, are nearly limitless. A single document—the yearbook of
the Department of Agriculture—contains more useful information in its pages than most newspapers report in a year.

The media are thus confronted with a dilemma. It is impossible for
any news organization, no matter how large, to cover fully the entire
federal government every day. And even if it were possible, no one
would want to sift through such reports. So the real question is not
whether the media are at fault for not covering the entire government all the time, or for printing only a small portion of what is
knowable about the government. The more appropriate questions
are: How good is the judgment of the Washington press corps as to
what parts of the government to watch and which of its actions to
record or to investigate? And how good is the judgment of the
Washington news bureaus and their outlets in deciding what
information to print and to broadcast every day?

These are two important questions—as important as any questions
we can ask about our official government in Washington; for, in a
sense, the two governments—the official government and the
national news media—increasingly form part of a single, symbiotic
unit. The major difference between the real government and the
media government begins with the conscious and deliberate action
by most officials to insert the image they desire into the media
process. The government nearly always attempts to create an image
of itself. Whether this will be successful depends on the reporter. In
some cases, the image of the officials vies with the reporter's own
concept of those officials. In other cases, the images are a match.

Ben Bagdikian, one of the most powerful media critics in the
United States, commented on the interrelationships between government image-making and press image-making when he made a
study of newspaper columnists. He talked to many federal assistant
secretaries for public affairs about how they briefed their bosses and
how they preferred to break government news. Bagdikian found that
the secretaries were heavily influenced by what they saw in the news
media, that they accepted this as what the media would respond to,
and that, as a result, they fashioned their output to serve what they
perceived to be the media interest. Thus, the work of the Washington columnists, Bagdikian speculated, "includes guessing what the
government is doing." This produces a double-mirror effect, in
which each side responds to what the other is doing, while at the
same time adjusting itself to the other side's anticipated needs.

Thinking about the mirrors of politics, John Kenneth Galbraith commented wryly: "Nearly all of our political comment originates in Washington. Washington politicians, after talking things over with each other, relay misinformation to Washington journalists who, after further intramural discussion, print it where it is thoughtfully read by the same politicians. It is the only completely successful closed system for the recycling of garbage that has yet been devised."

Viewed in the rawness of this circus of political reporting, government news seems very complicated—and dangerous. It is true that since the Vietnam War and the Watergate crisis, Washington correspondents are much more suspicious of the announcements of government officials. More and more correspondents every year are asking sharp questions of officials.

The questions are important because there have been times in the past fifteen years when *no one* in the official government knew what was true. Phil Goulding, assistant secretary of defense for public affairs in the second Nixon administration, once said: "In our office, the secretary's office, or the White House, we never knew how much we did not know." Again, in reference to the Nixon years and the Watergate scandal, Senator Charles Mathias has said: "The more a president sits surrounded by his own views and those of his personal advisers, the more he lives in a house of mirrors in which all the views and ideas tend to reflect and reinforce his own."

When it became evident in 1973 that Nixon had been living in a world of mirrors—that he saw only the image that he had manipulated—Dr. Edward Teller, who had developed the hydrogen bomb in strict secrecy twenty years earlier, wrote ruefully, "Secrecy, once accepted, becomes an addiction." He might also have noted that secrecy, once the routine practice and defense of the official government, had, by 1973, finally given way to the angry probings of the Other Government.

By the time the Watergate case had brought an end to the presidency of Richard Nixon, the Other Government was firmly in control. Contemplating the Washington cityscapes from the barely contained chaos of the *Newsweek* offices, one wonders if this is what the founding fathers had in mind.

2

The White House

A typical day for a White House correspondent begins at about 9:30 A.M. when news reporters are allowed to enter the White House grounds. They always enter through the southwest gate or the northwest gate, each of which is about one hundred yards from the press room. No one is permitted to enter the grounds without approved press credentials, and the correspondents must show their identification upon entering the grounds, no matter how familiar they are to the guards.

The press facilities are located in the west wing of the White House, adjacent to the offices of the president's press secretary. The press room is something of a cross between a television studio and the living room of a ranch-style house. The south wall and the north wall of the main room are appointed with leather couches and scarred wooden chairs. At one end are a little stage and a podium. At the other end of the room is a more elaborate stage ajumble with television lights and wires. Klieg lights hang from the ceiling.

To the right of the press room a doorway leads to a warren of small offices that house the secretaries, receptionists, and staff assistants for the press secretary and his deputies. Beyond this initial complex is a set of larger offices, each with its own secretary, that belong to the two deputy White House press secretaries and several chief assistants. Finally, beyond this area is the inner sanctum, the office of the press secretary.

As might be expected, the press secretary's office is the largest and lushest. It is also the farthest from the press room. Adjacent to the press secretary's offices, a wide corridor leads to the executive offices of the president's advisers and, at the southeast corner of the west wing, to the Oval Office itself.

To the left side of the press room, a doorway opens onto a couple of dozen tiny cubicles and studios occupied primarily by the correspondents for the nation's major newspapers, the two predominant wire services, and the television and radio networks. The basement floor just below is subdivided into even smaller spaces for the major radio news services, the lesser wire services, the government news agencies (Voice of America and the International Communication Agency), and some of the American and foreign newspapers that cover the White House less regularly. The walls of both the basement and the first-floor press rooms are lined with telephones for the correspondents, mainly foreign, who rate their own cubicles. A row of telephones in the basement, for example, is referred to as the "Avenue of the Rising Sun," because the phones "belong" to Japanese reporters.

White House cameramen spend most of their day waiting, either in their cubicles or in the press lounge. The press lounge, adjoining the first-floor press room, contains candy and soft-drink machines, a coffee maker, three teletype machines, a television set, and a large table at which a group of television technicians while away much of the day playing cards or watching soap operas. Each of the press rooms features three star-shaped lights that are used to inform the correspondents of the status of the news day. When one light is on, correspondents know that there is a possibility of news coming from the president or from the press secretary's office. Two lights mean a lid has been put on the dissemination of any news for a specified time, usually the lunch hour. Putting on the lid means there will be no news releases or announcements from the president or from the press office. The White House, for news purposes, has been shut down. Three blinking lights mean the lid has been put on for the day. On a normal day, the press office is shut down at about 6 P.M.

Thus, a typical day for White House correspondents consists of watching for the blinking lights and, in the meantime, making the most of a number of press handouts, the most important being the president's daily itinerary or a statement of opinion not significant enough for an in-person appearance. The highlight of the day is almost always the press briefing, which is usually made by the press secretary himself at 11 A.M. or at noon.

Not a very glamorous schedule for the most glamorous of

journalistic beats! Nonetheless, White House correspondent is the most prized of news positions. Despite the dullness of the daily routine, the White House always promises the possibility of generating more important national and international news than any other place on earth.

When the delegates to the Constitutional Convention straggled into Philadelphia in May of 1787, they agreed that drafting a new form of government, or shoring up the old one, would be an impossible task if their speeches were published piecemeal and debated on every village square. They took a pledge of secrecy. Thus, the president of the convention, George Washington, was stern in his admonishment of a delegate who had carelessly mislaid his copy of the day's proposals: "Gentlemen, I am sorry to find that some one member of this body has been so neglectful of the secrets of the convention as to drop in the state house a copy of their proceedings, which by accident was picked up and delivered to me this morning. I must entreat gentlemen to be more careful, lest our transactions get into the News Papers and disturb the public response by premature speculations."

By contrast, James Madison, the draftsman of the Constitution, held a less paternalistic view of the press (and of the governed): "Knowledge will forever govern ignorance. And a people who mean to be their own governors must arm themselves with the power knowledge gives. A popular government without popular information, or the means of acquiring it, is but a prologue to a farce, or a tragedy, or perhaps both."

Thomas Jefferson, the author of the Bill of Rights, valued public information about the federal structure itself: "The basis of the government being the opinion of the people, the very first object should be to keep that right: and were it left to me to decide whether we should have a government without newspapers or newspapers without a government, I should not hesitate a moment to prefer the latter."

Thus, the founders expressed the viewpoints that have defined White House-media relations throughout our history: In theory, all American presidents have wanted a free and independent press as a check on government; in practice, they have wanted no such thing.

Presidential control of information reached its zenith in 1829, during President Andrew Jackson's first administration. Jackson, who subscribed to twenty newspapers and dictated to almost as many, led "King Mob" to the capital and elevated journalism to a visible force in government. In the judgment of historian James Schouler, "Jackson was the first president who ruled the country by means of the newspaper press." The status of American journalism at that time was described by William Cullen Bryant: "Contempt is too harsh a word for it, perhaps, but it is far below respect."

President Jackson surrounded himself with newspapermen, among them Amos Kendall, an able Kentucky editor who became the leader of the president's "kitchen cabinet." A congressman later said of him, "He was the president's thinking machine, his writing machine, aye, and his lying machine." Another newspaperman, Duff Green, had proved his friendship for Jackson during the presidential campaign by fabricating a story that President and Mrs. John Quincy Adams had had premarital relations. Jackson asked Green to "remove to Washington and become the organ of the party."

The end of the era of presidential government and of presidential control of the press came soon after the Jackson presidency. Jackson's successors—Van Buren, Harrison, Tyler, Polk, Taylor, Fillmore, Pierce, and Buchanan—were seldom able to manage either the press or Congress. Powerful dailies had grown up in many cities, and their editors were sending probing reporters to Washington. By 1841, James Gordon Bennett, publisher of the *New York Herald,* was spending $200 a week to maintain a small corps of capital correspondents who were abler than the entire staff of any newspaper published in Washington. Bennett himself, who had earlier been a Washington correspondent, conducted the first presidential interview, a conversation with Martin Van Buren. As the dyspeptic commander of the powerful *Herald,* he was not a man a president could ignore.

With the newly independent and often irresponsible urban press of that era, it was almost impossible for any national political leader to promote a clear national image and policy.

Two events of 1860 marked the formal funeral of the party press. First, the Government Printing Office was established, all but destroying the printing-contract patronage that had fed so many Washington newspapers; and, second, President-elect Abraham Lincoln arrived in the capital. Lincoln apparently listened civilly to a number of Washington editors who tried to persuade him that their papers should be his official journal. Then he rejected all offers. He realized that the Washington papers were impotent and that tying his administration to one newspaper would restrict his dealings with others. Lincoln's decision was altogether characteristic of a shrewd new approach to the press and to the shaping of public opinion.

Primarily because President Lincoln had no party organ, historical writings tend to picture Lincoln at bay, with the press bent on bringing him down. It is, in fact, easy enough to find slashingly negative comments on his greatest speeches in the partisan journals of the time:

> *New York Express:* The president holds out, except in words, mere words, very, very little of the olive branch.
> *Richmond Enquirer:* . . . couched in the cool, unimpassioned, deliberate language of the fanatic.
> *Trenton American:* It is very evident . . . that he feels all the perplexity of his position and his incompetence to shape his own course.
> *Hartford Times:* This wretchedly botched and unstatesmanlike paper . . .

But it is also easy to find examples of high editorial praise for the same addresses:

> *Philadelphia American:* Its language is so direct, its tone so patriotic, its honesty so unmistakable, that all will feel the earnestness of its author and the significance of his words.
> *Buffalo Republic:* . . . certainly one of the most important addresses ever issued from Washington.
> *New York News:* . . . an able and statesmanlike document.
> *Washington Star:* . . . a state paper of great force and reasoning.
> *New York Courier & Enquirer:* The address is a noble one.

The truth is that in a time of strength and savagery for American newspapers—and a time of unavoidable and deep controversy for the American people—Lincoln came off quite well in the press, and largely because of his own insight. He knew the extent of the political power that resided in the great editors of the mid-19th century, and he pointed out: "In this and like communities, public sentiment is everything. With public sentiment, nothing can fail; without it, nothing can succeed. Consequently, he who moulds public sentiment goes deeper than he who enacts statutes or pronounces decisions."

None of this should suggest that Lincoln made the basic mistake of surrendering to the powerful editors. He granted many of their requests and demands; but just when it appeared that he had capitulated, he would refuse a favor and ignore their editorials. Few editors realized how subtly Lincoln used them and how well he understood the process of shaping public opinion through the press. The celebrated Emancipation Proclamation, for example, was as much a publicity weapon as it was a declaration of the national conscience, a fact that is emphasized by Lincoln's own account of issuing it two months *after* it had been drafted: "Things had gone from bad to worse, until I felt that we had reached the end of our rope on the plan of operations we had been pursuing; that we had about played our last card, and must change our tactics, or lose the game. I now determined upon the adoption of the emancipation policy." Thus, Lincoln acted like a shrewd publicist for his administration's policies.

None of the 19th-century presidents after Lincoln could match his subtle command of the press. Indeed, in the entire period from Lincoln's death to the beginning of the 20th century, there were so many discrete centers of press power throughout the United States that no public official could hope to master national public opinion for long. The nation was led, in the loosest sense of the term, by a coalition consisting of venal congressmen, of the new elite of wealthy industrialists and financiers, and of the princely overlords of the urban newspapers.

The press was still atomized, with many clusters of power scattered across the nation, when the era of Theodore Roosevelt began. As Colonel Roosevelt, commanding the horseless "Rough Riders" in their dash up San Juan Hill, he had demonstrated how a leader with a flair for drama could rivet public opinion through the press and overshadow the dull realities of a comic-opera absurdity like the Spanish-American War. (Years later, Roosevelt himself commented, "It wasn't much of a war, but it was the best war we had.") As the two-term governor of New York, Roosevelt had quickly learned to promote his many social causes through twice-a-day meetings with the small corps of Albany correspondents. When President William McKinley was assassinated in 1901—"Roosevelt luck," one of his despairing detractors called it—and TR became president, he was well prepared as a shaper of public opinion to reinstitute the authority of the presidency.

The new president fixed shrewdly on two important facts regarding the American press. First, the great press associations, which served many papers of varying political persuasions, had been forced during the latter part of the 19th century to develop more objective reporting so that any paper could safely use any story. Except for the remaining yellow journals, the giant dailies that used dispatches from their own reporters in Washington had also been shamed into reporting most political news impartially. The partisan publishers now relied largely on acid editorial columns to promote their opinions. This situation was ideal for the theatrical Roosevelt, who knew quite well that a strong president could promote an indelible image through the news, regardless of what editorials might say about him.

Second, the Age of the Reporter had been ushered in by romantic figures like Richard Harding Davis, Lincoln Steffens, Jacob Riis, and other "muckrakers"—a term Roosevelt himself had coined—with the result that some of the power that had resided in the thundering editors and publishers back home was now passing to the correspondents on the scene. The political reporters of TR's day were much more independently powerful than the newspaper reporters of 19th-century Washington.

So Theodore Roosevelt set about managing the news more adroitly than any president before him. The thrust of his method was both to court correspondents and to command them. Early in his term, for example, he noticed a small group of reporters standing outside the gates of the White House, interviewing departing visitors. He promptly ordered an anteroom in the White House set aside for them, and this became the White House press room. He developed an informal and effective press conference by regularly calling in the three Washington correspondents whose reports were most widely circulated: David Barry of the *New York Sun*'s Laffan Agency, Charles Boynton of the Associated Press, and Ed Keen of the Scripps-McRae Press Association (now United Press International). Everything the president said to these reporters was off the record, which allowed him a maximum range of comment and no responsibility for anything they used. (The day Keen joined the group, Roosevelt loosed an especially virulent view of his own party's old guard, then made the system clear to the newcomer: "If you even hint where you got it, I'll say you are a damned liar.")

Roosevelt's press relations were a fascinating mixture of apparent impulsiveness and tight control. He was, one correspondent wrote, "the master press agent of all time." He sometimes gave reporters the run of the White House, and he often overwhelmed them with news. When Lincoln Steffens had completed his exposés of corruption in municipal and state governments and turned to Washington, he was given open access to the executive offices and saw Roosevelt daily at the barber's hour. "I always came into the room," Steffens wrote, "primed with a question that I fired quick; and he went off." But one thoughtful correspondent, Charles Willis Thompson of *The New York Times,* also noted: "He was never interviewed, in any proper sense. He gave out many statements, some of them in the form of interviews, and sometimes, too, he was actually interviewed; but in such cases he always dictated the form the interview should take . . . he never said one word more than he had decided to say. Impulsive? The thousand reporters who have tried to catch Roosevelt off guard and make him say something he did not expect to say will laugh."

Guiding the correspondents whenever he could, Roosevelt often suggested news items and sometimes wrote them personally. Once, during a Senate fight over a railroad bill, a Standard Oil attorney telegraphed several senators to pressure them into voting Standard's way. Senator Stephen Elkins of West Virginia showed his wire to the president. TR not only gave the story to the press, but, according to David Barry, "wrote the preliminary item that was sent to the afternoon papers."

Roosevelt was generally understanding when a correspondent disagreed on political matters, but any reporter who abused a privilege was assigned to the Ananias Club. Oscar King Davis, who headed *The New York Times* Bureau in Washington during TR's presidency, recalled: "When he gave his confidence to a correspondent, he gave it completely, and trusted to the correspondent's judgment and sense of propriety as to the use that was made of it. Mr. Roosevelt trusted a confidant until something happened to make him think his confidence had been misplaced. Then he ceased entirely to give his confidence to the man who had not respected it. It was all or nothing with him."

In that heady time of growing strength for the Washington press corps, probably no other president could have used the news and the newsmen as adroitly as did TR. Dynamic, eruptive, vigorous of physique and intellect—he never seemed to tire physically or mentally—Roosevelt invested every issue with an enthusiasm for American life and democracy that made the opposition seem subversive. He was already famous too, as a forceful writer whose mark on the literature of public affairs might have lingered even if he had never become president. The correspondents, whose respect for any colorfully articulate politician is almost automatic, were naturally lured by a man whose sense of visual language led him to speak of "trust-busters" and "malefactors of great wealth," to announce intention to run with "My hat is in the ring," and to define his foreign policy as "Speak softly and carry a big stick."

It is clear that Roosevelt won the correspondents' support for his policies not only because of his own magnetism but also because of his respect for the power of journalism and his admiration for those who used it well. Most presidents have paid lip service to the press, but TR's sincerity was obvious. He castigated some newspapers and magazines for "mendacity, slander, sensationalism, inanity, vapid triviality"—which made the more genuine his tribute: "In our country I am inclined to think that almost, if not quite, the most important profession is that of newspaperman." This conviction helped make Theodore Roosevelt the first president since Lincoln, and the last for another quarter of a century, to manage the Washington press corps astutely.

With hindsight to make one aware of the later, dire repercussions of the League of Nations issue, one is inclined—perhaps rightly so—to condemn the correspondents for their sabotage of President Woodrow Wilson. But David Lawrence, Wilson's best friend and most devoted admirer in the press corps, suggested later that much of the fault for the continually bad relations between Wilson and the press was the president's. The bad feelings between the press and the president "constituted a series of misunderstandings and unfortunate clashes," Lawrence wrote. "The growing tendency in recent years in America to anticipate the news and to discuss future events or the processes by which conclusions were reached was deeply resented by Mr. Wilson. His theory was that nothing is news until it was completed."

Having discovered the full thrust of their power during the declining years of Wilson's presidency, the correspondents employed this power openly in revealing the ripe scandals of the Harding administration. The era was epitomized by the brilliant and erratic Paul Y. Anderson's chronicle of White House corruption, which won the Pulitzer Prize. First, Anderson's reports in the *St. Louis Post-Dispatch* pushed the Senate into a full-dress investigation of Teapot Dome. Then, during the hearings, he and other correspondents supplied many of the searching questions that were used by Senators Thomas J. Walsh and Burton K. Wheeler to cut through the evasions in the testimony of administrative officials. Through the press, Warren Harding's name became almost synonymous with presidential ineptitude and dishonesty.

This was surprising in a way; for Harding, an Ohio newspaper publisher and United States senator, liked being around reporters and was protected better by the press during his early days in the White House than any other president. He began well by restoring the press conference, and if he was a bit pompous in answering questions during the formal conference, he won the correspondents with warmth and friendly manner after hours. He was an attractive man—"No one ever looked more presidential," one reporter wrote—and one who privately confessed his limitations. He told correspondents that he knew he could not be the greatest president, but he wanted to be the best loved.

Unfortunately, Harding sometimes did not know what he was talking about. He had been in office only a short time when he was asked during a press conference whether the Four-Power Pacific Pact—drawn up during the Washington Conference for the Limitation of Armaments—involved the protection of the Japanese islands. The president said that it did not. Actually, it did, and Harding's answer raced around the world, creating an international sensation. Secretary of State Charles Evans Hughes, his chin whiskers bristling, rushed to the White House to get an official correction. Then he prevailed on Harding to agree that only written questions, submitted well in advance of press conferences, would be answered. It was a crushing backdown for a president who was warmest and most expansive in talking to fellow newspapermen.

The administration of Calvin Coolidge was a frustrating time for the Washington press corps. It is doubtful whether Coolidge, the inert beneficiary of national prosperity, could have been affected by anything. He presided over a time of repose, napping often and boasting of sleeping soundly for eleven hours every night. It was dismaying for reporters on the lookout for an angle. As Leo Rosten put it, "The most striking characteristic about the new president was his lack of a striking characteristic."

Although the president was a little man—it is almost unimaginable that Coolidge could have dealt with the tense and controversial times that faced his successor—it is also true that he calculated his actions. Much later, he revealed in his autobiography that a kind of philosophy dictated his tight-lipped image: "Everything that the president does potentially at least is of such great importance that he must be constantly on guard. . . . Not only in all his official actions, but in all his social intercourse, and even in his recreation and repose, he is constantly watched by a multitude of eyes to determine if there is anything unusual, extraordinary, or irregular, which can be set down in praise or blame."

Coolidge did little, and many members of the Washington press corps simply ignored him. Raymond "Pete" Brant of the *St. Louis Post-Dispatch* said that his group "never covered the White House in the 'Twenties. We covered the Senate. You wasted your time downtown." Those who were forced to cover presidential news used their imaginations to build the image of a president of silent strength. Henry Suydam, who was then a correspondent for the *Brooklyn Eagle,* recalled that President Coolidge would observe laconically, " 'I'm not in favor of this legislation.' The next morning Washington dispatches began as follows: 'President Coolidge, in a fighting mood, today served notice on Congress that he intended to combat, with all the resources at his command, the pending bill.' " Thus did the correspondents divert themselves in the quiet days of the Coolidge era.

The press corps reawakened during the administration of Herbert Hoover and, for a time, mastered both the president and the Congress. It had been the custom in the Senate since the time of George Washington for reporters and spectators to leave the chamber during the votes on nominations submitted by the president. But Paul Mallon of the United Press and his assistant, Kenneth Crawford, decided to destroy the system. They began checking with friendly senators after the executive sessions and publishing the secret roll-call votes.

In 1929, President Hoover sent up to Capitol Hill a highly controversial nomination: Senator Irvine Lenroot of Wisconsin was nominated for a federal judgeship. The senatorial votes on Lenroot's nomination were certain to affect the election in a number of states in 1930; therefore, the Senate took extraordinary precautions to ensure secrecy. But Mallon made his usual rounds after the vote and published the complete senatorial box score. It showed that several senators had been talking one way in public and voting quite another way behind closed doors. Mallon was subpoenaed and questioned sharply by a Senate committee, but he would not reveal the sources of his information. The Senate gave up then, virtually abolishing executive sessions. The Senate has gone into executive session fewer than a dozen times in the five decades since.

Hoover entered the White House on a wave of respect and liking, and then promptly changed all that. Instead of continuing his impartial news policies, he began to play a few favorites among the correspondents so blatantly—Mark Sullivan was a particular pet—that they became known as "trained seals." To combat such favoritism, a few of the correspondents silently declared war on the president.

Through much of his presidency, Hoover's relations with the men who covered his actions were strained and humorless. The president invited publishers to the White House to complain about their Washington men and caused several correspondents to be transferred or fired. When leaks from his disenchanted subordinates reached print, Hoover announced that "only such news as is given out through the stated channels of the executive offices should be printed by the newspapers of the country." This was actually an effort to cut down on the leaks, but the clear implication was that the chief executive was seeking to rule the press as well as his administration.

Finally, unable to exert any control, Hoover began to lie. He required that press-conference questions be submitted twenty-four hours in advance. Then, when he bypassed the pointed questions and was asked about them, he would say that they had not been received. During the London Naval Conference, the president stated that the United States was holding up the building of three cruisers. Harold Brayman of the *New York Post* and Phelps Adams of the *New York Sun* did a minimum of investigative work and proved that construction on the cruisers was continuing.

When the financial panic mushroomed after the Great Crash of 1929, Charles Michelson, a former *New York World* correspondent who had become publicity director of the Democratic National Committee, fired broadside after broadside at the hapless Hoover. Considering the president's ragged relations with the men who wrote about him day by day, it is not at all surprising that, having the option of using Michelson's charges or ignoring them, the reporters played them up. The consequence was that in Hoover's abortive reelection campaign of 1932, crowds booed him, men ran into the streets to thumb their noses at him, and the most widely reported remark ran, "If you put a rose in Hoover's hand, it would wilt." The president became morose. Driving to the Capitol with his successor, Franklin Roosevelt, on inauguration day, he said nothing.

Like his cousin Theodore, Franklin Roosevelt both courted and commanded the news correspondents. It was sometimes a testy relationship; but, all in all, Roosevelt was a firm friend of the Washington press corps, winning scores of reporters for his policies and programs and employing this loyalty to his great advantage. Far too much has been made of the influence FDR exerted among the American populace through his few "fireside chats." Too little attention has been given to the fact that this president held 998 press conferences and that, from the very beginning, he was over-poweringly effective at press-conference management.

The initial press conference with President Roosevelt, on his fourth day in office, proved that he intended the conferences to be an instrument of presidential statecraft. His opening remarks began:

> I am told that what I am about to do will become impossible, but I am going to try it. We are not going to have any more written questions; and, of course, while I cannot answer seventy-five or a hundred questions simply because I haven't got the time, I see no reason why I should not talk to you ladies and gentlemen off the record in just the way that I have been doing in Albany and in the way I used to do in the Navy Department down here. . . . There will be a great many questions, of course, that I won't answer . . . because they are "if" ques-tions—and I never answer them. . . .
>
> And the others, of course, are the questions which for various reasons I do not want to discuss, or I am not ready to discuss, or I do not know anything about. There will be a great many questions you will ask that I do not know enough about to answer.
>
> Then, in regard to news announcements, Steve [Press Secre-tary Steven Early] and I thought it would be best that straight news for use from this office should always be without direct quotation. In other words, I do not want to be directly quoted unless direct quotations are given out by Steve in writing. That makes that perfectly clear.
>
> Then there are two other matters we will talk about: The first is "background information," which means material which can

be used by all of you on your own authority and responsibility, not to be attributed to the White House, because I do not want to have to revive the Ananias Club.

Then the second thing is off-the-record information, which means, of course, confidential information which is given only to those who attend the conference.

The remarkable contrast with the moody, monosyllabic answers of a Hoover press conference thrilled the correspondents. They gave Roosevelt the first standing ovation any president had ever received from the White House press corps. The reporters did not seem to realize that for all of Roosevelt's informality and apparent accessibility to the press, he was also laying down the rules for his mastery of news dissemination.

President Roosevelt was so thoroughly professional in his approach to news that Arthur Krock, then Washington bureau chief of *The New York Times,* declared: "He could qualify as the chief of a great copy desk." The president was, in fact, more sophisticated about news reporting than many in the White House corps. Responding to a question about reorganizing the National Recovery Act, FDR admonished the reporter: "Now you are getting too definite. I don't know. That is the trouble: You haven't got a spot-news story. You have an interpretive long-range story." That kind of reporting was so new that some of the correspondents simply shrugged in bewilderment.

When Harry Truman succeeded to the presidency, he moved the press conference setting from the Oval Office, where Roosevelt had held forth, to the Indian Treaty Room in the old State Department building. The difference was stark. Instead of chatting informally while sitting at his desk, as Roosevelt had, Truman looked down on the correspondents from a podium. And his relations with the press were always, if not hostile, at least clearly adversarial. The result of Truman's meeting with the Washington press corps was some of the testiest press-conference prose in American history.

REPORTER: Could you tell us anything about your conference with the secretary of state and the secretary of the treasury?
TRUMAN: No, it's none of your business.
REPORTER: Would that mean, sir, that you would shake up the individual civilian and service heads of the Navy Department, if this fight continues?

TRUMAN: Not necessarily. I think it will work itself out. Just wait a little.
REPORTER: I'll bet you two to one.
TRUMAN: I'll take you on that. I'll take you on that.

Truman won over fewer reporters—many fewer—than Roosevelt; but even those who considered him inadequate, or who had felt the cutting edge of his tongue, were reluctant to fault his behavior toward the press. Truman was reserved and feisty, but he was also fair—and he was unintimidated by the media's insatiable demand for information and its propensity for criticism and negative news reporting. Instead of trying to clamp the lid on executive branch activities, Truman shrewdly increased the number of federal press agents from 270 under Roosevelt to 3,632 employees working under the "information" and "editorial" classifications, or with titles like "deputy assistant secretary for public affairs," "administrative assistant," "executive assistant to the assistant secretary." The talk in the National Press Club was approving when, a decade after Truman's retirement, a poll of leading American historians named him a "near great" president, well ahead of Eisenhower and just behind Washington, Lincoln, Franklin Roosevelt, and a handful of other great leaders.

How astute public relations can overwhelm the Washington press corps is best revealed by the Eisenhower presidency. When the Eisenhower administration took over in 1953, most of Truman's publicists were locked into place under Civil Service. Not trusting them with the Republican merchandising, Eisenhower's lieutenants added their own men. Thus, during Eisenhower's first four years, executive information personnel nearly doubled: In 1957, the Civil Service Commission was listing 6,878 "information and editorial employees." The increase continued during the second term; and Christian Herter, who had been aghast at the size of the Truman administration's propaganda machine, eventually became Eisenhower's secretary of state and presided unprotestingly over one of its largest units.

James Reston made the mission of this publicity complex clear in a speech before the national conference of the Public Relations Society of America: "PR people are not doing their jobs in terms of serving the public but for the men who appoint them." Government public relations specialists, Reston charged, "have become personal press agents for their employers."

Eisenhower's men went to unprecedented lengths to protect him and to divert and to mislead reporters. It is no accident that the phrase "news management" was coined during the Eisenhower era. Much more than euphemistic "management" was involved, of course. Joseph and Stewart Alsop, who were then writing a newspaper column together, described the "insidiously indirect censorship" of the Eisenhower administration.

> A reporter obtains and publishes nationally significant information about, say, the grave lag of the American air program behind the Soviet air program. He has seen no secret papers. He has written nothing which was not already fully known to Soviet intelligence. He has merely posed a major public issue, with a vital bearing on the nation's future.
>
> Nowadays, however, even the most trivial information has been classified by someone or other, in some dim Pentagon corner or other. Furthermore, the reporter has given no pleasure whatever in high quarters, by posing this major issue which the leaders of the administration have been hoping to keep under the rug. So a "security investigation" is ordered.
>
> The fact that a reporter is the subject of one of these investigations does not mean for one moment that he has broken the law. Even less does it mean that there is the slightest danger of prosecution. . . . The security investigation, in truth, is nothing but a kind of indirect reprisal against the reporter who shows inconvenient curiosity about facts of national interest.
>
> The reprisal takes three forms. First, while the investigation goes on the reporter must assume that his telephones are tapped and that listening devices may be planted in his house and office. . . .
>
> Second, the reporter's official acquaintances and friends are subject to the most shameless harassment. It does not matter whether there is a tittle of evidence that they are the source of the reporter's information. It does not even matter if it is well known that they have never discussed the subject in question with the offending reporter. The real object is not to locate the reporter's source, but simply to strike at the reporter through the men he knows in government.
>
> Then third and finally, the word is passed in government that the offending reporter lies under the grave displeasure of the powers that be; and that it is therefore a risky thing to see him. Thus the attempt is made to prevent the reporter from doing his job as a reporter thereafter.

The charges of "news management" that were born during the Eisenhower presidency became more intense during the Kennedy administration. But there was a stark difference that blunted any media displeasure with Kennedy. That difference could be foreseen during the 1960 campaign, especially as retold in Theodore White's *The Making of the President, 1960.* White reported that the three Democratic party press assistants were also solicitous with the press, that they gave off a sense of joy when they greeted a correspondent joining or rejoining the circuit, as if they had waited for him, and had for him alone, a little nugget of color or some anecdote that his particular magazine or newspaper would especially want.

White's report reveals the little touches that endeared the Democratic candidate to the correspondents:

> Kennedy would, even in the course of the campaign, read the press dispatches, and if he particularly liked a passage, would tell the reporter or columnist that he had—and then quote from its phrases. . . . He would ask the advice of newspapermen—which, though he rarely followed it, flattered them nonetheless. Most of all he was available for quick exchanges of conversation—whether getting on his plane, or in his plane, or by the side of the road where he would stop to drink a Coca-Cola and then chat with the correspondents who clustered around. When presented, say, with a box of apples, he might fling one of them in an underarm pitch to a correspondent, to test whether the man was on his toes. He would borrow combs and pencils from the press—or accept chocolate bars (early in the primary campaigns) when his meal schedule also went awry.

Typical of the chumminess and interdependence of the Kennedy-media relationship was an incident during the 1960 campaign for the presidency. In the course of a flight, Kennedy dropped down beside White, pulled out the draft of a campaign pamphlet and said: "Read this. Isn't it lousy?" White agreed that it was. Kennedy then said, "Fix it up for me, will you, Teddy?" White rewrote it. Kennedy read it, then edited White's writing. "You write soft copy, Teddy," Kennedy explained. "This has to be harder." Kennedy treated White as though they were partners.

This partnership with the press flourished during the brief Kennedy presidency. Unlike Hoover, who grew aloof from his journalist friends after entering the White House, Kennedy drew even closer to the newsmen. Only two presidents had ever granted private, on-the-record interviews to correspondents: Franklin Roosevelt had given Arthur Krock of *The New York Times* a single exclusive interview, and Harry Truman had granted Krock a single session. In both cases, other news correspondents had brewed such a violent storm that neither Roosevelt nor Truman had ever tried it again. Nor had President Eisenhower.

When Kennedy came to the White House, he was warned by the old-time Washington hands of the importance of impartial and *distant* relations with individual journalists. He was also warned by many correspondents themselves about the venom of *other* correspondents. He nodded shrewdly, and then, the very day after the inaugural ball, showed up at the home of columnist Joseph Alsop. A few days later, the president drove to the home of Walter Lippmann, then went to dinner at the home of Rowland Evans, Jr. When President Kennedy took a weekend holiday in Hyannisport, he invited columnist Charles Bartlett, an old family friend.

All of this made it quite clear that presidential relations with the press had changed dramatically. President Kennedy was amazingly accessible, not only to his liberal friends in the press but also to conservatives, such as columnist George Sokolsky, who eventually became a warm supporter of the Kennedy administration. Kennedy drove to the homes of Washington reporters for parties and meals; he was interviewed and photographed endlessly; he brought television crews into the White House for a network special featuring Jackie and her new furniture; he established, for the first time since Andrew Jackson, an open White House. Never before had the press been granted so close a view of a president at work.

Correspondents attended the White House press conferences by the hundreds, and it is noteworthy that *they* were filmed while the president answered their questions. John Kennedy won them over with flattery, attention, and an appealing, empathetic, intimate style. An example:

> Q: Mr. President, have you given any thought to some of the proposals advanced from time to time for improving the presidential press conference, such as having the conference devoted all to one subject or having written questions at a certain point?
>
> THE PRESIDENT: Well, I have heard of that, and I have seen criticism of the proposal. The difficulty is—as Mr. Frost said about not taking down a fence until you find out why it was put up—I think all the proposals made to improve it will not really improve it.

> I think we do have the problem of moving very quickly from subject to subject, and therefore I am sure many of you feel that we are not going into any depth. So I would try to recognize perhaps the correspondent on an issue two or three times in a row, and we could perhaps meet that problem. Otherwise, it seems to me it serves its purpose, which is to have the president in the bull's-eye, and I suppose that is in some ways revealing.

That was the Kennedy style—bright, astute, witty, and poised. But Kennedy could also be tough and demanding of his friends in the press corps. He once said to Benjamin Bradlee, then the bureau chief of *Newsweek:* "When I was elected, you all said that my old man would run the country in consultation with the pope. Now here's the only thing he's ever asked me to do for him [appoint an incompetent judge] and you guys piss all over me."

The most important thing about the Kennedy style, however, was the style of presidential power and news management perfected by JFK. While Kennedy kept the press enthralled with his apparent intimacy and openness, governmental secrecy rose to a dizzying height. Not until much later did the correspondents realize what had been going on behind their collective backs—not only in matters of state but also in Kennedy's personal affairs.

Lyndon Johnson as president was at least in part the victim of the successes of his predecessors in charming and bamboozling the press. Arthur Krock once observed that the only law requiring the president to hold press conferences is the political law of self-preservation. Nothing illustrates the point better—or makes it more obvious that presidents use the mass media for their own ends—than the stark difference between the press conferences of Kennedy and those of Johnson.

Johnson, whose widely known ego was not quite so inflated as to interfere with his political acumen, knew better than to match himself immediately against the memory of Kennedy's glittering performance. The kind of press conference Johnson preferred was apparent from the first. Two weeks after he became president, twenty-five of the regular White House correspondents went to the office of Press Secretary Pierre Salinger for what had been announced as a routine briefing. Suddenly, they found themselves ushered into the president's office. It was a highly informal conference. Navy mess attendants served coffee; the president sat in a cushioned rocking chair at the head of two semicircular couches; the correspondents sat on the couches, sipping coffee and asking occasional questions to further the rambling flow of Johnson's conversation.

Ten days later, Johnson held another surprise press conference that was almost as informal as the first. Then, during an extended work-vacation at the LBJ ranch in Texas, he held no fewer than four impromptu conferences, one of them beside a haystack, another at a party given by the correspondents. He became wildly experimental. There was a conference in the old White House theater; another in the spacious East Room; another on the south lawn. The conferences became mobile: seven laps around the White House grounds. They became expansive: the reporters' wives and children were invited. Finally, the Baltimore *Sun* asked somewhat plaintively, "Will the next press conference be tonight, tomorrow or next week? Will it be held on horseback? In the White House swimming pool? Will the public be invited and the press excluded?"

The great value for Mr. Johnson of his spur-of-the-moment press conferences was that he faced only the White House correspondents, avoiding questions from the specialists who covered the rest of Washington—specialists who did not have a vested interest in remaining on good terms with the president. Another was that the intimate atmosphere of small conferences discouraged embarrassing questions and allowed the president to control the content and the length of the meeting.

The importance of this latter factor became evident one Saturday two months after Johnson took office, when a rumor ran through the press corps that another impromptu presidential conference was likely. By 2:30 that afternoon, more than one hundred reporters were milling about. The president waited until 5:00 to call them in. He alluded to the fact that he had heard complaints about "quickie conferences" and invited questions with what sounded like a warning: "I never enjoy anything more than polite, courteous, fair, judicious reporters, and I think all of you qualify." Then, after responding to a tentative question, he swerved into the Bobby Baker case and explained that his own involvement was innocent. Before the correspondents could pin down his exact relationship with Baker's deals, the president turned and walked out. Not until his hundredth day in office did he schedule a traditional mass press conference, after which James Reston commented: "President Johnson achieved his major objective in his first live televised press conference. He survived."

Contrary to the deep belief of some Republicans, various correspondents had been pointing up Johnson's flaws from the beginning— his massive ego, his cornball sentiments, his occasional inclination to treat the truth casually. Few political reporters could be entirely drawn to a man who flew a personal flag and stamped his initials on everything he touched. Several pointed out the flapdoodle in Johnson's proposal that Washington build "a memorial to God." Some noted the paradox of his saving pennies on the White House electric bill and planning to spend thousands to equip a presidential television studio. A great many pointed to the falsity of Johnson's melodramatic announcement in 1964, not long before the election campaigns began, that a railroad strike had been averted. The president considered the settlement such a coup that he would not wait for television to come to him. He drove out to the CBS studio in Washington to go on the air as soon as possible. In concluding the announcement, he read a letter from Cathy May Baker of Park Forest, Illinois, who had appealed to the president to stop the strike so her grandmother could travel to Park Forest from Yonkers, New York, for Cathy's first communion. Johnson's whole-souled happiness that Cathy's grandmother would now be able to make the trip no doubt won him more than his share of the grandmother vote. The trouble was that the letter had been written two weeks earlier, and Cathy had experienced her first communion, with grandmother on hand, the Saturday before.

Johnson suffered the worst press relations of any president since Hoover. He was a devious, egomaniacal man who seemed determined to enhance his reputation as a mendacious, bullying operator. In dealing with the press, Johnson employed—and sometimes stooped to—every trick or gimmick that any president had ever tried. In the end, hardly a reporter in Washington believed much that Johnson said; and, eventually, correspondents stopped using euphemisms like "news management" and stated quite frankly that the president was lying. Toward the end of the Johnson presidency, a cynical joke made its way around the Washington press corps: "Do you know how to tell when Lyndon Johnson is not telling the truth? Well, when he goes like this—finger beside his nose—he's telling the truth. When he goes like this—pulling ear—he's telling the truth.

And when he goes like this—stroking chin—he's telling the truth. But when he starts moving his lips, he's *not* telling the truth."

David Broder of the *Washington Post* has written: "I do not believe that the press of this country ever made it clear to the readers and viewers what the essential issue was in the 'credibility gap' controversy. It was not that President Johnson tried to manage the news: all politicians and all presidents try to do that. It was that in a systematic way he attempted to close down the channels of information from his office and his administration, so that decisions could be made without public debate and controversy."

For the first time, the "press management" issue was utterly clear: No correspondent during the Johnson administration was fully free to report. The correspondents, again for the first time, broke through every Johnsonian obstacle to the free flow of information. President Johnson failed, and he determined not to run for office again. The ire and the opposition of the press were surely instrumental in his decision.

During the early months of the first Nixon administration, most of the news correspondents seemed too exhausted and dispirited from their jousts with Johnson to take on their old adversary Richard Nixon. Or perhaps they were simply holding back in the hope that Nixon might have experienced a sudden conversion along the road to the long-sought office of president. But whether the reporters were dispirited or merely self-restrained, it was clear that they would be viewing the new administration with a jaundiced eye. Witness this salute, of a sort, written to the new president by James Reston, in his *New York Times* column, just before Nixon's inauguration:

> Mr. Nixon has had more than the normal share of trouble with reporters, because, like Lyndon Johnson, he has never really understood the function of a free press or the meaning of the First Amendment.
> Ever since he came into national politics, he has seemed to think that a reporter should take down and transmit what he says, like a tape recorder or a Xerox machine. He has learned to live with interpretive journalism more comfortably in this campaign [1968] than he did in the campaign of 1960, but he still suffers from this old illusion that the press is a kind of inanimate transmission belt which should pass along anything he chooses to dump on it.

Before he became president, Nixon had been the focus of

controversy within the press for more than two decades. On one side were those elements, most of them editors and publishers, who had always promoted what must be termed a "sweetheart relationship" with the man and his supporters. On the other side were those elements, mostly reporters, who had been Nixon's adversaries from the days of his demagogic anticommunist campaigns for the Congress in the late 1940s and his involvement with the Alger Hiss hearings in the early 1950s.

The editors and publishers bestowed their most impressive valentine on Nixon by their reporting—or lack of reporting—of the "Nixon Fund," which was a vital issue in the presidential campaign of 1952. Nixon, who was then a senator and the Republic candidate for vice president, had been accepting thousands of dollars from wealthy Californians. Although Nixon claimed that the money was used to pay extraordinary expenses of his senatorial office, it was nonetheless obvious that the Californians making the payments had unusual leverage with a United States senator. The issue became so heated that Dwight Eisenhower, the Republican presidential candidate, considered naming another vice presidential candidate. Nixon saved himself only by going on national television with an emotional appeal ("the Checkers speech") that became the single most memorable event of the 1952 campaign.

Arthur Rowse, then a copy editor on the *Boston Traveler,* subsequently examined the reporting and display of news of the Nixon Fund in thirty-one U.S. dailies. The title of the book that grew out of his study—*Slanted News*—suggests the results. As Rowse points out, the Nixon Fund story was voted by Associated Press editors at the end of the year as one of the top-ten news stories of 1952; yet it received some very peculiar play from many proud papers of the day:

> Any review of the way thirteen evening papers displayed the Nixon story makes it clear that editors were in no hurry to get the news into the paper. They were even less enthusiastic about getting it onto the front page. Of the thirteen evening papers studied, only four put the story on the front page at the first opportunity on Thursday afternoon. . . . The four papers using the report on the front page included only one pro-Eisenhower paper, the *Chicago Daily News,* which spotted the newsworthiness of [Peter] Edson's column and played it up with a three-column headline on the first page. . . . Three other evening papers used the story the first day but buried it inside the

paper. . . . Five evening papers apparently did not use the Nixon story in their editions of record until the next day. . . . One paper, the *New York Journal American,* could not find room on the front page for the story until Sunday, the fourth day the news was available.

Of the eighteen morning papers studied—all pro-Eisenhower on their editorial pages—only eight allowed the Nixon affair on the front page of Friday editions of record. Of the remaining ten morning papers, seven used the story somewhere in their edition of record on Friday. But three omitted it entirely from the issues studied.

Newspapers that were "giving their readers the first glimpse of the story," Rowse points out, "should have included more than just three or four words to describe the cause for all the disturbance." But, Rowse adds, some readers undoubtedly "got such a one-sided picture from the first few stories that they might have wondered what all the defensive statements were about. Thus, the first headline to greet readers of the record edition of the *Chicago Herald American* was: NIXON DEFENDED BY EISENHOWER. The natural reaction of readers might be 'Why not?' as they passed on to another story."

Nixon's relationships with most of the reporters in Washington were quite different from his status with their publishers. Many reporters who had watched him during his successful anticommunist "smear" campaigns for the House and Senate were unable to forget his tactics and his opportunism. His performance as vice president did not reassure them, and there was a continual, tangible antagonism between Nixon and the media reporters throughout his two terms in office and during his unsuccessful campaigns for the presidency in 1960 and for the governorship of California in 1962.

As a much-scarred veteran of the frequent battles between contemporary politicos and the national press, President Nixon was wary and careful at the beginning not to adopt Johnson's ruinous press policies. It is nonetheless clear that he was on his own collison course with the media. This was in part because Nixon, who had attacked White House secrecy under Johnson, had promised regular meetings with reporters and had emphasized during his campaign that, "It's time we once again had an open administration—open to ideas from the people and open to communications with the people—an administration of open doors, open eyes and open minds." Yet Nixon managed to schedule only six press conferences during his first six months in office (less than half as many as his two immediate predecessors in similar periods). More than half of Nixon's cabinet members held even fewer conferences during this period, and Attorney General John Mitchell, who was to head the administration's much-heralded "law and order" campaign, did not meet with the press until 11 July 1969, nearly six months after he took office.

The lack of regular conferences was forgivable at that point—the media were agreed that the new Republican administration needed time to feel its way. But the press corps was becoming uneasy about an apparent effort by the White House staff to shield even routine activities from the oversight of the press. Despite Nixon's harping on the Johnson credibility gap during the presidential campaign, the Nixon administration showed few signs of having learned any lessons from Johnson's worst failing as president.

On 17 April 1969, Secretary of Defense Melvin Laird had told the American Society of Newspaper Editors: "I am fully aware of the special responsibility of those in this audience and others in the communication media to inform the people about what we in Defense are doing and call us to account when we make mistakes. . . . As long as I am secretary of defense, there will be full and free access to all information that can be made available without danger to the nation's security. There will be no coverup, no concealment, no distortion. We intend to put a lot of fill in the credibility gap."

But six days later, correspondent James McCartney revealed just how devoted to concealment both Laird's Pentagon and Nixon's White House had become: "Now, a full week after the EC-121 shooting [off the coast of North Korea], the Pentagon continues to refuse to furnish exact times for key incidents in the crisis, or to describe [the incidents] in detail. . . . Both White House and Pentagon officials have wrapped a mantle of secrecy around the time that Henry A. Kissinger, President Nixon's national security adviser, was notified of the incident at home."

By mid-August 1969, so much doubt had arisen among the news media that *Newsweek* published a long catalogue of cases proving that Nixon's "open administration" was "suffering from an advanced case of closed doors." There were signs, too, of a rebirth of the tough stance many reporters had adopted toward Nixon many years before. After watching the administration bow in quick succession to the American Medical Association, the American

Pharmaceutical Association, and the Automobile Manufacturers Association—actually reversing decisions already made—one journalist remarked that Nixon would be in trouble with working reporters for a reason that has always been at the root of his policies: "He worries too much about the problems of people who own yachts."

Then, in the first year of his second term, there was the scandal identified simply as Watergate. The Nixon scandal occurred exactly a century and a half-century after the other great White House scandals of American history, the Grant scandal of 1873 and the Harding scandal of 1923. But Watergate was quite different. Both of the earlier scandals were measured by the definition of politics in Ambrose Bierce's *The Devil's Dictionary:* "the conduct of public affairs for private advantage." The difference with Watergate was stated well by Senator Sam Ervin of North Carolina: "What they are seeking to steal was not the jewels, money, or other property of American citizens, but something much more valuable—their most precious heritage, the right to vote in a free election." Because of the tireless and courageous investigative reporting of Carl Bernstein and Robert Woodward of the *Washington Post,* the Washington press corps was responsible for the unprecedented resignation of a president in mid-term.

The Other Government had become firmly institutionalized in the mind of the public, and many members of the press now viewed themselves differently. Gerald Ford's press relations and the drastic change in the authority and in the demands of the post-Watergate Washington press corps can be defined by one incident: On the night of 23 January 1975, President Ford was asked by a reporter to comment on the belief that he was too dumb to be president. He answered that his school grades had been so good that he was in the upper third of the class. The next day, correspondents demanded that the White House produce Ford's transcripts.

Because the Johnson and the Nixon presidencies had been mightily attacked and finally brought down by the press, Jimmy Carter knew from the beginning that the news media had, in fact, assumed the mantle of the Other Government. He therefore began his campaign for the presidency by directing his aide, Hamilton Jordan, to prepare a long document that focused almost entirely on the Washington news correspondents. More important than political deals and guesswork, Jordan wrote, was a careful publicity campaign: "Stories in *The New York Times* and *Washington Post* do not just happen, but have to be carefully planned and planted." He added, "A disproportionate number of national political writers are Southerners by birth and harbor a strong, subconscious desire to see the South move beyond George Wallace and assert itself as a region and as a people in the political mainstream of this country." Carter decided to adopt Jordan's report as *the* campaign document. He also read such books as Timothy Crouse's *The Boys on the Bus,* a detailed analysis of campaign reporting in 1972.

Although Carter sometimes stumbled along the campaign trail, he put his reading to good use. That he could control neither the media nor himself became evident as his lead in the polls began to slip with the approach of the November 1976 election. But as a newcomer to national politics, an outsider and an unknown, he would never have won the Democratic nomination if he had not understood a great deal about how the media operate.

Carter promised an open administration in which the public again would participate in their own governance. Barry Jagoda, who became his special assistant when Carter was elected, reported that "President Carter asked us to open up the government through television." But Carter made one colossal mistake: He publicly set standards for himself that correspondents considered impossible for a politician, and particularly for a president. Carter promised the nation, on television, that he would never lie. Thus, even a hedge or a white lie delivered in good faith to protect the nation would be a black mark on Carter's credibility and character. The promise never to lie attracts skepticism; the press inevitably interpreted Carter's promise as a literal challenge to catch him in an untruth, rather than as a sincere effort to alter the pattern of White House-press relations during the previous twenty-five years.

The correspondents caught Carter in several minor instances—but especially when he supported Bert Lance, a longtime friend and a fellow Georgian, who was forced to resign as director of the Office of Management and Budget. In the late spring and summer of 1977, the news media, and eventually the Senate, had begun to unravel the shadowy personal finances and past business practices of Lance—practices that included long overdrafts by himself and members of his family, the use of the same collateral for two loans, the use of his bank's plane for personal and political trips, and many other actions that, at best, did not seem to recommend Lance's judgment or ethics. Serious charges, including suggestions of illegality, were given wide currency by the media.

The thrill of pursuit among the press was evident in the headlines and in television spots. The rather wild scandal reached crisis proportions if for no other reason than that it was being treated by the media as a crisis. Russell Baker of *The New York Times* observed: "The papers were covering it like a crisis, television was displaying it as a crisis, reliable sources were leaking at crisis rates, and normally sensible men were behaving with crisis foolishness."

When Carter came up for reelection in 1980, he faced the future with optimism, because his Republican opponent was a near-70-year-old, Ronald Reagan. After the single Carter-Reagan debate at the close of the 1980 presidential campaign, the *San Francisco Chronicle* (which, like most of the daily newspapers around the country, endorsed Ronald Reagan's candidacy) featured this front-page headline: CARTER WAS DOMINANT. The reporter for the *Chronicle,* Larry Liebert, began his analysis of the debate with these sentences: "President Carter clearly dominated last night's presidential debate, putting Ronald Reagan repeatedly on the defensive on questions of war and Reagan's conservatism. Although Reagan is always a top-flight performer in such encounters, he seemed slightly off his pace last night, most often battling on Carter's chosen turf." Only a few newspapers and reporters around the nation disagreed with this assessment of the debate.

A week later, Reagan astonished all of the pollsters and most of the voters by winning the election with a margin of 8 million votes. What happened? James David Barber, a highly respected political scientist, may have the answer: "I think the media in the United States are the new political parties. The old political parties are gone. What we now have are television and print. Jimmy Carter may have dominated the debate, but in four years of media performances as president, he was at best lackluster, and at worst dull, disconcerting, and even depressing."

Ronald Reagan, on the other hand, walked onto the public stage with the security of a man who had been striding the boards successfully for more than forty years. If his cue cards of statistics, one-liners, and gibes are dog-eared and often simplistic and irrelevant, his voice, his timing, and his style have been honed over the years into a forceful instrument. Regardless of what Reagan is saying, he projects an easy confidence and determination, and an appropriately modest certainty that he has a handle on the public good. That Ronald Reagan is a consummate public performer—and the first *professional* performer to attain the White House—is an unmistakable indication that the news media, and television in particular, have become the most powerful force in American politics.

Consider the halls of Congress, which are gradually being filled with astronauts, actors, preachers, and professional sportsmen— people who know how to use television. Consider the ever-increasing importance of television commercials in election campaigns. In early 1980, for example, during the Iowa primary campaign, President Carter telephoned each of the Democratic county chairmen in the state. According to one of the chairmen, the conversations went like this: "Actually, we didn't say much. The president said he'd like to have my support in the Democratic primary, but he didn't really go into any issues or campaigning. Mainly, he said he wanted me to watch the TV ad he had put out about the White House, and he said that would sort of say what was important about the election and what he has been doing." Senator Ted Kennedy took the same tack. In a speech in eastern Iowa a few days after Carter's phone calls, Kennedy began: "First of all, we want you to remember to tune in on our television program next Monday night at 6:30. That will tell you why it is that we're running for the presidential nomination, and what some of the important issues are."

If President Reagan really wants to understand his chief competitor, the Other Government, and to live in peace with this disparate but powerful institution, he should keep this datum in mind: Every president since John Kennedy has been assaulted, two of them mortally, by the news media. The correspondents decided that Kennedy was bright, strong, and a charming liar; that Johnson was overwhelming, effective, and a vulgar liar; that Nixon was manipulative, paranoid, and a congenital liar; that Ford was open, honest, but dumb; that Carter was private and honest, but also fuzzy and ineffective. These estimates have already passed into popular wisdom.

Reagan should also reread a letter written to him by Edmund G. (Pat) Brown, the man he defeated in the 1966 California gubernatorial campaign. This was among Pat's tips to the new governor: "As you may have noticed by now, the press fires the first real bullets at new governors. And the hardest lesson to learn is that it is futile to fire back. Never get into an argument with a newspaper unless you own it."

3

The Bureaucracy

*J*ust before the accession of Dwight Eisenhower, President Harry
Truman was relaxing with some of his cronies in the White House.
Truman said at one point: "When Ike gets in here, he'll say, 'Do
this. Do that.' And *nothing* will happen." No other president has
stated so succinctly the problematical powers of the bureaucracy,
and none has so clearly indicated why the story of government-press
relations encompasses much more than the relationship of presidents
and the correspondents.

When a new president attempts to get things done, he is suddenly
confronted with the vastness and complexity of the federal government. Colonel Robert Burke, the former director of information for
the enormous Department of Defense (it employs more than 2
million uniformed military, more than 1 million civilians), describes
the difficulties: "If the president asks, for example, that we land a
battalion in Guatemala tomorrow, we can't do it. First, where are
the weapons? Second, we have no air cover. Third, what are the
weather conditions? Fourth, we have to construct a supply line.
Finally, we must study how we are vulnerable to submarines.
There's always complaining, but the information is not fed up to the
president. Everything's blamed on the bureaucracy."

Colonel Burke is right to a degree, but the bureaucracy itself can
also block, distort, or simply lose information that should go to the
president. Even if the nearly 3 million employees perform flawlessly,
the information must make its way through 3,300 political appointees, nearly all of whom have ambitions intimately linked to the

successes or failures of their department heads, of the political party, or of the president himself. The problem is formidable.

When Richard Nixon was attempting to tame the bureaucracy in the course of his first term, he called for a "complete reform of the federal government, because the federal branch has become a hopeless confusion of form and function." He envisioned the creation of four super agencies closely supervised by the White House. But despite the fact that Nixon made the proposal in his State of the Union address in 1971, when he was at the peak of his power, the reforms were never seriously pursued. Foreseeing the ferocious battle he would have to wage with the federal unions, with the social welfare establishment, with the Congress, and with the small army of lobbyists that profit from an unwieldy government, Nixon gave up the fight before it had begun.

Ironically, even as Nixon was planning to reshape and to trim the government, his administration created more new executive branch agencies and units, fifty-three, than any other first-term administration in history. Then, in 1973, the first year of Nixon's second term, *another* twenty-three offices were created. Herbert Kaufman of the Brookings Institution noted (in his book *Are Government Organizations Immortal?*) that of the 175 federal agencies that existed in 1923, 148 of them were still functioning at that time—and 246 new agencies had been created.

To get a sense of what occurs in the federal bureaucracy—who leads it, how it operates, and who covers it—we can refer to the expert commentary of a former assistant to a member of the Federal Communications Commission:

> The bureaucracy plays a decisive and necessary role even in the formation of general policy. The real power centers in Washington are the so-called subgovernments that create policy and make key decisions for the large, regulated segments of our economy—communications, transport, agriculture, labor, and so on. Within these subgovernments, the president of the United States and the Congress, collectively at least, have remarkably little influence. The key power groups in the various subgovernments are usually three:
>
> * the regulated industry's lobbyists and the industry's trade press;
> * the relevant agency charged with regulating a particular aspect of the economy, such as agriculture or communications;

• the U.S. House and Senate subcommittee chairmen whose committees oversee the agency's regulatory work.

For practical purposes, virtually all relevant decisions and policies are determined within this governmental subgroup—generally without regard to what the president, the Congress, or even the courts or press have to say about the matter. If any two of these three power groups agree, then [a policy] is likely to be accomplished. If they don't agree, then there is likely to be a stalemate—even if the president, a majority in Congress, and the *Washington Post* are demanding that something be done. It won't be, unless two of the three power blocks in the subgovernment agree—and usually the two are the agency and the industry itself through its lobbyists and trade press.

Although this can be illustrated with examples from agriculture, labor, or transport regulation, the easiest to use for illustration is the communications regulatory game. The subgovernment's power groups are roughly as follows:

• the broadcasting industry's trade press, *Broadcasting* magazine, and the industry's trade association, the National Association of Broadcasters;
• the Chairman of the Federal Communications Commission and a half-dozen bureau chiefs in the FCC, such as the chief of the Broadcast Bureau, chief of the Common Carrier Bureau, chief of the Cable TV Bureau, the General Counsel, and so on; and
• the chairmen of the two relevant congressional subcommittees, the Senate Subcommittee on Communications and the House Communications Subcommittee.

In the first power block, *Broadcasting* magazine is an institution of enormous influence within these circles. It has more influence on the FCC's commissioners, bureau chiefs, and staff than *The New York Times* has on the presidency. Correspondingly, *The New York Times* has no influence on the decision makers in this subgovernment on communications matters.

There are many reasons for this, but basically, the *Times* does not cover communications issues with any sophistication, and it is not read by the decision makers to gain insight into what ought to be done. However, *Broadcasting* magazine is read precisely for these reasons. It covers communications issues exceedingly well in an exhaustive and balanced matter. Its vigorous editorial pages reflect the strong biases of the broadcasting industry itself. If those who want to have influence on a key communications policy issue—say, the future of cable television—the message must be in *Broadcasting* magazine; forget *The New York Times* or the *Washington Post*.

The second power group, the agency or bureaucracy itself, is usually run by a key commissioner or two or by a strong chairman in concert with the powerful agency bureau chiefs. Over the years, the bureau chiefs at the FCC have emerged with an enormous authority and power. These are the chief of the Broadcast Bureau, chief of the Common Carrier Bureau, chief of the Cable Bureau, and the general counsel. They are powerful primarily because they are long-standing civil servants. They have built up years of expertise and knowledge in difficult policy areas, such as domestic satellite transmission, telephone regulation, cable television, broadcast licensing, and programming problems. These chiefs are also powerful because the commissioners or chairmen of the agencies are usually so weak. The commissioners come to the agency, stay a short while, and leave. They don't stay there long enough to master even the basics of a complicated issue—say, a policy issue such as our domestic satellite policy ought to be. But the bureau chiefs have always been there—ten years, twenty years, thirty years. They grew up with the issue. They know more about the issue of deceptive children's advertising than any six FCC commissioners put together, and nothing will be done on the issue unless the bureau chiefs agree and help.

The third power group, the congressional subcommittees, exercise their power through legislative oversight hearings. They can often play a key role, especially when a sophisticated subcommittee chairman has been around awhile. Such a chairman and the bureau chiefs have been known to conspire on a particular issue to force the FCC chairman and the industry to do things that the chairman of the agency and the industry did not really want to do.

Most of this governmental activity is largely unnoticed by the big national metro newspapers—the *Washington Post* and *The New York Times*. Occasionally, the *Wall Street Journal* would develop a good policy issue story; but this is because the *Journal*'s audience is different from [that of] the *Post* and the *Times*. The *Journal* aims at the business class and its interest in economic decisions. The *Post* and the *Times* are still built primarily on a geographic interest—what could be called a superficial interest in the personalities of politics, rather than its economic substance.

Moreover, government doesn't often announce its most important happenings—they just happen in tiny little steps of the bureaucracy until they add up to something important without anyone really noticing until it is much later than anyone thinks. This has been happening in the U.S. Department of Agriculture for years in its grain inspection programs. The deterioration has been setting in for years—until we have a major world-wide grain scandal. The general press has not covered this sufficiently, but the agricultural trade press has.

This trade press coverage has put the heat on the department to the point where *something* had to be done, and as soon as Secretary Butz did *something* after years of scandal, *The New York Times* finally published an article or two and an editorial on that which had been vigorously covered and debated in the trade press for years.

Much of the problem is that the national news media never cover so much of what is *really* going on in the bowels of government where the decisions are made. For example, the big grain companies and a few key regulators in the U.S. Department of Agriculture are primarily those who decide if Russia is to get large shipments of corn next year. This is not a policy decision made by Congress or the White House or the State Department. The trouble with the national media is that the editors still think that Congress, collectively, and the White House and the State Department really do make these important decisions. Unfortunately, they don't.

Confronted by the explosion of new federal agencies and the intricacies of bureaucratic decision making, news correspondents are understandably reluctant to attempt to cover the day-to-day operation of the *whole* government. Moreover, regardless of the significance of bureaucratic activities, the press will rarely view these activities and their progenitors as newsworthy. Most correspondents depend heavily on bureaucrats for information, but they will seldom quote them. Checking one week's issues of the *Washington Post,* I found in all the many columns of government stories only one bureaucrat: Dr. David W. Gavior, the chief biostatistician at the National Center for Toxicological Research. Of the nearly one hundred government officials who were named in news stories, all except Dr. Gavior were members of Congress, Supreme Court justices, the president, or presidential political appointees.

Dr. Robert Kupperman, chief scientist of the U.S. Arms Control and Disarmament Agency, explains this situation:

One reason is the fact that well-known names are more newsworthy. The fact that Joe Blow was GS-15 in the government, unless he has gone out and embezzled 2 million bucks or more, is not very newsworthy. The second thing is that political-level people are very obsessed that the bureaucratic people are not out in front at all. The political-level people want to capture anything that is good. They are *all* news-hungry. These two main things combine to shove the bureaucrats deeper into the shadows. I mean, they do get quoted periodically, but it is normally more in the middle of an article, just a side reference.

Joe Jones, chief of Blankety-Blankety, answered something. That's it.

Kevin Flynn, who worked for the Interstate Commission on the Potomac River basin, points out another reason for the "silence" of the bureaucracy: "Almost every person working in the government has an inherent desire to protect himself—and this extends from the lowest levels right through to the top. It is no wonder that the bureaucracy is invisible."

When NBC devoted much of a three-hour program in 1976 to explaining the place of the United States in the world, it tried also to explain how the government makes foreign policy. The process was explained by Secretary of State Henry Kissinger, who said, "There's no great mystery how foreign policy is made. The final decision is, of course, made by the President. Before you reach a final decision, there are a series of committees which examine various options. Eventually, they lead to a meeting of the National Security Council." There he stopped, as though he had said everything in four sentences.

The correspondents who covered Henry Kissinger were granted so many backgrounders and interviews that they seemed to have broken through the foreign policy bureaucracy and were content. Most of them failed to understand the kind of bureaucracy at the State Department about which the German sociologist Max Weber warned long ago: "The insinct of the bureaucracy was to increase the superiority of the professionally informed by keeping their knowledge and intentions secret." The addiction to secrecy is pronounced in foreign affairs. Thorstein Veblen argued many years ago, "In proportion as the nation's statecraft is increasingly devoted to international intrigue, it will take on a more furtive character, and will conduct a large proportion of its ordinary work by night and cloud." Kissinger seemed to be candid—articulately explaining relationships, explaining possibilities, tracing out clear directions— and only very slowly did it become clear that although he almost never said, "I don't know," he seldom did know. The bureaucrats often *do* know.

A case in point is Thomas Williams, who served as director of the Technical Information Staff of the Office of Solid Waste in the Environmental Protection Agency from 1971 until 1977, when he became deputy director of EPA's Office of Public Affairs. Williams is a bureaucrat who manifests everything that is ideal in government—dedicated, articulate, hard working, a writer who can say precisely what he wants to say—yet he found himself and his office in serious trouble during the Nixon and Ford administrations. It is a remarkable story of what happens to a man who believes that the public must be told what is going on in government.

Williams began his environmental career with the federal government's air pollution program more than twenty years ago. He was director of the public information and education activities for the Department of Health, Education and Welfare's air pollution programs from 1958 until 1968. His many years in air pollution effort were saluted in the book *Vanishing Air:*

> The legislation enacted during these early years was at best only palliative; the problem was increasing steadily at an alarming rate. No one knew this better than Thomas Williams, the public information officer for air pollution activities at HEW. Williams realized that pollution was a threat to life and health but was also aware that most members of the public—difficult as this may be to comprehend today—did not know what air pollution was or what its dangers were. To be sure, many people had had some experience with what they called "smog," a contraction of the words smoke and fog. But there was no outpouring of concern. After all man had lived with smoke and fog for centuries. A massive program of public education was needed.
>
> To this end, Williams spearheaded a public information effort that did much to make Americans conscious of the dangers of air pollution. In the mid 1960s, stories began to appear in magazines and newspapers around the country. They drove several points home: (1) Air pollution is more complicated and dangerous than a simple combination of smoke and fog. (2) Air pollution is more than an inconvenience; it is a danger to human life and well-being. (3) Air pollution can and should be controlled.
>
> Very few people outside of professional pollution control circles know who Thomas Williams is, but they nevertheless owe him a debt of gratitude; much of their knowledge and concern about air pollution today is a direct result of his lonely campaign to drum up public support for stronger action.

Mainly as a result of Williams's successes under two Democratic administrations, he was almost immediately marked as a dangerous figure after Richard Nixon came into office in 1969. Williams, who was then director of the Office of Public Affairs of the Environmental Health Service, which contained all the environmental programs of HEW, continued to distribute information on air pollution as well as on many other environmental programs—information that was, of course, largely unpleasant and that inherently and inevitably revealed the need for governmental action. The new Nixon-appointed political hatchet-man, Deputy Under Secretary of Health, Education and Welfare Frederick Malek, tried to shunt Williams into a less public, make-work position in the department.

Malek's role is revealing. A self-made millionaire, he quickly became known as the chief political ramrod in HEW during the first Nixon administration. (He was then promoted to the infamous Committee to Re-Elect the President, and later to the number-two position in the White House Office of Management and Budget, which is always the cutting edge of the executive branch.) Within a few months of Nixon's inauguration, Malek had produced a 133-page primer entitled *Federal Political Personnel Manual,* which is also called the "Malek Manual." The manual was to serve as a guide for skirting civil service regulations and laws to make it easier to place politically motivated and malleable persons in key federal jobs. Williams was in a key job; he had to go.

Malek attempted to dismiss Williams grandly. He was "pleased" to be able to inform Williams that he would be promoted to the position of assistant director of Extra Departmental Relations. Williams resisted strongly. After an exchange of memoranda in which Williams documented the false and extralegal tactics Malek was employing* to politicize Williams's career position, Williams was granted a meeting with John Veneman, a Nixon appointee who was under secretary of HEW, and met with him in February 1970. The meeting was supposed to be private, but as Williams was entering the under secretary's office, Malek suddenly appeared and asked, "You won't mind if I meet with you, will you?" Williams agreed, remarking that his arguments would remain the same, whether Malek was present or not. The following is Williams's recollection of the proceedings:

> I told Mr. Veneman as I had told Mr. Malek before, that from the very beginning, I had been worried about the nature of

---

*These memoranda were published in their entirety in the *Final Report on Violations and Abuses of Merit Principles in Federal Employment* of the Committee on Post Office and Civil Service, U.S. House of Representatives, December 30, 1976.

the unstated accusation against me, that I had suspected very early that I had been, as I put it, "fingered" by a young fanatical partisan, who in my opinion, could not be trusted to know enough to determine which persons should or should not occupy which positions in the Department. I explained that since the time I had first met with Mr. Malek, I had received various pieces of rumor and information which suggested that my original suspicion was right, that a young man named Alan May, employed in Mr. Patrick Gray's office, was, indeed, the prime source of information employed by Mr. Malek in making determinations such as those which had affected me.

I told Mr. Veneman that while I knew he had not invited me into his office to receive public relations advice from me, I felt it nonetheless necessary to point out that no matter how exalted the ultimate purpose or objective, the use of means to the end, would, in the long run, place an unnecessary and potentially hazardous shadow over the secretary and perhaps even over the president. I explained that I had recently learned, for instance, that Mr. Alan May was directly harassing Dr. Marston, the administrator of the National Institutes of Health, telling him that he ought to hurry and remove his information director, so that Mr. May could replace him with someone Mr. May had in mind. Mr. Veneman looked somewhat shocked by this piece of information. He turned to Mr. Malek, who said that he didn't know that Alan May was going that far, or something to that effect.

Williams also told Veneman that, in addition to changing his position, Malek was attempting to reduce Williams in grade, even though he had been assured that his professional competence was not in question. Williams said to Veneman: "My supervisor and my co-workers could never be fully certain that I was fully acceptable to the secretary if I were obligated to accept a reduction in grade. This would inevitably have a subtle but certain and profoundly adverse effect on my chances of being able to contribute fully in the new position." Veneman agreed that Williams would remain in the Environmental Health Service and be given a new position with no loss of grade.

In a letter to a friend at about the same time, Williams lamented:

> I have always found it possible to explain matters honestly as I see them in my past years in the government, and I will stay with the government only if I am allowed to continue enjoying that ordinary human right. It would be a horrifying happening if either of our major political parties were able to place its own

partisans in all the key public information spots of the federal establishment.*

Let me give you a concrete example of something that happened last week when I was unable to carry out my normal responsibilities. We put out a news release notifying the public that the manufacturers of microwave ovens are being called to Washington next week to meet with the secretary because, as you know, there are about 100,000 of these ovens in commercial and home use which are hazardous by even the most conservative definition of the word. Although I was hardly in any position to assert myself in the way that I normally do, I saw to it that the news release was not totally innocuous when it left our organization. But that is not the point of this little story. One of my assistants called the secretary's information office to find out the exact time of release so that we could make a secondary distribution on the mailing list that we have in our Bureau of Radiological Health. These secondary distributions are extremely important since the Department deals only with the Washington-based press corps. My assistant was told that the White House did not want a secondary distribution made, that they had chosen a slow news day deliberately to insure that this matter got as little public attention as possible. Well, if by some miracle I'm allowed to retain my present position, I would tell the secretary's information officer to go straight to "Hell" in a circumstance such as this.

Almost prophetically, Williams said in that letter, "I think my chances are about 50-50." He wrote that in 1970, but he survived.

Shortly afterward all the functions and people of the Environmental Health Service were removed from HEW to become part of the newly created Environmental Protection Agency. Williams lost the grade he had saved in HEW and was made head of the Editorial Division of EPA's Office of Public Affairs, which was, of course, headed by a political appointee. Williams found the experience of working under inexperienced and untrained people so frustrating that, nine months later, when he received an offer from Sandy Hale, the head of EPA's Solid Waste Office, to become the director of that program's technical information operation, he accepted gladly. Ironically, the offer came from a person who had been one of

---

* Although he could not have known it at the time, this is precisely the enduring blow to professionalism in federal public information work that Nixon was bringing about. Both Carter and Reagan followed the new precedent of placing their own partisans in all the key information jobs.

Malek's key lieutenants in HEW, during the time when Malek was pursuing Williams! Before accepting that job, Williams told his new boss that he would not confine his efforts to technical information, that there would doubtless be an overlap into public information. Because information for the public and the press was supposed to come from the central public affairs office only in EPA, Hale advised Williams to keep his head down.

Within a short time, the information and citizen participation activities of the Office of Solid Waste were so effective that they were periodically a prime target for elimination. For example, in April 1975, after Hale had left the government, Arsen Darnay, the new deputy assistant administrator, called Williams into his office and said that in the new year he would have no money for citizen activity and no money for producing public information. Hardly had Williams recovered from that shock when a memorandum came from Mary Blakeslee, an EPA program analyst, recommending that citizen training grant work be transferred away from the technical information staff.

Writing a twelve-page, single-spaced report in response, Williams said that Blakeslee's memo was so illogical that it would be regarded as "frivolous, were it not for the fact Ms. Blakeslee's memorandum is merely the most recent in a series of attempts to deprive the Office of Solid Waste Programs of the capacity to effectively communicate with the various segments of the public concerned with the solid waste management issue."

From 1970 to 1975, Williams was coping with the frustration that nearly all of the well-meaning bureaucrats face: warring with other bureaucrats. Although some other bureaucrats understand what the selfless bureaucrat is trying to do, they must cope with the next-higher-level bureaucrats, who must cope with political appointees who may or may not be primarily concerned with implementing the laws administered by their agencies.

By July 1976, Williams was facing the destruction of his own program, which would have closed the door to the public and the press. Where would he go? None of the Washington correspondents took notice of his dilemma. Williams was only one of three million employees of the federal government, yet his story was clearly important. Where was the press as that story unfolded? Stephen Hess of the Brookings Institution answers that question: "If we draw a scattergram of Washington reporters, we are likely to find that all the dots are bunched around certain institutions or events, such as the White House and the presidential campaigns; few reporters would be located at the regulatory agencies, with the special-interest lobbies, or anywhere beneath the top layers of the bureaucracy. A major Washington press conference, for example, represents more wasted manpower than any event since the Egyptians built the great pyramids. Think of all that high-priced talent writing exactly the same story!"

If the *real* decisions and the *permanent* power and the *human* drama of government reside within the bureaucracy, then why are so few members of the press corps assigned to cover it? The question is difficult and can be answered best, perhaps, by examining the lives of reporters who do cover various aspects of the Washington bureaucracy. Mike Conlon, a reporter on consumer affairs for United Press International, provides a good example. Although Conlon's beat and office are in the HHS building, his working day always begins with an early morning visit to the House press gallery, where he can get an advance copy of the *Federal Register*. "It takes the *Register* a day to arrive over at HHS. Every now and then they slip something in and don't do a press release. Tuesday, for instance, they published the final results of iron content in white bread. Five years ago this was headline news, but this time they didn't do a release on it."

Conlon enters the gallery in a morning huff, his blue blazer flapping behind him. He offers coffee to a colleague and retrieves two styrofoam cups from the vending machine that sits snugly just inside the door to the gallery. A lukewarm sip confirms once again that the "coffee" is horrible stuff, contrived by some degenerate chemist in the dark corridors of fast-food research.

The gallery is divided into three sections by partitions. Along the interior wall, the wire services and the major newspaper bureaus have niches that are closed off by other, smaller, chest-high partitions. All manner of teletypewriters, video terminals, and other journalistic paraphernalia are crammed into these little bunkers. Along the outer wall are telephone booths and a row of typewriters on a long shelf-desk.

In the narrow central portion of the gallery, there are chairs and a table around which the reporters can sit. Like almost every reporter's office in Washington, there are bits and pieces of hilarious bizarreness hanging around affixed by pins or by tape. On one partition is a newspaper photo of Mrs. Richard Nixon being grasped at the breast by a mop-headed five-year-old boy. He looks sly; she looks astonished.

The United Press International cubicle has four video terminals and one old UPI ticker. The day's *Washington Post* and *The New York Times* are already neatly shelved along with other back issues. UPI correspondent Bill Clayton is sitting at a video terminal calling up text and editing it. Conlon and Clayton exchange pleasantries and a little shop talk while Conlon skims the *Federal Register* and endures his coffee. Then, he takes off for the Department of Health and Human Services (HHS), using one of the many underground trollies to get to the Rayburn House Office Building, then walking across the street to the HHS building. This is the new structure, the one that looks a little like a stack of egg crates rearranged by a high wind.

Conlon's office is on the sixth floor of the modernistic building. As he waits for the elevators, he amuses himself by watching passers-by walk in wide arcs around an exhibit of sectioned lungs from lung-cancer victims. A machine is nearby for testing lung power. Nobody uses it. It menaces people with its certain conclusions.

The wire services have a special office all to themselves on floor six, alongside the HHS Public Affairs Office. UPI and AP have four rooms between them, a big one that is used as a foyer and three back rooms, two of which are used by UPI. Old wire stories, clips, press releases, and other printed matter lie around in great profusion. Everywhere there are piles of paper. The walls are covered with posters.

At 10:42 A.M., the typewriter in the small AP office is already clicking away. Conlon sits down in his own small office and turns on the video display terminal. The terminal is hooked into a complex, interactive communication system for all of the UPI journalists in Washington. With the system, Conlon can recall notes stored in the computer's memories, exchange messages with other UPI correspondents or with the bureau headquarters, and take care of all of his writing chores.

Conlon punches the appropriate keys and immediately begins translating an HHS release into a short piece for the UPI wire. The release concerns an FDA ruling on a drug called ipecac. No telephone calls or other queries seem necessary. The release is filed as a rewritten story, with several of the quotations in the release lifted verbatim.

The news story completed, Conlon reviews the HHS Greensheet, a daily compendium of consumer affairs articles from the previous day's newspapers. Conlon is primarily responsible for news issuing from the FTC, EPA, and the FDA, as well as any other more general consumer topics that come along. The Greensheet makes it easier for Conlon to know what is being reported in these areas— and what he is missing. Today's Greensheet is twenty-three pages long.

At 10:53, the little matrix printer starts to sputter, giving Conlon a hard copy of the story he just filed. He scans the story and then returns to the Greensheet to ponder a story on the American Meat Institute (AMI) reaction to the nitrite ban being proposed by the FDA. He calls an editor at UPI headquarters in the National Press Building. UPI hasn't covered the story yet, so Conlon jumps on it immediately.

At 10:54, he is on the telephone to the AMI "to see if the *Post* story is accurate." He begins taking dictation over the telephone from someone at the AMI. His hands fly over the terminal's keys, which make mushy sounds unlike any typewriter. He finishes the transcription at 10:57 and then asks: "There's a quote in the *Post* that says, 'regulation is . . .' Is that accurate?"

His query answered, Conlon hangs up and begins working on the new story. By 11:16, Conlon has finished his nitrite piece and is reviewing it on the display terminal. He edits, rearranging phrases here and there to make the story flow. Satisfied with his rewrite, he swings around from his desk; he can take a break now. But not for long, he says, because he has his rounds to make.

Federal agencies often schedule their most important hearings and press conference reports during the season when Congress is out of town. That way, Conlon says, the agencies can count on getting some attention. All such hearings and conferences are unusually solicitous to the press, particularly to the major wire services. "They'll always save us testimony and a place to sit at the hearing," Conlon says. He also mentions that Joseph Califano, secretary of Health and Human Services at the time, is expert at getting his name into every release that comes out of the department.

Conlon frequently attends these hearings or meetings, but it is also sometimes possible for him to cover them via telephone: "When you know what the agenda is, you can call the press person or someone you know on the staff to get your story."

There is no set consumer beat, but his work does end up

concentrating on a few agencies: "There are certain agencies that tend to produce more paper than the others, and these are the ones I have to worry about." Conlon regularly contacts the Environmental Protection Agency, the Interstate Commerce Commission, and sometimes even the Civil Aeronautics Board. The lines of beat jurisdiction aren't always clear, and two UPI reporters can end up trying to work the same territory.

Most of the agencies go out of their way to help stretch the reporter's time. The Federal Trade Commission, for example, drops releases for the wire service reporters at their press offices in the Health and Human Services building. Agency news sources, Conlon says, tend to bear down on the reporter, making the journalist more of a reactor than an actor. "On any given day, it's largely reactive; and maybe in the course of a week, 10% or 20% initiative."

Different agencies take different approaches to distributing information and handling press inquiries. The Federal Trade Commission, Conlon says, often refers a reporter directly to a source that can best deal with the subject matter. The Food and Drug Administration, though, is more reluctant to refer. It will take a question at the press office, it will get the answer, and then it will funnel the answer back through a press officer.

Conlon says agency press releases are a help and a hindrance at the same time. "Sometimes they're done for obvious purposes, and you're at their mercy. Sometimes they're incomplete. I think the agencies I deal with generally have a pretty good record." The main problem he has with releases is "incompleteness." Often a release will cover only one side of an issue and will leave it to him to get the other side.

There is a steady turnover of reporters in Washington, and a lot of them end up becoming flacks. "They don't all go to work for the government, though. The guy that covered HHS last year for us went to work for the American Dental Association. One guy just quit to go to work for the *Washington Star*. Somebody went to work for Bruce Caputo, who's running for lieutenant governor of New York. It really varies. Obviously the Washington beat is a source of other kinds of jobs for reporters. My personal feeling is that I haven't run into any government agency that I'd want to work for. I might work for a congressional committee, but not flacking. I'd want to investigate, not write releases."

How did Conlon get along with Eileen Shanahan, a former *New*

York Times reporter who was at that time the director of the Health and Human Services Public Affairs Office? "In my opinion, she has not done that good a job. She's a little overprotective of the secretary. I had a shouting match with her shortly after she came here. I'm not covering HHS as an institution, so I don't have to deal with her that much. It was a stupid argument."

The incident started with an off-hand remark from Shanahan, who told Conlon that the Carter administration was about to name a new commissioner of the Food and Drug Administration.

> I knew one of the Carter transition team who helped pick the commissioner, so I called this guy up and said, "Hey, I hear they're gonna announce the commissioner. Who is it?" He told me, and I put it on the wire. Anybody would do the same thing. She came storming into the room and said, "That's the last time I'm ever gonna tip you off to anything." She called me a smartass and various other names.
>
> [HHS Secretary Joseph] Califano likes to play things close to the vest and doesn't like advance publicity on anything unless he controls it completely. He apparently jumped on her, and she jumped on me.

Conlon smiles a thin, tight smile; he's satisfied he had the upper hand in this conflict: "I thought it was absolutely unforgivable and insensitive and—you name it. I wrote her a letter and told her I thought she owed me an apology, and she never replied. She grates on people. She was that way when she was a reporter. There's no reason to expect she would be otherwise. Maybe she's doing some very good things I don't see." Conlon isn't confident she is, but like the good diplomat many Washington reporters must be, he is balancing his criticism, covering his tracks enough to stay clear.

What was the best story he had done lately? It had been written two weeks earlier, when he broke the story that the Food and Drug Administration was going to recommend banning the use of nitrites in prepared meats: "One of Nader's people called me and said he heard the FDA was going to ban sodium nitrite. They had filed a suit on this about two weeks previously, saying the evidence was so strong they had to do it. I called the FDA, and they said, "Well, we're putting this MIT study on the record, but there's gonna be no announcement or news release." I had never heard of the MIT study, so I called somebody else at Nader's organization, and they told me about the study. It was the first time nitrites had been linked directly to causing cancer in laboratory animals."

Conlon launched into several off-hand but clearly knowledgeable references to the chemical processes involved in the cancer-producing food additives. He referred to amines, nitrosamines, carcinogens, and such, and then continued with his narrative:

> This went on all afternoon, with me trying to find out what was going on. In the meantime, their chief flack at FDA is headed down here. Word finally came out, actually via the Department of Agriculture, which is involved in this, that there was going to be an announcement around six o'clock. That's the absolutely worst time you could announce anything—6 P.M. on a Friday night—you're talking about the Saturday A.M. papers, which are not widely read.
>
> At six we got a very weasel-worded statement. Halfway through it, the FDA commissioner is quoted in a very strong way as saying, this is very serious evidence we have against this, and we are probably going to have to do something about it. I guess both wires at that point filed urgent stories.

Rumors about a press conference, though, had been rampant before the weakly worded statement came out. Conlon could not recall a specific source for the information about the press conference, but the Nader people thought there was going to be one, he said, and the fact that the head flack for the Food and Drug Administration was headed downtown from his suburban office was taken as confirmation of the conference. No conference was held, however, and nothing further happened after the press release, which Conlon considered inadequate.

On Monday morning, Conlon continued to pursue the issue with a series of calls and visits. Nobody wanted to talk, and Conlon was stymied. But then, as is typical in a reporter's dealing with the executive branch, Conlon received an unexpected and unsolicited phone call:

> The following Tuesday I got a call from a person who has a very high position in the government right now, who said, "I would like to leak to you the stuff on sodium nitrite." He said the Agriculture Department and the FDA had drawn up an action plan banning nitrites and phasing them out. He said he had all the info, and if I came to a certain place I could pick it up. I did, and it was in an envelope with my name on it. I went back and called this person up and said, "This is a hell of a document." He said, "I wanted it out because they've been playing games with it. It's been on Califano's desk for a month and now the Justice Department and the OMB [Office of Management and

Budget] have got their hands involved in it. They're writing comments on it, and it was supposed to have been released at a news conference Friday night or Saturday morning."

Conlon wrote a follow-up story based on information in the document that proclaimed the evidence against nitrites was so damning that the additives would have to be phased out of the national meat supply. Conlon's story was an exclusive and made front-page news in most of the nation's papers. He explains the circumstances of the leak: One trick used by companies who know they are about to get some bad flak from a government agency is to issue a preemptive press statement, hoping to put forth an interpretation of things first, perhaps giving it more credence and making a better defense.

> The reason this person leaked to me, among other things, was that he thought the meat industry had it and was probably going to do something with it. I don't think they did, though, because the American Meat Institute called me yesterday and asked me for a copy of it, which I gave them. I figured it was in the public domain by then anyway.
>   I'm told Shanahan was intimately involved in this whole thing [the FDA foot-dragging], but she may just have been reflecting Califano's desires. My person feeling is that last year's saccharin fiasco caused so much bad publicity for FDA that they're being more careful now. This goes on in *any* administration. It has to be that there is a feeling that you don't want rinky-dink publicity. People are worried about overregulation.

Conlon explains that it is relatively rare when agency releases are issued at times that almost guarantee that the media will not cover them. "It is not done that often—only when they have to put something out but they don't want publicity, and that doesn't happen that much. Usually they want it." Conlon cites Representative Les Aspin and Senator William Proxmire as being especially good at garnering publicity through their releases. "They'll issue something for release at 6:30 P.M. Sunday, because they know there's always a hole in the Monday paper."

Conlon is not troubled by the frequent use of unattributed sources in stories he writes: "You can always get around it by saying 'it was learned . . .' if somebody wants to give you something or say, 'this is off the record,' it's fine. I have no trouble with that. If it's something you're gonna have to get on record, you can usually go back and ask for some kind of attribution." In general, Conlon says that when news gets as far as the wire services, it is usually "up front" on attribution. Of course, Conlon's story about the nitrite leak is a direct contradiction of this, pointing up not his inconsistency so much as the inconsistencies of the working situation.

The embargo, or "hold-for-release" date, is one of the more interesting folkways that have developed between the Washington press relations establishment and reporters. The day Conlon was interviewed—a Friday—a release was available from Representative Les Aspin detailing junkets that Coast Guard generals had taken outside the prescribed rules. It was marked for release on the following Tuesday. Conlon was asked how reporters—who supposedly compete fiercely for the first lead on a story—could always sit on this kind of embargoed news until the marked release time. "Aspin figures, 'Who's going to read the paper on Labor Day [the coming Monday]?'" Conlon replies. "These embargoes are always set by the person who issues the story, and it's become part of the system. Usually you don't even question them."

Conlon points out that he has already written a story on Firestone tires, which was not to be released until 6:00 the following morning. Because he received the embargoed story early, he was able to do the background work necessary to round out the story. However, "The *Post* got around the embargo by calling Firestone in Youngstown, Ohio, and getting something out under a Youngstown dateline. But if you break too many of these things, you never know when somebody else is going to do it to you." Conlon notes that the AP and UPI have an agreement to alert one another when either breaks a standing embargo.

We can learn more about press relations with the bureaucracy by visiting two correspondents who work for the *Los Angeles Times:* Ron Ostrow and Penny Girard. Ostrow sits at his desk with the telephone cradled against his ear and neck. His voice rises and falls as he expresses amusement or outrage or skepticism; he is a maestro of the telephonic device. Part leprechaun, part logician, and part father-confessor to his enviable covey of inside sources, Ostrow appears to be the archetypical fun-loving Washington reporter. He smiles a lot, which goes nicely with his friendly blue eyes, and he is eager to make you laugh.

Everybody seems to like Ostrow and to think him fair, trustworthy, and funny. Is Ron Ostrow a Boy Scout out on a journalism jamboree? "I'm like a kid," he agrees. "I love it." Ostrow is the Justice beat correspondent for the *L.A. Times,* and he also works on investigative projects.

It is equally easy to imagine Penny Girard as a popular reporter among male government officials, for she is a beautiful woman. She is also bright, forthright, not a bit bashful. Penny Girard covers regulatory agencies for the *Times.* Over lunch in a downtown Washington restaurant, Ostrow and Girard talk about their jobs.

Girard says she arrives at work between 9 and 9:30 in the morning. When she has finished reading the papers—like everyone else, she reads the *Wall Street Journal,* the *Washington Post, The New York Times,* and her own paper—she begins working her contacts at the regulatory agencies. "I usually start contacting my agencies by telephone to see what's on the agenda for the day. First, I'll call the press offices, and then I'll talk to other people who are involved in specific stories I'm working on. During the day, there might be a news conference to attend, there might be an interview, there may be a hearing on the hill. If I eat lunch out—which is most of the time—it's usually with someone from an agency. We've usually got all our information by 4 P.M., and our schedule is out by 4:30. We write for deadline, usually anywhere from 6 P.M. on."

Ostrow says his routine is a little different from Girard's. "I get to the office between 9:30 and 10 A.M., and I usually begin by calling the Justice and the FBI press offices to see if they have anything outside of what I knew was coming anyway. But what I try to do, especially in summer weeks, is to figure out some things that are perking—that are right for doing—and try to break out something on them."

As Ostrow concludes the last sentence, Girard offers an emphatic, "Yes!" Ostrow laughs and continues:

> There're some things going on right now that haven't been in the news. I know there's something going on behind the scenes at Justice now. I just know the clock has kept ticking on these things, and they gotta do something with 'em. For example a foreign terrorist, fleeing Europe, recently crossed into the United States via Canada, and the Justice Department is considering prosecuting three Americans who helped her across the border. Nobody's doing much with that story, but it's still

going along. There's a whole set of people I'll call this afternoon that are related in one way or another to the case. I'll spend most of my day doing this, because Justice doesn't have anything.

Ostrow pauses and thinks. He remembers something at the Department of Justice: "They have a report on a draft of a bill that isn't gonna make anything in our paper. I'll glance at it to be familiar with the context, but that's all now."

Girard notes that a reporter's beat determines how many long pieces he or she will do. Ostrow, she says, depends more on spot news, while she writes more long pieces on regulatory agencies. Her beat is called regulatory agencies, but it is limited in scope. "There must be at least ten or so regulatory agencies, but I don't cover them all. They're broken up. The energy reporter watches the nuclear regulatory agencies, for instance. The business reporter watches the SEC [Security and Exchange Commission] and to some extent the airline regulators. I concentrate mostly on the FDA [Food and Drug Administration], the FTC [Federal Trade Commission], the ICC [Interstate Commerce Commission], and the FCC [Federal Communications Commission]."

Both reporters play down the role the press release plays in their work. Girard says, "The press releases I get at the agencies or from the pick-up services. I usually know pretty much what's in them before I get them from the agencies."

Ostrow agrees. Asked whether they use quotes directly from agency releases or try to "get something live," Ostrow defends the people he quotes: "When the attorney general says something that's attributed to him in the release, he *said* it," Ostrow says emphatically. "I know how the system works, and they don't just sit there and write them and then put 'em out. They run them through the guy, and they get changed and changed and changed. The FBI crime report, a quarterly, usually has some comment and the AG [attorney general] makes in it, and there's usually enough in there if you need to use a quote in the story. You'll want to get into the analysis of why crime is up or down, and you're not going to get that out of [former Attorney General Griffin] Bell. You're going to get that out of the people who work with the figures."

Both Girard and Ostrow say they take materials home to read, but they both emphasize the social aspects of Washington reporting.

Even when they are not at work, they are often working. "For example, I'm supposed to go to dinner tonight," Ostrow says. "She's having over some White House people. Number one, I'll be careful not to have more than one glass of wine, and to keep the ears open. I mean, I just know the way I'll behave."

Ostrow says he has found many stories that way. "Sure. For instance, secret efforts by the Nixon administration to spring Jimmy Hoffa. I got that from a drunken official."

Girard remembers a similar incident. "Last fall, long before there was trouble with something called liquid protein diet, they had all the deaths. I learned that at dinner and did a story before anybody else did."

Do Washington officials or bureaucrats conspire to influence certain reporters? Do they sit in their private offices and analyze which reporters are with them, which ones are not? "Yeah," Ostrow says. "I think there is a lot. I think there is a lot of attempted psychoanalysis that does go on."

Does it work? "In some cases, yes," says Girard. "It's just being tipped off early that something's happening. You have a personal rapport with someone. They think you've dealt with them fairly and honestly. They're likely to call you and tell you something's happening."

"But sometimes," Ostrow says, "they speak in purposefully obfuscated language, and you take it to mean one thing, and they meant another; and you might throw in an interpretive sentence afterwards, saying presumably this means so and so—that can be a problem." Much domestic political language has become almost diplomatic in its nature, being ambiguous, equivocal, and dense. "Ambiguous is the key," Ostrow says. "There's always this great fuzz." Removing the fuzz is part of the reporter's job, but it has to be done "without making something black and white that isn't black and white."

Both Girard and Ostrow emphasize the importance of personal trust between the reporter and the sources. Girard says, "Reporters in this town, those working for major publications, all have reputations. The people at the agencies very much know who is a fair reporter and who isn't."

"That's right," Ostrow mutters. "That's right."

Even though there is a definite grading of reporters, Girard says this does not give reporters power as such. "I don't think it's power.

I think it's access. If you work for a major organization, you have much quicker access to the officials."

Before Girard came to the *Times,* she explains, she worked for the chain that publishes *Women's Wear Daily.* Her ability to "get the quote" from the highest officials in an agency is much greater now that she works for one of the largest daily papers in the nation.

Ostrow, according to other Washington reporters, is a great pro at cultivating sources, opening up the channels of communication that give him exclusive stories. "I have never yelled at a person who works for the government in my life. I just bite my lip, because these people, one, don't deserve it usually. Their high-paid, martini-lunch bosses are always out. Aside from that, these people are crucial. They know. They can save you a whole afternoon at a time—time that allows you all sorts of hours to do something else or to pursue another angle. I rely on that a lot."

Ostrow says most of these people turn out to be women. "I kid with them. I ask them how their families are. I try to take a personal interest. It kind of grows over time."

Girard says it is not quite so personalized in her beat, which is broader than Ostrow's. "I'm spread out a lot more than you are. When I can or when someone's free, we'll have lunch." Because she spends time with the press people of the agencies she covers, "If I need something, I don't have to go over there all the time now."

On the other hand, it is normal for reporters to bypass the press people and go "right to the source. I don't usually tell the press office I'm going to call so-and-so," Girard says. "I usually go right to the person."

Ostrow says the regulatory agencies are harder to penetrate than the Justice Department beat he covers: "Regulatory agencies were always a problem—I used to do some of those stories—they're so bureaucratized that they're protected by these layers. It's tough cutting through. It's enough for most of these people if they know you're going to give a straight report and that you're not going to be satisfied with one-dimensional types of information."

As you can judge, it is both crucial and difficult to cover the bureaucracy well. The print media are doing that job better than they used to, as they more and more realize its importance. The impressions of Rich Jaroslovsky, a correspondent who recently joined the Washington bureau of the *Wall Street Journal*, provide a fitting conclusion:

> The first thing that impressed me when I arrived in Washington was the sheer physical size of government. Not just the White House and the Capitol, but also the three House and two Senate buildings, the Library of Congress and the Supreme Court, the massive Commerce Department building, and the labyrinth of the Pentagon. In every conceivable nook and cranny, some sort of decisions are being made that affect my life.
>
> Washington has been derided, somewhat unfairly, as a town of "Southern efficiency and Northern charm." But the fact is that many of the government buildings, massive and impenetrable, reflect the goings-on within them.
>
> While the civics books say that Congress makes the laws, the fact is that the various agencies, departments, and administrations—the agglomeration generally known as "the bureaucracy"—make a great many vital decisions. Yet to a newcomer (as well, I suspect, as to many old hands), it's nearly impossible to tell precisely what the bureaucracy is up to.
>
> One problem is its size. Say you have a question on the safety of jet planes. Whom do you talk to? The Federal Aviation Administration? Civil Aeronautics Board? National Transportation Safety Board? Some agency is deciding whether banks can offer interest on checking accounts. Is it the Federal Reserve Board? Comptroller of Currency? Treasury Department? Federal Deposit Insurance Corporation?
>
> Still another problem is that so much of what the bureaucracy does is hidden from day-to-day public view. When an agency proposes a new regulation of some sort, it is usually in close-to-final form. But that regulation is often the result of weeks or months of staff work and internal deliberation within the agency—the records of which aren't often released to the public.
>
> The simple fact is this: If you don't know how the bureaucracy operates, you don't know how Washington operates.

4

Congress

*T*he press and the broadcast galleries at the Capitol are like supermarkets. Correspondents come in with shopping lists and pick their stories right off the shelf. Some stories are more processed than others. Some are fresh, and some are rancid. The press offices in the House and in the Senate offer by far the greatest source and the largest range of "goods" to be found in Washington. A flood tide of daily news releases arrives in the Capitol press galleries from the individual members of Congress, from the congressional committees, from the party leaders and caucuses, and from the various outside agencies and lobbies that want to comment on something under consideration in one house or the other.

The Senate broadcast gallery, runt child of the Senate press gallery, is on the third floor of the Capitol, down the hall from the spacious facilities for the print media. The broadcast gallery is a small, L-shaped room with a loft above the bottom leg of the L. The loft is clearly an afterthought and has been crammed in among other, older fixtures in the building to provide a place for the wire-service ticker tapes. Toward the rear of the room, below the loft space, are three small sound studios from which radio correspondents file their "actualities." The studios are only a bit larger than telephone booths. In the other leg of the L, past the secretary-receptionist's desk, one encounters the expected line of typewriters on a long shelf against one wall. On the opposite wall are rows of shelves stacked full of telephone books and other oddly assorted directories and government reports. The ceiling is arched and has been lined with acoustical tile that has taken on the color of old cigarette smoke. Stacks of bright blue videotapes are scattered everywhere.

Max Barber has been overseeing this shop since 1953, and the place has never been altered in that time, despite the fact that the number of radio and television reporters in Washington has jumped from 35 to 1,000. Barber, a kindly, gentle-voiced man with flowing gray hair, is a little bitter about the bridesmaid status of the Senate broadcast gallery: "We just asked for airspace over part of the press gallery so we could put in a balcony, but they wouldn't hear of it," he says. "We have practically nothing here. We have just what we had in 1939."

The problem began when newspaper correspondents refused to let radio correspondent Fulton Lewis into the gallery in 1939, forcing the creation of a separate and unequal broadcast gallery down the hall in a storage area. Barber believes, quite rationally, that the press and broadcast galleries should be combined, as they are at the White House and in most other federal buildings, so that the broadcast personnel would have at least a token of the space befitting their number and the importance of their services to the public. The Senate, however, moves like a mollusk on even the most urgent of public issues. Except for salary increases and office budgets, the housekeeping problems of Congress are always well down on the agenda for action. Both houses are also handicapped somewhat by the bureaucracy they have created to preserve the historic integrity of Washington's more illustrious structures. Changing the position of a light switch or a doorknob in the Capitol can require more paperwork and discussion and analysis and fuss than anyone cares to contemplate.

Barber has four people on his staff, none of them a journalist. The main job of the gallery is to serve as a funnel for news from the Senate and from its committees. "If something really earthshaking comes in, we'll call the network reporters and let them know something's up," Barber says. Otherwise, as the press releases come in, one of each batch is posted on a bulletin board, and the rest are filed away in a numbered drawer. Every now and then, probably once a year, according to Barber, the files are purged. Releases from federal agencies and from lobby groups are seldom posted and are never filed. Instead, they are piled on top of a filing cabinet, where reporters can sift through them.

Between fifteen and twenty releases a day come from senators and Senate committees. The largest number are produced on Fridays, many times with Monday release dates so that the reporters can work ahead and take the pressure off for their weekends. "William Proxmire is the release champion," Barber says. "He puts out more than any other senator right now." Are the releases necessary? "It would be difficult to do the job without them. It's a form of spoon-feeding, but how do you get the word out?"

The staff of the gallery also does a lot of informal work for reporters, Barber says. "We answer all kinds of questions about bill status, parliamentary procedures, you name it. We try to be helpful and show them the ropes." "Showing them the ropes" usually means referring reporters to the right staff members, the second-echelon people who do the hard work on a given issue.

What would Barber do if he could renovate his operation? "We'd need one large studio for news conferences, and we need more room and facilities for individual crews. Right now we don't even have facilities for the networks. Soon every city with more than 500,000 will have a minicam crew up here. The number is increasing monthly."

Barber also thinks correspondents have changed in Washington, and not for the better: "I don't know whether it's the times or what, but it seems to me that a younger bunch has come in whose idea of news is how you can embarrass someone. I hear some of these kids bragging that they've zapped a congressman. What kind of journalism is that?"

Just down the hall is the Senate press gallery. Perhaps four times larger than the broadcast gallery, the offices are elegantly appointed with leather furniture and feature an anteroom that opens directly onto the Senate floor. This direct access in itself puts the Senate press gallery into a different league from the broadcast gallery.

Security is supposed to be tight in the press galleries of the Congress, but all you really have to do is look the part. One day, a researcher put on his worst, most tattered polyester suit. He stuck a long, skinny reporter's notebook in his coat pocket, so that it was displayed prominently, and he carried a small portable recorder in one hand. He stalked through the third floor of the Capitol trying to look distracted, bored even. The security guard at the door of the

Senate press gallery looked him over. The researcher tried to assume the mien of one who is bored, on the one hand, and harried and hurried on the other.

"Press?" the guard asked. The visitor nodded and walked by. Some security.

One enters the Senate press gallery to find a large room dominated by typewriters, desks, stacks of paper, and a lovely, ornamented ceiling that must be 15 feet high. This is the room where Max Barber requested balcony rights for his broadcasters, but it would have been a shame to lower its ceiling. The room, despite the typical newsman's crowding and clutter, seems spacious and elegant, primarily because of its proportions. Off to the right is a space where the administrators of the gallery make their offices. At the left rear, the room opens into a hall bedecked with more typewriters. The hall opens into the anteroom that opens into the Senate chambers. A bank of telephone booths stands along one wall of the anteroom, and several luxurious leather couches are in the room's center. Another wall supports a big bulletin board covered with the day's press releases. At the window wall there is a large display table with a slanted top that holds additional copies of the day's releases. An adjoining rack supports a dozen or more daily newspapers from around the country.

This place has journalistic class. The leather on the couches is faded and soft and misshapen, like a favorite pair of old shoes. Reporters are photogenically clustered about the room, telling each other inside jokes and trading tips. Edward R. Murrow's ghost seems to be stalking around, puffing cigarette smoke and hacking cancerously. Why is it that reporters slouch so? Nobody seems to stand up straight or to move crisply. Everyone appears to be trying to look bored or jaded.

One young reporter opens the door to the Senate floor below, listens a minute and exclaims, "Shit!" He runs over to a typewriter, grabs a note pad, and is gone again through the door. Forty seconds later, he is back in the anteroom and into a telephone booth. No one else in the room so much as twitches a mustache. Whatever moved the young reporter to action is of no concern to the others.

Don Womack has directed the Senate press gallery since 1951. Squat and powerful, gravelly of voice, he reminds one of a Mafia henchman. Seven people work on Womack's staff, and the reporters elect another advisory group of five. There are 1,245 correspondents

registered at the gallery, and Womack is proud of his evenhanded-
ness: "*The New York Times* doesn't get a bit better treatment here
than the *Biloxi Gazette.*"

The biggest changes in the gallery over the years, in Womack's
opinion, have been mechanical. Now, he says, senators don't have to
make a speech; they can just turn a statement in to the typists and
have it printed in the *Congressional Record.* Legislation doesn't
make news, but colorful politicians do.

The nitty-gritty work for Womack and his staff is handling
releases, and it is done in about the same way as it is at the
broadcasters' gallery: one copy on the bulletin board, one copy to
each wire service, one copy to each correspondent known to be
interested in a given subject. Additional copies are placed in a rack
where the correspondents can pick them up. Extras are filed for a
month, then thrown away. Like Max Barber, Womack respects the
institution he works for: "We get releases from lobbyists and other
groups outside the Senate, but a lot of them go into the cubic file—
the trash. If we get anything in here at all that is derogatory to the
Senate or a Senator, it goes in the trash can."

Womack is especially proud of the new congressional computer
system. Its bill-reference service, he says, is wonderful. Just call
them up, ask them your question and they'll have the answer in a
minute. "Here—take the phone and ask them anything, anything at
all."

The visitor asks the information service whether the lower Rio
Grande Canyons in Texas are in this year's National Parks authorization bill.

"Ummmm," says the voice, and in the background there is the
soft mushing sound of a computer keyboard in operation.

"Do you know what committee that would be in?" the voice asks.

"Try Interior," the visitor asks.

"How about the subcommittee?"

"Try National Parks," the visitor says.

"Ummmm."

The visitor feels uneasy. Womack, looking generally like a drowsy
pit bull, is beaming. See how great this system is?

"Ummmm," says the voice.

"Yes, well, thanks very much," says the visitor, opting for
graciousness over truth. "That's been very helpful."

"Well, if you can wait just a minute. . . ."

"Thanks again," and the visitor hangs up. "Marvelous system you've got here, Mr. Womack, just amazing."

Covering Congress, perhaps even more than covering the White House and the executive bureaucracy, is like reporting the movements of a living organism—of a gigantic, antediluvian, crotchety, and set-in-its-ways organism. Even its individual organs, its committees, have independent personalities. Reporting seldom gets us close to the personality of the legislative branch, yet a rudimentary apprehension of it is essential to any comprehension of the special difficulties faced by the correspondents on Capitol Hill.

The media-Congress relationship can be almost unbelievably complicated. Because Senator Lowell Weicker of Connecticut was coming up for reelection in 1976, he was especially attentive to correspondents, including those he did not know. As a consequence, something occurred which is now known as the "Brenda Brody caper." It started early in 1976, with the arrival in Senator Weicker's office in Washington of a reporter named Brenda Brody. When she had interviewed Weicker for half an hour, the senator's assistant for the interview session came out of his office in search of two other assistants, Bob Herrema and Fred Mann.

Brody was then questioning the senator, concentrating on his 1970 campaign contributions, and especially on contributions to Gulf Oil. She insisted that a complete listing of 1970 contributors was not on the public record because some contributions had been lumped in the account and reported to Connecticut as one sum. Weicker and Herrema were explaining that, under 1970 law, D.C. accounts did not have to be reported at all. They had gone beyond the legal requirements by reporting the D.C. total to Connecticut. Some donors at that time wanted and had the legal right to contribute anonymously. They could not, therefore, unilaterally make public their names and gifts. Finally, the entire issue of Weicker contributions in 1970 had been scrutinized by themselves and the Watergate special prosecutor when the Nixon White House tried to impute that Weicker had received illegal money.

Senator Weicker was clearly unhappy while the interview was progressing. He emphasized that his records were open to anyone; he had stood squarely for full financial disclosure. The UPI stories on Gulf Oil contributions of a few weeks back had been thoroughly negated by the attorney general himself, the Senate Ethics Committee, and the special prosecutor's office. Weicker also said that there were a lot more important issues to discuss than contributions from 1970.

Brody switched to energy, asking, with a strong disclaimer that the question did not mean to accuse, if contributions from oil companies or energy concerns were a conflict of interest, or could be seen as having influenced his votes. Weicker responded no, it did not influence anything in his thinking. She then asked for heat and electric bill totals for his house in Alexandria, Virginia, his condominium in Florida, and his house in Greenwich, Connecticut.

Brody closed by passing Senator Weicker a card bearing a number of names. She said those persons had contributed to his 1970 campaign, and could he please identify who they were—some of the names were familiar to her, but she couldn't place them. The first was Ab Siebel, a former Connecticut congressman from the 4th District; Bob Smith, Weicker's old college roommate was also on the list, along with a number of others. Herrema seemed to know most of them.

Brody then thanked Senator Weicker for his time, put her pad back in her briefcase and got up to go. The most striking thing, Mann said later, aside from her manner, which was rather aggressive, and her unusual question selection, was the fact that Weicker talked to her in great detail and she did not take a single note. Before she left, Senator Weicker called his wife in Greenwich and got a heating bill total for her. She asked Mann to point her to Democratic Senator Abraham Ribicoff's office, which he did.

Senator Weicker was perturbed. He believed that he had been had—somehow. Mann said to him, "As one who has conducted more than a few interviews, I saw very clearly that she was out to do a number on you. She did not seem to be a reporter. She was equipped with very little correct information on issues, lots of names on financing, and a desire to find an exploitable opening."

Senator Weicker asked Mann if she was really from the biweekly *Westport News,* as she had said. He stressed the need for Mann to screen people who want to have interviews. Mann assured him that he would. Later, Weicker called Herrema and Mann back to his office and stressed that he was extremely tired of going back over 1970 contributions and having to defend all that was legal. Not another minute was to be wasted on that.

Mann called the *Westport News* to ask whether Brenda Brody was a reporter. No, she didn't work in the office, but she did write for the paper sometimes. Asking how he could send information to her, Mann was told that he could send it to the editor and that Brody would receive it. "I was bothered that she was a free-lance writer," Mann said, "rather than the staff writer she had appeared to be. But, having free-lanced myself, I understood the situation." He asked friends in Washington, however, who told him everything. She was a member of the state central committee for the Democratic party. One friend added that she was "an asshole, and you shouldn't talk to her. She'll do a hatchet job on you."

Senator Weicker, a Republican, was gloomy until Mann told him. He checked the most recent Blue Book and found her listed as the Democratic state central committeewoman from Westport. Mann called to ask whether she was still a committeewoman. She said that she "had been." "Are you still a member of the state central committee?" Mann asked. She responded, "Well, yes," then added that she was just beginning to write again for the *Westport News*. She planned to write an original piece on the Senate election and had interviewed only Weicker, but also planned to interivew "whoever the Democratic nominee is and possibly also Senator Ribicoff."

Senator Weicker then wrote to William O'Neill, the chairman of the Democratic state central committee and complained, "I did not spend two years risking a career as a member of the Senate Watergate Committee to defend the right of a political party, specifically yours, to be free from that kind of bat guano only to have it practiced on me by a prominent Democrat."

In the end the *Westport News* column by Brenda Brody, raising questions about Weicker, was posed against the overwhelming questions about Brody that appeared in *The New York Times,* the Connecticut News Service, the *Boston Globe,* the *Hartford Courant,* the *Hartford Times,* and an indeterminate number of newspapers and broadcast stations that picked up the long report on her, filed by the Associated Press. At first, the *Westport News* published a short editorial that ended, "It seems to us that both politics and journalism have been enriched by the combination." Two days later, another editorial capitulated. It concluded: "To preserve a civil dialogue and promote communication, rather than impede it, it is better if all their labels are plainly in evidence."

Most of the real news in the legislative branch is made in committee. Yet even committee meetings, however much the bargains are struck there, are often only "fronts" for work done, not by congressmen at all, but by congressional staffers. They are to Congress, more or less, what bureaucrats are to the cabinet. On Capitol Hill, the assistants to a congressman are almost never identified in news reports, even though ideas originate with them and are executed by them, all in the name of the congressman. An example is a case involving Congressman Jake Pickle of Texas and his administrative assistant, Michael Keeling. Congressman Pickle had opposed most of the early investigative moves against President Nixon. At the same time, he represented a district with a growing liberal constituency that wanted to unseat him. Congressman Pickle needed badly to put distance between himself and the Republican administration.

Earlier in that session of Congress, there had been some publicity about the merger of International Telephone and Telegraph (ITT) with Hartford Insurance. The merger was achieved through a foreign intermediary, Mediobanca of Italy, and because of that, the Internal Revenue Service (IRS) awarded the merger a tax-free status, thus saving ITT several hundred million dollars, or thereabouts.

Michael Keeling was aware that Pickle had helped investigate that merger as a senior member of the House Commerce Investigating Subcommittee. Pickle had voiced the opinion that ITT had been awarded the tax-free status as a political reward from the Nixon administration. The committee took no action either condemning or endorsing the merger, however, because of Commerce Chairman Harley Staggers's fear of any publicity. Keeling developed the idea that pursuing Pickle's criticism of the ITT merger could put quite a lot of ground between Pickle and Nixon, so he began to work on it.

Keeling simply wrote a series of letters to the IRS protesting the tax-free status and demanding that it be revoked; press releases were based on each of these letters. Ned Kenworthy of *The New York Times* became interested, although, as far as anyone knew, the protests would have no practical impact on the ITT case. The releases and letters were simply a way for Pickle to criticize the Nixon administration on a specific point that fell short of an impeachment. A man from the IRS then read Pickle's press secretary the press release it had just issued, saying the ITT decision had been reversed and that ITT would be liable for the full sum of back taxes.

Pickle was motivated by the knowledge that the tax ruling was a means of helping ITT and, most important, by the knowledge that the ITT publicity would harm any liberal opposition in his district. Pickle and Keeling collaborated on every letter and release, making sure they keyed the statements to the liberals in Pickle's district.

At the same time, other political motivations in the Nixon bunch may have been responsible for the IRS moving on Pickle's protests. At any rate, Pickle ended with a good deal of news space in the national press, and ITT had to pay off its tax bill, all because Pickle needed some anti-Nixon press in his district. Keeling was not mentioned in any of the press reports.

Indeed, it seems that many of those who work for congressmen and senators are as closed off from publicity as those who work for the executive branch.

The most remarkable Congress-media story of recent years occurred in 1975, when the Child and Family Services Act was introduced by then-Senator Walter Mondale of Minnesota. Senator Mondale had, earlier in 1975, won the first award of the American Academy of Pediatrics for excellence in public service because of his legislative concern for children. In 1971, both the Senate and the House passed legislation that would build on existing programs to provide health, education, and child care services to families seeking help. President Nixon had vetoed it. After Nixon's resignation, Senator Mondale and Congressman John Brademas of Indiana introduced a more limited version of the legislation. The bill seemed rosy, for it had as cosponsors ninety-six representatives and twenty-eight senators. The media in Washington paid almost no attention to it. It seemed to be a bill destined to become a law.

But by the time the senators had completed their hearings, Senator Mondale felt the need to declare: "A vicious and totally inaccurate propaganda campaign is currently being waged. It [the Child and Family Services Act] is being subjected to one of the most distorted and dishonest attacks I have witnessed in my fifteen years of public service. Wild and completely false allegations are being made that this legislation would somehow give children the legal right to disobey their parents; somehow prohibit parents from giving religious training to their children; somehow give the government authority over child rearing; and somehow give children the right to complain about their parents and teachers without fear of reprisal."

These charges were false. The bill simply offered to families access to the health, education, and welfare services that they want for their children but that they cannot afford. The bill specifically limits eligibility to "children whose parents or guardians request such services," and it does not change the legal relationship between parents and children.

The most curious of the many flyers that became, for want of a name, the opposition, was a one-page, unsigned specimen. It spelled "those" as "thoes" and "superiority" as "superiorty." Moreover, it represented a four-year-old argument, based on paraphrases of Senate speeches against the very different bill of 1971. The flyer was also based on a British charter, which has nothing whatever to do with the bill of 1975. Those who circulated the flyer in 1971 were never identified. They sent the flyer, unsigned, to churches, religious organizations, and schools everywhere.

Although Nixon had resigned in disgrace, the flyer proclaimed the Nixon veto of the 1971 bill: "The bill passed both houses in 1971 and was vetoed by President Richard M. Nixon with the following remarks: 'This bill would weaken the American family by committing the vast moral authority of the National Government to the side of the communal approaches to child rearing over and against the family-oriented approach.'" Actually, Nixon had said that the bill was too costly.

Senator Mondale's staff of four in Minneapolis as well as his staff in Washington were inundated with letters and telephone calls. Every senator and representative was likewise besieged. For example, Congressman Gillis Long of Louisiana said that the result of this opposition "was one of the most massive mail campaigns ever launched against a piece of legislation, and it flooded congressional offices for weeks."

No investigation has revealed who was behind the opposition. In April 1976, Geri Joseph, a contributing editor of the *Minneapolis Tribune,* tried to track it down. Joseph finally gave up and added: "The situation is particularly frustrating because a careful reading of the bill reveals that it contains none of the dreadful proposals critics are quoting in letters to the editor or distributing in mimeographed handbills all over the country. Their charges that the bill is Communist-inspired and that the 'Reds' in our government are 'trying to take our children away from us' are the typical, fearmongering jargon used by extremists."

The opposition sent information about the bill to newspaper editors and broadcasters who were not represented in Washington.

For example, the *Thermopolis Independent Record* of Wyoming editorialized:

> What is at issue is whether the parent shall continue to have the right to form the character of the children or whether the state, with all its power and magnitude, shall be given the decisive tools and technique for forming the young lives of the children of the country.
>
> As a matter of the child's right, the government shall exert control over the family because we have recognized that the child is not the care of the parents but the care of the state. We recognize, further, that not parental, but communal forms of up-bringing have an unquestionable superiority over all other forms. Furthermore, there is serious question that maybe we cannot trust the family to prepare young children in this country for the new kind of world which is emerging. . . .
>
> The proposed bill as detailed above defies belief in the United States. It is unthinkable that such a bill could be introduced in the Congress of the United States. Such a law might even be considered liberal in the Soviet Union or the People's Republic of China.
>
> Americans who take the view that "such a bill could not possibly pass Congress" may be "selling their souls to the devil." Before you decide that such a bill has no chance for passage and you won't write your Congressman, reflect on the fact that the men who introduced that ridiculous piece of legislation are representatives of people who voted for them and sent them to Washington. Write your Congressman and Senators and urge them to defeat the bill.

Although the editorial was wrong, the editor wrote as though he believed it. It turned out that he was relying on the publication called *Good News Broadcaster,* which was relying on the Emergency Committee for Children, which was relying on a quotation from an unsigned flyer, which paraphrased the *Congressional Record* of 1971. As a consequence of the flyer and of other publications (such as the magazing published by Bob Jones University of Greenville, South Carolina; the *Christian Crusade Weekly,* a publication of an organization called Christian Crusade, with offices in Tulsa, Oklahoma; and publications of the Church League of America in Wheaton, Illinois), some broadcasters and newspapers picked it up and spread the misinformation without checking the accuracy of the allegations. Local journalists wrote columns for the hometown paper, at times adding their own embellishments. Even the good reporters in the many cities added to the flames by reporting them. In Texas, for example, page 1 of the *Victoria Advocate* headlined THE MYSTERIOUS FLYER—FACTUAL OR FANCIFUL? Nick Bournias of the *Advocate* wrote, "A mysterious unsigned flyer attacking an obscure bill in Congress is being widely circulated in Victoria, particularly in the school system." He questioned five elementary school principals, four of whom had reproduced the flyer for teachers. One principal said that there was no reason to question the information. "If DuPont puts it out, it has to be right," the principal said. The manager of the Victoria DuPont plant said that it did not come from him. While such headlines and stories gradually worked their way to the metropolitan areas, radio commentator Paul Harvey of Chicago, who is heard by millions of listeners, broadcast a segment expressing outrage over the purported intent of the bill.

Significantly, both the official government and the Other Government were neatly encircled by a four-year-old false argument. The opposition skirted Washington as the flyer appeared in Ohio, then appeared throughout the Midwest, then surfaced in Wyoming, and elsewhere. Nothing that was quoted in the hundreds of thousands of protesting letters bore any relation to the bill. As a consequence of the campaign, the bill died.

Although legislative staffers had been working almost ceaselessly to forestall the campaign against the bill, the Washington news correspondents hardly ever mentioned their efforts or the scurrilous campaign against a worthy and innocuous piece of social legislation. The story helps to explain why the Other Government has developed: A powerful, respected, professional, knowledgeable, and courageous press is the best and perhaps the only means of keeping the public well informed and of protecting the public from the misinformed and the malicious. The story is also a cautionary tale of what can happen when the news media fail to observe their new responsibility.

5

The Supreme Court

Just before the dedication of the new Supreme Court building in 1935, one of the justices quipped about that grandiose marble mausoleum: "What are we supposed to do, ride in on nine elephants?" Anyone who visits a session of the Supreme Court for the first time will find that the Court's procedures are also rather more Byzantine than one would expect of an American governmental institution in the late 20th century. For the neophyte reporter who is attempting to cover the Supreme Court, this formal, anachronistic style can be unnerving and confusing. But even the experienced correspondent, who has learned the jargon and become accustomed to the ritual, finds the imperial aloofness and silence of the justices a bewildering and frustrating phenomenon of contemporary government. The justices of the Supreme Court almost *never* speak publicly or critically of one another or of the cases before them. The Court's deliberative process—its internal debates, the tentative positions taken by the justices, the preliminary votes, the various drafts of written opinions, the negotiations, confrontations, and compromises—has always been hidden from public view.

The Supreme Court is the only branch of the federal government in which news correspondents are left almost entirely on their own to discern and report the news. The correspondents are almost never assisted by interviews with the justices or by press conferences, by

Let me thank the authors of the *Guide to the Supreme Court,* published by Congressional Quarterly, for explaining so well the many press–Supreme Court encounters.

briefings, or by press releases. A single public information officer serves the Supreme Court by releasing unadorned copies of the justices' opinions and orders (the releases are given to the correspondents at the same time they are announced from the bench). The correspondents must then attempt to translate the language of the law into concepts that millions of people will understand.

For example, in a 1956 bus-segregation case, the Supreme Court's order read:

> No. 511 *South Carolina Electric & Gas Company* v. *Flemming*. Per curiam. The appeal is dismissed. *Slaker* v. *O'Connor*, 278 U.S. 188.

For a UPI correspondent who had covered the Court for fifteen years, the Court's dismissal of the appeal seemed to outlaw bus segregation, with the case of *Slaker* v. *O'Connor*, decided in 1929, cited by the Court as precedent. The AP report concurred, and this reading of the case was splashed on front pages all over the country.

Actually, the opinion was not nearly so sweeping. The Supreme Court had refused to consider the appeal merely because the trial court had not reached a final judgment, which had also been true of *Slaker* v. *O'Connor*. Bus segregation per se was neither accepted nor disallowed. Because of this misinterpretation by the UPI and the AP reporters, hundreds of millions of people around the world read and heard mistaken information. When many of these people protested the sloppy reporting, an editor of the *New York Herald Tribune* had his telephone operators quote this statement written the previous year by Justice Felix Frankfurter: "The secrecy that envelops the Court's work is not due to love of secrecy or want of responsible regard for the claims of democratic society to know how it is governed. That the Supreme Court should not be amenable to the forces of publicity to which the Executive and the Congress are subjected is essential to the effective functioning of the Court."

Although this quotation does not entirely explain why the wire service correspondents were so wrong in reporting the case, other factors explain why the correspondents are sometimes confused. First of all, the complex Court opinions are often too difficult even for trained lawyers to understand. Yet news correspondents must give their interpretations under deadline pressure. Although in a few cases there is some personal interaction between the press and members of the Court, this interaction is usually limited to providing background information or explanation which can *never* be attributed to the justice or even to an unidentified member of the Court or its staff. Moreover, such assistance is invariably defensive and extremely cautious. A justice once sent this note to a correspondent: "You didn't read Page 11 of my opinion." Keep in mind that the page referred to is found in one of as many as nine Court opinions, which can add up to hundred of pages for each case.

Second, the Court deliberately attempts to shut out the news media from its deliberations to keep the justices free from external pressures. The leak of a Court decision can adversely affect the administration of justice by allowing people to act before the Court has officially stated its position. Here are some examples:

- In 1973, *Time* magazine predicted much of the historic abortion decision and its 7-2 vote more than a week before the decision was announced by the Court. As a result, Chief Justice Warren Burger invoked many new security measures, including orders that all of the court clerks (top-ranking law school graduates who serve each justice for a year as part of an exclusive apprenticeship) were not to speak to or to be seen with news correspondents.
- In 1977, National Public Radio violated the secrecy of the Court by reporting that the justices had voted, 5-3, against reviewing the convictions of three defendants in the Watergate cover-up case. The NPR report, made by Nina Totenberg, came a week before the Court announced its decision.
- In 1979, ABC-TV correspondent Tim O'Brien correctly reported in advance the outcome of a Supreme Court hearing regarding the right of the federal courts to question newsmen about their thoughts while writing stories. After that story, a Government Printing Office linotypist was reassigned out of the Court's printing unit, despite his protestations of innocence. The Court's public information officer, Barrett McGurn, issued new rules governing the press's access to the Supreme Court Building:

> Parts of the building are, of course, closed at all times to all but Court personnel. These include the garage and the basement area in general, the ground floor section beyond the ladies' restroom, the Justices' chambers and access corridors on the first floor, and all of the second and third floors including the

Library. Where members of the media need access to these areas, escorts will be provided by the Public Information Office, the Marshal, or other Court officers. . . .

During nonpublic hours all visitors to the Building are required to sign in and out at the Building entrance desk. Accredited news personnel may use the press area (rooms 30, 31 and 32) and the adjacent food machine section and restrooms from 8 A.M. to 10 P.M. seven days a week. Where additional time is required, arrangements may be made through the Public Information Office. During the nonpublic hours, all other areas of the building are closed.

Nonetheless, these rules do not seem to imprison Supreme Court documents, which seem to wander into the correspondents' hands. For example, Betsy Olson, a UPI correspondent, found on her desk one day, early in June 1981, a document that said that the U.S. Supreme Court would rule that women may ask the courts to enforce demands for higher pay for traditionally female jobs. The time was a full week before the Supreme Court would announce its decision. Was it a true statement of what the Court would do?

Although Olson believed that someone left it on her desk accidentally, like many other correspondents, she asked her editor what to do. The editor asked her to try to make certain that the document was authentic. As a Washington correspondent, she had long known that it would be fruitless to ask the Supreme Court justices and their aides whether this was a Supreme Court document. The Court policy barred comment on pending cases.

She decided to show the eight-page, legal-sized document to five constitutional scholars and sex discrimination experts. All of them agreed that it followed the form for court opinions, and that it seemed to be in line with the Court's expected action. Moreover, the document seemed genuine.

Olson's editor asked her to write a story for the review of the other editors and to place her story in a secure computer file. She fashioned a story that began, "There are indications the Supreme Court will only slightly open courthouse doors to suits seeking higher pay for women in traditionally female jobs."

While Olson was writing her story, Fred Barbash of the *Washington Post* spoke to one of her experts, who mentioned that Olson had a seemingly authentic document from the Supreme Court. The *Washington Post* reporter asked Olson if she had such a document. She replied affirmatively and said that she was writing a weekend story. Barbash promptly wrote a story for his paper, quoting Olson. He also wrote in his story that there apparently was a new leak at the Court, referring to the furor that was stirred up two years before when ABC reported on two cases before the Supreme Court announced its decisions.

When Olson's editor called Grant Dillman, the Washington manager, they discussed Olson's story at length, but they always came back to the leading point: Although the document seemed genuine, how could UPI prove that it was authentic? They also explored other questions: Was it a draft opinion written by a justice that was circulated among his colleagues searching for reaction and perhaps support for his opinion? Or was it—worst of all—a "plant" designed to embarrass UPI, the court, or both?

Dillman said: "It was a close decision and might have gone the other way had it involved a coverup of scandal or official wrongdoing, or even some critical decision. But our information—if it was authentic—shortly would be made public anyway. I told Ronald Cohen (the Washington news editor) my inclination was not to carry the story but that I wanted to read the papers and talk to the reporter. She was convinced that it was real and that we should carry a story."

While the UPI was discussing the Olson story, Barrett McGurn, the Supreme Court's press official, read the short *Post* story, which was published on a Saturday morning. He then attempted to call UPI President Roderick W. Beaton in New York to protest the story that seemed imminent. Although McGurn did not reach him, Beaton eventually heard about the call and sent word to McGurn that this was an editorial matter for Washington to judge.

On Saturday afternoon, after Dillman completed reviewing the Olson story, he called McGurn and told him that UPI had the document but had been unable to determine whether it was actually a Supreme Court document. Dillman said there would be no UPI story. Dillman also said:

> Anticipating inquiries, I drafted a three-line statement repeating what I had told McGurn. Both the *Post* and the *Washington Star* obtained it. The Sunday *Post* ran a brief story limited to the statement. Lyle Denniston wrote in the *Star* that "a new 'leak' at the Supreme Court may add fuel to an intensifying dispute between the Court and news reporters who cover it."
>
> Denniston also raised a question: In view of McGurn's calls, did UPI bow to pressure in deciding not to run a story?

"Absolutely not," I replied, pointing out that the decision was made before I talked to McGurn.

The following Monday, 8 June, the Court handed down the decision. The dissent was identical to UPI's document.

Almost from the beginning of the Supreme Court, inaccurate reporting and misinterpretation of the Court decisions by the press were serious problems. In 1819, for example, several newspapers printed an erroneous account of the Court's ruling on a challenge to the constitutionality of a New York State bankruptcy law. Because no federal law governed bankruptcy at the time, the issues in the case were critically important to businessmen as well as to ordinary citizens. The Court invalidated the state law, insofar as it enabled a debtor to free himself from a debt that had been contracted before the statute went into effect. But the first newspaper accounts of the confused opinion reported that the Court had held that states had no right to pass bankruptcy laws generally.

"This opinion has given much alarm to many persons," the *Niles Register,* a newspaper of Baltimore, announced. According to a New York paper, the inaccurate version "caused a very considerable sensation in the city, and we do not wonder at it." Another Baltimore paper reported that "nothing but the publication of the entire opinion can possibly allay the fermentation that is excited." Nearly two weeks after the decision, an accurate story was printed in another newspaper, and the furor began to subside. For several weeks, the full text of the opinion of the Court in the case, *Sturges* v. *Crowninshield,* was not published. At the same time, a period of economic distress in the nation compounded problems that were created by the first mistake.

The principal characteristic of press coverage of the Court during its first years was political partisanship. The parties—the Federalists or the Republicans during the first years, later the Jacksonian Democrats or the Whigs—were closely allied with many of the newspapers. The newspapers' accounts leaned this way and that, according to the party they favored. In reporting arguments before the Court by famous lawyers or in presenting the facts behind a controversial decision, objectivity was not the style of the time. The newspaper correspondents, the staffs, or the publishers seemed to feel little restraint in publishing the most virulent attacks on the Supreme Court and on its decisions.

The dream of every Supreme Court reporter—having an informant actually on the bench—was realized at least once. Nearly two weeks before the Supreme Court gave its decision in the *Wheeling Bridge Case* in 1852, the *New York Tribune* reported that the majority opinion would require removal or elevation of a bridge across the Ohio River because it interfered with interstate commerce. The *Tribune* story later proved accurate.

Later in 1852, the *Tribune* provided its readers with a running account of the Supreme Court's secret discussions of the controversial *Dred Scott* case. Observing that the *Tribune* "seems to have had a trustworthy pipeline to the Supreme Court," Carl Swisher wrote that the paper was "well served by its new source—from the nature of the comment apparently one of the dissenting justices." One of the two dissenting justices was Justice John McLean, who sympathized with the *Tribune*'s antislavery position.

The Supreme Court did not play a major part in governing the country during the first thirty years of the 20th century. As a result, the Court received little attention from the newspapers and magazines. With the beginning of the depression, when President Franklin Roosevelt persuaded Congress that government action was necessary in the nation's economic and social affairs, the legal challenges posed to the resulting legislation focused a strong spotlight on the justices and their work. As U.S. citizens realized that the New Deal hung on the responses of the Court, press coverage broadened and deepened.

The clash between the executive branch and the Supreme Court spelled good news for the media at the time. The relatively conservative Court, which had been almost unseen during the terms of Presidents Calvin Coolidge and Herbert Hoover, made its decisions news by consistently finding the New Deal laws unconstitutional. The president then launched an unprecedented attack against the Supreme Court. Roosevelt proposed that the Court be enlarged, with the expectation that his appointees would shift its philosophical stance. The controversy that followed turned Supreme Court reporters into combat correspondents. The justices, who were completely unused to such an adversary role, tried to defend their Court. They were upheld by the editorial pages around the nation, which printed fuming articles charging that Roosevelt was running roughshod over the Constitution. Nonetheless, the Court changed its mind and began upholding New Deal legislation. For the Supreme Court correspondents and the nascent columnists, it was a journalistic field day.

Since 1953, the Supreme Court has made news more consistently than at any other time. Under Chief Justice Earl Warren, the Supreme Court became a strong engine of government and social change in a way it rarely had been before. The sixteen years of the Warren Court made news that tested the press's journalistic ability: the end of public school and other institutionalized racial segregation; the requirement that members of Congress and both houses of all state legislatures be elected from districts balanced as to population; and many rulings guarding the constitutional rights of criminal defendants against abuse by law enforcement officials.

Because of the sweeping and controversial nature of many of the Warren Court's decisions, the current press coverage has continued to be among the most intensive that the institution has ever received. The Burger Court's decisions on abortion, obscenity, capital punishment, and affirmative action presented as great a challenge to reporters and editorial writers as had the rulings by the previous Court. In addition, the second half of the 20th century had introduced a new dimension to coverage of the Supreme Court: television. Although television cameras were and are barred from the Court (even though admitted experimentally to some lower courts), network news departments began to hire reporters with legal training, and they worked to clarify and to illustrate major Court decisions for the broader audience their new television medium commanded. Newspapers, now more aware of television competition, tended to compress and to analyze the exhaustive coverage given landmark cases of the past. They also followed the example of the networks in seeking out reporters with better legal knowledge to cover the Court's overall activities more thoroughly. As a former *New York Times* Washington bureau chief has remarked, the lawyer-reporters have brought "a dimension of expertise that the non-lawyer-reporter simply doesn't have."

For example, consider the case of John Connally. Over the years, a silent battle has developed between the trial reporters and the lower courts. Moving ponderously, the courts have attempted to close off the media. In the case of Connally—former secretary of the Navy, governor of Texas, longtime friend and protégé of Lyndon Johnson and Richard Nixon—the courts won. Connally was charged with accepting a bribe from lobbyist Jake Jacobsen. When Con-

nally's case was ended, all the news media announced, "CON-
NALLY ACQUITTED." Even the more deliberate magazines,
such as *Time,* writing for its five million subscribers, had the same
story. It developed a full-page report headed, "Big John Connally
Acquitted." As the three-column article paid homage to Connally,
nothing hinted that anything was amiss. In the 21 June 1975 issue of
The New Republic, however, an article entitled "The Secret Trial of
John Connally" showed vividly how the courts had been fighting
with the Other Government to maintain their authority. The article
charged that:

- On 31 March 1971, Connally, then secretary of the Treasury,
  promised to give President Nixon discretion over "a very
  substantial allocation of oil in Texas."
- Milk lobbyist Jake Jacobsen once offered to give criminal
  evidence against former President Lyndon Johnson, but
  Attorney General John Mitchell ordered his staff not to
  pursue the matter.

Until *The New Republic* published this article, *no one* had
reported either of these charges. There were two Connally trials.
One took place in open court, closely covered by scores of
journalists, and one took place secretly in the chambers of Chief
Judge George L. Hart, Jr. There, Connally's attorney, Edward
Bennett Williams, and Special Prosecutor Henry Ruth argued the
charge that Connally promised Nixon control over a substantial
amount of oil in Texas. In nearly every argument, Williams won. For
example, he complained about the predominantly black juries in the
District of Columbia. And the prosecutor, Ruth, was not allowed to
comment on such arguments to the news media. Williams asked the
judge to put a total gag order on the prosecutor's office. Judge Hart
agreed, observing that the press has "had a license to lie . . . and
they use it frequently."

Special Prosecutor Ruth told his staff: "In response to Chief Judge
Hart's command, I am conveying to you his order that no member of
this staff speak in any way to any member of the media about any
aspect of the John Connally trial." The result was that nothing
appeared about the secret trial until *The New Republic* article was
published several weeks later. Most of the public is convinced that
John Connally had a fair trial and was acquitted and that is thanks to
Time, the networks, the many members of the Associated Press and

the clients of United Press International: magazines, newspapers, and the broadcast stations. Only the 70,000 subscribers of *The New Republic* have had anything like a chance to judge Connally in another light.

Legal action during the long forty years between Walter Lippmann's observation about public and private trials and Connally's secret trial makes it seem as though the courts and the media have been dancing a very intricate and symmetrical minuet. The courts move to secret trials. The media, stalemated, decide to employ attorneys as reporters. CBS News reporter Fred Graham, who wrote "The Secret Trial of John Connally" for *The New Republic,* is himself an attorney and is thus better qualified to cope with the courts than are most reporters.

But the dance has not ended there. When Graham filed a request, under the Freedom of Information Act, for the text of the gag order that the court had placed on the special prosecutor's staff, he found that Judge Hart had instructed the prosecutors to delay their compliance with the text for as long as the law allows. As Judge Hart observed, "If you put it off for the maximum length of time, I think the case will be over, and who cares?"

For nearly two hundred years, Washington news correspondents generally understood and respected the Supreme Court's need for a pool of silence, beyond the reach of journalism, to make its decisions. The post-Watergate era and one of the Watergate hero-reporters, Robert Woodward, changed this tradition when he and Scott Armstrong, also of the *Washington Post,* published *The Brethren* in 1979. In that book, the authors revealed, for the first time, how the Court worked, including rather intimate biographical information about each of the justices who served on the Court between 1969 and 1976. The chief victim of *The Brethren* is Chief Justice Warren E. Burger. The book begins with a statement Burger made about the Supreme Court in September 1968, eight months before he was appointed chief justice: "A court which is final and unreviewable needs more careful scrutiny than any other. Unreviewable power is the most likely to engage in dispassionate self-analysis. . . . In a country like ours, no public institution, or the people who operate it can be above public debate."

The news correspondents who applauded these words were no doubt surprised when, in 1970, the new Chief Justice Burger refused to allow television cameras to cover his public appearances and turned away almost all reporters' questions and requests for interviews.

The focus of Woodward and Armstrong's book was not so much Burger's obsession with privacy and secrecy as it was his opinions and his managerial failures as the presiding officer of the Court. For example, when Burger wrote an opinion in 1969 about desegregation in the schools, Justice Potter Stewart complained that the draft read like a press release from the Nixon administration. It was a confused, rambling document, listing all the administrative problems involved in desegregation, lauding the Department of Health, Education and Welfare, and flattering the administration.

Moreover, *The Brethren* revealed that unless Burger could get at least one other justice to go along with his views, he always moved to the center, joining the most conservative written opinion. A number of the clerks of the other justices worked out a theory of the chief justice's jurisprudence: Burger would never be alone in dissent. "Always to the right, but never alone," the clerks said. Not until Burger had been on the Court for nearly two years and had voted on many cases did he vote alone in dissent.

Early in 1980, Fred Graham of CBS said in a speech that Justice William J. Brennan (who, like the other justices, has read *The Brethren)*, had warned that unless the press toned down its rhetoric, it might find itself stranded in "shrill and impotent isolation." Graham warned his audience about the cumulative impact of a series of actions by the Burger Court. "Even at this point," Graham emphasized, "there are signs that it has caused a dangerous erosion of this nation's unique heritage of press independence." Graham then cited this checklist:

- The Court has ruled that reporters may be subpoenaed before grand juries and sent to jail if they refuse to disclose their sources.
- The Court has let stand a lower court's imprisonment of a reporter for forty-six days for refusing to obey a fishing expedition subpoena filed by a defendant in a criminal case.
- The Court has permitted lower courts in libel cases to order defendant journalists either to go to jail or to suffer huge default judgments for refusing to reveal their sources.

- The Court has ruled that police armed with search warrants may raid newsrooms for confidential information.
- The Court has let stand a lower court's ruling that law enforcement officials may secretly subpoena journalists' telephone toll records in efforts to discover their sources.
- The Court has ruled that journalists sued for libel may be placed under oath and questioned about the inner thoughts and discussions of the editorial process.
- The Court has held that pretrial criminal hearings may be routinely closed to the press.
- The Court has ruled that journalists' constitutional defenses should be narrowed in libel suits brought by newsworthy private citizens.

Although most of the lawyers who heard Graham speak seemed to think highly of what he said, the same lawyers were disapproving of the 467-page exposé, *The Brethren*. But most of the correspondents who read *The Brethren* loudly applauded the authors. For the first time, they now understood what was going on in the Supreme Court chambers. Again, for the first time, the Supreme Court was revealed as a body of men who don their judicial robes one sleeve at a time.

6

Government Flacks

*I*f you talk for as much as ten minutes with a Washington correspondent, it is almost inevitable that he or she will make some comment, usually uncomplimentary, about the federal executive's own press people—the public relations representatives derisively known as "flacks." These staff officers serve on the front lines in the government's efforts to control or at least to outmaneuver the information-gathering strategies of the Other Government. Consequently, the executive press reps are not much loved by Washington correspondents.

Still, the often-bitter frictions between the two groups are rather surprising, as the federal government's public relations people are almost always recruited from the ranks of the Washington press corps. Moreover, the press representatives for government agencies play an essential, a fundamental role in the Washington economy of information. So what is the problem? Perhaps we can begin to answer that question by visiting one of the flacks, Matthew Cooney, who is deputy director of public affairs for the Department of Commerce. He was previously a Washington correspondent for Westinghouse Broadcasting.

The old commerce building is a comfortable one, baroque and homey. It makes the new structures in Washington—the new Health and Human Services Building, for a horrible example—look like the inside of an intestine after a heavy fiber feed. The upper-floor offices of Commerce seem even more hospitable because of the plants hanging in most of the windows. And, of course, there's leather everywhere, which adds immensely to the clubby, elegantly comfortable ambiance of the building. (The fact is, there must be more leather on wooden legs in Washington offices than on the hoof at the entire King Ranch in Texas. If one has a sardonic sense of the world, one cannot help imagining all of this Washington furniture richly upholstered with the skins of American taxpayers.)

Today, Matthew Cooney is in a hurry. One gets the impression that he usually is. With his small frame, thinning black hair, and luxuriant mustache, Cooney looks a little like Groucho Marx as he bounds through one door and backs out another, talking, always talking. On the wall beside Cooney's impressively big desk are framed photographs of Cooney with dignitaries, or of dignitaries who have signed their pictures "To Matt." One of the frames holds an original sketch of the Watergate hearings by a CBS sketch artist. Cooney had covered the proceedings for the Group W (Westinghouse) stations.

Cooney and the thirty-two people who work for him are responsible for gathering and disseminating information from and about the U.S. Department of Commerce. There are 38,000 employees in the department, divided almost equally into two independent branches, each of which has its own public information section. Cooney's office, the Office of Communication, monitors the entire Department of Commerce organization. The other public information agencies coordinate their releases through Cooncy's office: "We review everything that comes out through the secretary," Cooney emphasizes. "If one of the agencies has something, they get in touch with us."

Cooney says much of the work is routine: "The economic information is the most important. We're required to put out the gross national product statistics, housing starts, trade figures, and so forth. These data are more or less standardized in form. They really are the most important things to come out of this place."

In addition to the statistical releases, the Office of Communication puts out a steady stream of answers to correspondent queries. The public information employees can refer the correspondent to the proper authority, or they can gather answers and funnel the information to the correspondent. Cooney's assistants usually try to refer the correspondent to a "substance person" (someone working on a problem) whenever possible: "Having been a reporter on the outside, and knowing what you feel like when you're referred to two-dozen people, we'll take the name and number and say we'll get back to them."

Cooney's public information staff does not routinely monitor what the departmental "source people" (people who know something newsworthy because of their jobs) tell news correspondents. But, Cooney adds: "Obviously, if something sensitive comes up, the person will usually contact public affairs. There's no requirement that that be done, though." Cooney also notes that his staff does not include an "internal reporter," who would have the task of probing the Department of Commerce for information that news correspondents might find interesting. Cooney is thinking of hiring such a reporter, however. As things stand, ideas for feature-oriented releases must filter their way up through the ranks of the department. Obviously, many good ideas never make it.

How many releases and "actualities" (taped press releases for radio) are produced each week by Cooney's office? "We put out forty-five or fifty releases a week, mostly statistics. And we put out twelve to fourteen actualities a week. They're networked by calling the networks and the radio wire services and making the tapes available by telephone. Sometimes they take actualities; sometimes they don't."

When Richard Nixon was in office, Republican congressmen always seemed to get the word about a big grant from an executive department several hours ahead of their Democratic colleagues. When the Democrats held the presidency, were Democratic members of Congress informed first about Department of Commerce grants? Cooney pauses thoughtfully at this question. He speaks carefully. "The policy is that we make the information available to the congressional delegations at approximately the same time. Sometimes, one will get it before another."

So politics cannot really be separated from government in the dissemination of information? "Everything you do is political. It has to do with the flow of power," Cooney says. "[But] we try not to be political."

Why are Washington reporters generally so critical of what they call "flacks"? Cooney shrugs: "The reasons are as varied as the individuals." He notes, however, that of thirty-two employees in his communications office, only eighteen could be described as "professionals" in their attitudes and work habits. About 90% of them have had some experience as journalists. Cooney says that the need for "a challenge and the need for a higher income are the chief reasons for the switch from journalism." A *challenge* for those journalists who type out statistics from some officials who have figured them out? He shrugs again.

Cooney thinks Washington needs more reporters, but he's not sure how many it would take to do the job. He says he's surprised that the major newspapers and networks don't have full-time reporters working agencies as large as the Department of Commerce: "We find the major newspapers will come by every so often, especially when they see some conflict," Cooney says. "That's not necessarily bad, either. Inevitably, that's what is news." But Cooney holds that not nearly enough investigative reporting goes on:

> There is far too little sleeves-up investigative reporting at the agency level—especially by the networks, where the crews and reporters spend most of their time racing to news conferences. Mob journalism isn't necessarily bad, particularly at the presidential level. Every local news medium wants its people there. The problem is that reporters seldom follow up leads that surface in news conferences. One reason this is not done— especially by the television networks—is that investigative reporting often yields non-stories. A lot of information is harvested, but not much is used, and that is not profitable.

Like most Washington journalists and publicists, Cooney is skeptical about stories of wily politicians manipulating reporters: "It's my view that, if you have information that's newsworthy, you get a story. I used to read about Nixon's people conspiring to manipulate the press, but I never ran into it personally."

This doesn't mean that friendships won't affect the source-reporter relationship: "If a cabinet officer knows a particular correspondent and has had a relationship with that person in the past, he would want to make sure that person gets in on the story. If that's currying favor, I don't know how you'd avoid it." Cooney insists, however, that his staff give every reporter the same access to information. Playing favorites is no way to run an effective public information office.

Does Cooney devote much of his time to the cultivation of the Department of Commerce secretary's image? Not on the standard-ized statistical stuff, he says, but policy and feature releases are another matter: "We obviously think about how we can cultivate a positive impression of the Cabinet officer for whom we work. And when we are making policy judgments as to what kinds of things we want to attach her name to in terms of announcements, that is a consideration."

Cooney considers himself a professional, however, which to him means that these considerations must be balanced by the need to be fair and accurate: "It's also true that we work not only for the secretary, but that we are the top public affairs people in the department, with the responsibility to make sure that information is made available. It may be negative. It's a creative balance, if you will. There is a tension there that is at work all the time. We have *two* clients. Although it's a paradox, we try to treat both fairly and honestly." The two clients Cooney refers to are, clearly enough, the press (and the public, by extension), on the one hand, and the secretary of commerce, on the other.

This division of loyalties is even more intense and more paradoxical for the person who serves as the presidential press secretary. The career of Jerold ter Horst, President Gerald Ford's first press secretary, is instructive. As Washington correspondent for the *Detroit News,* ter Horst knew Michigan Congressman Jerry Ford very well. Ter Horst also knew the presidency well; he had covered the White House for sixteen years. When he was appointed press secretary by President Ford, ter Horst expected to become an honest secretary for an honest president. Ter Horst served for almost a month, then learned after the fact that President Ford had granted "a full, free, and absolute pardon" to Richard Nixon. Ter Horst resigned.

Some Washington correspondents claimed that ter Horst had quit primarily because "he was being kept in the dark about White House decisions" and because "he had been misled by high administration officials on a number of different matters, and that this caused him to issue misleading statements to the news media." But some reporters have said that it was not the handling of information that precipitated ter Horst's resignation, but the pardon itself. Ter Horst said: "I knew that giving a pardon in advance of any confession or accusation of a crime flew in the face of the Constitution. . . . Critics have said I turned my back on the president at a time when he needed me most. But I would have made his problem worse in the long run by trying to defend something I could not possibly defend. An act of mercy to me just represented an act of favoritism."

Ter Horst's situation points up the fundamental dilemma faced by any presidential press secretary of good conscience. How closely must the press secretary's views mirror the president's? What does the press secretary do when his views are not a reflection of the president's? How far should he go to put the best face on the president's words and actions? Does he owe the public an obligation to deliver at least the nearly unvarnished truth? Ter Horst believed that the primary allegiance of the press secretary must be to the president and that a press secretary is necessarily a presidential image maker. "But," ter Horst explained, "in order to do that you must pretty much believe in what you're doing. I couldn't be an image maker to the extent of pretending a problem didn't exist when it did."

When Ron Nessen succeeded ter Horst as presidential press secretary, he left a position as Washington news correspondent for NBC television. Why did he take a job for the official government? Even though he was working for the most powerful medium in the Other Government, Nessen felt constricted, as do most television news correspondents, by the limitations of air time. Television correspondents must attempt to explain most news stories in fifty-five seconds or, for the "big story," in one minute and fourteen seconds. That camera time represents about seven sentences. All responsible television reporters are frustrated, even embarrassed, by the superficiality of television news. They are also frustrated by the limited personal exposure for most television correspondents in Washington. A network bureau may employ two dozen correspondents, who must compete for stories and air time, often working ten to twelve hours a day for weeks and never getting on the air. A presidential press secretary is on the air often, probably more often than even the most ambitious would wish.

Most incoming press secretaries, are well aware of the compromises involved in joining with the official government, but none of them anticipate how far they will have to go in "adjusting" the truth. When reporters become flacks, they soon learn, usually to their surprise, that they must serve not The Truth, but a Higher Truth.

To portray what happens to a reporter-turned-flack, Ron Nessen, no longer presidential press secretary, and Lou Cannon, a correspondent for the *Washington Post,* put on a "demonstration" in 1977 before two hundred journalists in a San Francisco hotel. Very few of the spectator journalists had ever been in Washington. Nessen played the press secretary and Cannon took the roles of many of the Washington correspondents. Even with the laughs from the audience, they re-created the daily briefings astonishingly well.

*

CANNON: The first example we are going to comment on represents these sorts of annotated briefings, as we call them. I'm not sure of the year, but there was a time when we had learned that President Ford was going to play golf in Florida. It went like this.

> PRESS: Is the president going to be playing golf with Jackie Gleason?
> NESSEN: I think that you know we announced the president is attending one of those public forums around the country. One of them has been scheduled for Fort Lauderdale, where various members of the public and community leaders come and ask questions. Whether there is going to be any time to play any golf or not while he is down there, I really can't tell you right now.
> PRESS: Ron, it was reported that the president wrote a letter last fall, accepting an invitation to play golf. Of course, the forum has been scheduled since then.
> NESSEN: Well, I don't go through every letter that comes in. As you know, a lot of invitations come in from people. I think, in this case, what you may be referring to is probably the standard answer; if he can fit the event into his schedule, he probably would like to.
> PRESS: Isn't it a fact, Ron, that the only reason that forum is scheduled at all is to give the president a cover for playing golf?
> NESSEN: Look, Lou, I think that I have answered your questions. The answer is that the president is going to Florida to take part in a long-scheduled public forum, and if there is time, he would like to try to play golf.

CANNON: And that was very close to what actually took place in the White House. Perhaps you would like to tell us your memory of that.

NESSEN: That is horrifyingly close to the briefing. I guess that Lou and I agree that this episode may have been in the spring of 1975. It was about as close as I ever came to not telling the truth at briefings. It sounds so terrible because it was such a minor issue. All I can say at this late date is that it was based on what I think on my part was oversensitivity. Instead of coming right out and saying that the president liked to play golf and he had accepted an invitation to play golf in Florida while he was there, we would see if we could work up some other event.

But I guess that confession is good for the soul, so I am confessing that that is really over the line to not telling the truth.

CANNON: He is paraphrasing Sam Ervin, who, after watching the David Frost show, said, "Partial confession." But I will not grovel.

. . . The next example occurred in 1975 or early 1976. There was a report in *Newsweek,* exclusively, that the president was not going to run again. And, of course, we wanted to know about this.

> PRESS: Ron, there was a story in *Newsweek* today that says the president has decided that he is not going to run again. We would surely like the White House response to that story.
>
> NESSEN: You can quote me as saying that that story is totally untrue. In fact, there are some people on the White House staff who use stronger language than that. If you have a family newspaper, you can quote me as saying that that is totally untrue, the *Newsweek* story that the president will not run for reelection.
>
> PRESS: Are you suggesting that *Newsweek* just made this story up?
>
> NESSEN: I haven't any idea what their source is, and I don't have any idea what the motive for that story was.
>
> PRESS: Do you think it is a plot by Ronald Reagan people or by the people who are supporting Reagan to discredit the president?
>
> NESSEN: If you want to, you can quote me as saying that some people in the White House believe it is an effort to sabotage the Ford campaign.
>
> PRESS: Do you absolutely rule out the fact that Ford might not run again?
>
> NESSEN: Well, I hate those questions that ask, "Will you rule out?" because there may be some unforeseen circumstances. Right now, his present plans are to run for election.
>
> PRESS: You sure left the door wide open, Ron.

NESSEN: Well, that was pretty much how the questioning went. I guess it was on a Monday that the *Newsweek* article came out. The fact is that *Newsweek* had called the White House on Saturday. In fact, the White House reporter came to see me on Saturday to tell me that his story was running and to get our reaction. I, and Dick Chaney, who was at that time the president's chief of staff, and the president spent a great deal of that day issuing unequivocal denials of the *Newsweek* article. *Newsweek* changed the wording slightly, but ran the story.

As subsequent history has proved, it was a bad story. I think the point that Lou and I wanted to illustrate here was that once a story like that floats out in a journal like *Newsweek,* it is very difficult to erase doubt completely. Maybe there is some element of truth in it. I believe that this is partly a legacy of the Watergate/Vietnam period. Reporters up until then were perhaps willing to give the benefit of the doubt. The things that they never thought could happen—that they never thought could be true about their government and their government officials—were true. Consequently, it has affected, I think, the atmosphere in Washington. Nobody is really ready to dismiss any idea, no matter how far-fetched, including the one *Newsweek* wrote about, that he wasn't going to run again, but he was going to go through the charade of being in the primaries, and even go right up to the convention before announcing that he would not run again.

I think in conclusion, my point of view, I always found it very difficult to answer honestly questions that began, "Can you rule out?" In the real world there are very few things that you can completely rule out as never, ever, under any circumstances, happening. So if you want to answer that question honestly, you would really have to say, no. There may be a one-in-a-million chance that I can't rule out.

In the shortening of the headlines and leads that often get translated, as in Lou's final comment, "You certainly left the door wide open," it would have been a perfectly legitimate headline. That was the question that I often had trouble with. You want to knock down the story completely, but you then have to violate, I think, my understanding that far-fetched things can come true. If I said I would completely rule out that the president would drop out of the race, I would be really dishonest. You can't ever completely rule out anything.

CANNON: Would you like to give us the background of this third episode?

NESSEN: This was an episode that happened in the spring of 1976. It was a day when there were several news developments, I thought. The day after the president had been on a trip to Hartford, Conn., as he was leaving the hotel on the way to the airport, his limousine was

struck at an intersection (two or three blocks from the hotel) by a car
crossing the intersection, which had not been blocked off by the local
police. At my briefing the next morning, I began with this statement:
"Today, as you know, a few hours ago, the Commerce Department
announced the gross national product of the United States in the first
three months of this year went up by 10%. That is a sizeable growth
of the national product, and I would like to tell you the White
House's reaction to that news."

> CANNON: Are you now taking questions? I want to know if there
> were any seat belts?
> NESSEN: Lou, I'm trying to tell you what the White House
> thinks of this important economic development. If you have any
> questions about the accident last night, I suggest that you check
> with the Secret Service.
> CANNON: We called them, and they are not returning their calls,
> Ron. We have a few things that we would like to know. Were
> the seat belts buckled? There were seat belts?
> NESSEN: I'd like to try to read you what I prepared here about
> the reaction to the very large increase in the gross national
> product for the first three months of the year.
> CANNON: There was one report, Ron, that there weren't any
> seat belts. You know the president of the United States doesn't
> just get hit by a car any day.
> NESSEN: All of the details about his protection are handled by
> the Secret Service. They have a press office there. I suggest that
> you check with them. Now, the present economic advisors feel
> that the important thing about this growth increase in the first
> quarter was . . .
> CANNON: Are you now answering questions? I'd like to know
> who pays for the insurance? We would like to have a few basic
> facts.
> NESSEN: Lou, if I had any basic facts to give you, I would give
> them to you. But all the details about the president's limousine
> and how it is paid for, insurance, and the seat belt, are handled
> by the Secret Service, and you ought to call Jack Warner over
> there.
> CANNON: Well, we have called Jack Warner, but we would like
> to get a reply from the White House why that intersection
> wasn't blocked off. If you are willing to tell us.

NESSEN: That will give you an idea pretty closely approximating
the actual exchange that morning that we were talking about. It
demonstrated to me the problem that I encountered often in my
briefings, and that is the concentration that I felt and still feel, the

concentration on trivia, to the exclusion (sometimes at least) of the serious news.

The country was coming out of a very deep economic recession. The fact that the gross national product had gone up 10% was a major news story that day. President Ford often felt the same way. And I often walked back to the office with him after his news conferences, and he would frequently comment, "Why wasn't I asked about this?" or, "Why weren't the questions tougher on that subject?"

On looking back, I think the primary example of a serious and complex subject that came up at my time at the White House that was trivialized by the coverage, had to do with President Ford's energy program. This energy program was announced in a fireside chat in the library of the White House, on 15 January 1975. Afterward, the reporters were let into the library, to take pictures and ask questions.

The president had just unveiled his complex, thirty-one-point energy program, and there were only two questions from the press. Helen Thomas asked why the president had decided to do the broadcast in the library, and Gaylord Shaw asked how the president liked using a teleprompter.

It seemed to me that the coverage of the president's energy program, which is a complex subject, was trivialized and over-simplified, and really concentrated almost entirely on a single emotional situation, "How much are gasoline prices going up?" I have a sense of that as I watch the Carter administration attempting to obtain a serious coverage of *its* energy program. I sense that there is a trivialization there, too, in a concentration on a single emotional subject of how much our gasoline taxes are going to go up.

[This is] like the one that we demonstrated to you, where an increase in the gross national product is ignored and the seat belts in the back of the limousine are concentrated on. This springs from two reasons: One, I think that there is a lack of experts covering the White House. The White House reporters, by and large, are generalists; they very often don't know the right question to ask. And I certainly think that was true with the energy program and perhaps the day that Lou and I just illustrated to you.

Also, a second reason, it seems to me, is a lack of newspaper space and television and radio air time. It is difficult to deal with a thirty-one-point energy program in a thirty-second radio spot. Or even in a minute-and-fifteen-second television spot. Consequently, there does have to be simplification and oversimplification. Sometimes there does have to be simply a shrug, and the simplification and oversimplification.

There are people in Washington who believe that trivialization of the news comes from the fact that the country and the professional journalists have been through ten or fifteen traumatic years in which the news has been traumatic. Assassinations of our leaders, an unpopular war, a scandal at the highest level of government, and the resignation of a president. Really, there is a kind of a recoil from any more serious trauma, and both reporters on the one hand and viewers and readers on the other hand, are seeking escape in trivia. It is not only my own idea, but what others have suggested.

CANNON: We just struggled through three examples [of problems in executive-media relations]. The problem with White House briefings—and our re-creation cannot be completely faithful—is that there are different people there with different legitimate purposes. Sometimes a digressive law operates in the briefings; the bad questions drive out the good. Often, you get kind of a shrill and inconclusive situation, where the press secretary has his wits about him, is very much in control.

What happened in this country—the power was concentrated in the White House; so were the informational functions that were related to it. The White House began announcing things in the Johnson administration, the Nixon administration, that had previously been announced by departments and by agencies. Ron and I were talking about this coming out, and I felt that always when the news was bad, Ron would say, "Why don't you ask the Department of Commerce about that?" When the news was good, the White House wanted to announce it.

I remember that day as rather a good-humor day, because most of the people who wanted to write about the gross national product, or the people who were assigned to write about it, in fact did have that information and did write about it; that was the major story the next day. But you did have some people there who were very frustrated about not being able to get any information out of the Secret Service.

I can recall one wire-service reporter who said (we had asked a series of questions and Ron had given a series of these nonanswers), "That is not funny, Ron!" And it wasn't, to her, because that was the story that she was assigned to write.

NESSEN: President Ford made a trip to China, and other places in the Far East at the end of 1975. There was, frankly, a good deal about the lack of information during and after the trip by the press office on the progress of the talks in Peking as they went along.

What Lou and I would like to do for you now is re-create what I believe is a typical exchange that took place during that trip, in my briefing room, which was on the top floor of the hotel. Usually, the briefings were held late at night because of the time difference:

> PRESS: President Ford and the Chinese have been meeting for several hours. Have they made any progress toward further normalization or improvement of relations between the United States and the People's Republic of China?
> NESSEN: Lou, you can quote me as saying that the talks are continuing, in a businesslike and sincere atmosphere.
> PRESS: Well, the Shanghai communiqué was going to be the subject of one of his latest talks. We know there are real obstacles as far as Taiwan is concerned. Are they going to issue something that will be part of the Shanghai communiqué, that will give a further understanding of the relationship between the [People's] Republic of China and the United States?
> NESSEN: I can't at this time tell you whether there will be a communiqué at the conclusion of these talks or not. In the past I have not said that there will be, or that there won't be. I don't want you to take this statement today to mean that there has been a decision one way or another. I just don't know.
> PRESS: As you do know, Ron, there are a number of people writing that the talks have failed, and there is a kind of a showcase thing to bail out a couple of leaders of two countries who were rather shaky, and it seems to me that you are confirming it. Are you saying that the talks have failed?
> NESSEN: I'm saying that the talks are continuing in a businesslike and sincere atmosphere. If you want a little more, I can tell you that this afternoon's meeting was for three hours and nineteen minutes. The two sides have met in the great hall of the people. The table was about twenty feet long and black lacquer. The representatives sat on one side. It was fairly warm in the room, and they took off their suit jackets and met in their shirt sleeves. Bottles were on the table.
> PRESS: Now we are out here—we have come a long way. We are kind of captives here in the hotel. We are getting less from you than we are getting from the officials from the other groups— from the officials of China.

NESSEN: All I can say is that the talks are continuing in a sincere atmosphere.

NESSEN: Well, I think that is a very accurate depiction of what happened in Peking. That little re-creation demonstrates a couple of things. I guess the main point of that is, on occasion the necessities of foreign policy outweigh the necessities of full and open press conferences. It was decided on that trip that if the talks were going to have any chance of success, any chance of improving relations between the United States and the People's Republic, then they needed to be conducted without daily reports of progress or lack of progress. As you can see quite clearly, we did issue very ambiguous statements in Peking and in the next ride to the next stop, which was Jakarta.

Let me take that a step further, and go into a subject that you and I have discussed a great deal. That is the fact that my experience in life was that information about foreign policy was handled really quite differently from information about domestic policy. It's really only a reflection of the fact that the foreign-policy decisions are handled differently in the White House. The number of people who have asked for opinions and advice is smaller. In my opinion, some issues that are called foreign-policy issues have a very large domestic component to them. I can think of a number of occasions when, say, the congressional liaison office, the press office, the people who govern politics, people with the special interest groups, have been asked for an opinion or a view, instead of only the State Department, the Defense Department, the Central Intelligence Agency, and the National Security Council. The decisions would have turned out differently, and perhaps better.

Initially, the controversy was treated as a foreign-policy decision, when in fact those who dealt with the domestic part of the matter should have been asked for an opinion. I think the shortcomings in the handling of foreign-policy information are illustrated by the fact that even the organization for handling foreign-policy information is different. I had a person on my staff, my liaison with the domestic council and the domestic departments and agencies, who went out and soaked up all the information I needed. He represented my interests and the interests of the press, I thought. On the other hand, information about foreign policy was brought to me by a liaison person who was on the staff of the NSC. His interests were the interests of the NSC, not the interests of the press.

When Jody Powell and I had a long transition talk after the election, one of the areas that I pinpointed for him, that I thought he ought to think about, was that particular job. And whether his liaison with foreign policy, national security information should not be on his staff, instead of on the staff of the United States. The fact is that that job is now held by Jerry Schecter, a very good reporter for *Time* magazine. But organizationally it is exactly the way it was with the Ford-Nixon White House. Which is that Jerry Schecter worked for the NSC. And whatever shortcomings that may indicate are being handled organizationally the very same way.

CANNON: I was critical of Ron, to put it mildly, on that China trip. I am very much in agreement with the analysis that he has presented here. It was, in fact, true that for those who were covering that trip, that we were getting reports with more information from the Chinese than was being given out by the White House to American reporters.

Ron has pinpointed something. I quoted him once in the *Columbia Journalism Review* as saying that he was a much better press secretary on domestic policies than he was on foreign policy. I think that the reason that that was essentially true was that he was very dependent upon the information that Henry Kissinger thought ought to be given out to the American people in the area of foreign policy.

Mark Russell, who is a comic in Washington, has said that the title of Dr. Kissinger's book is going to be "Presidents Who Have Known Me." I think that captured a view Kissinger has about what ought to be printed and what shouldn't be printed. Kissinger knew publishers, he knew editors, he had ways of getting his views into print. I don't think that Kissinger was ever covered well or as critically as the president. Now I think that it showed very much at these sorts of critical things, in the different issues that came up, relating to foreign policy—where the White House secretary had really a lot less latitude to speak (I think that that is a fair statement) than he did on domestic affairs.

I think, however, the press shares in having created the conditions under which the period of the presidency that Nixon so abused flourished—we didn't create it, that is giving us too much credit and blame at the same time. But essentially the people that work in Washington and covered Washington during the Johnson and Nixon years were people who grew up in a time, fought in a war that most of us thought was a patriotic war, felt that politics stopped at the water's edge. There was kind of an ethical imperative about foreign policy in which our country was involved, more than there was about domestic policy. I don't think that that point of view served our country very well. It seems to me that not reporting that people were counting dead buffalo instead of dead Vietcong and not reporting what this meant and doing the kind of deceptive things that happened and wound up deceiving, in my point of view, certainly Johnson himself, was very harmful to the kind of understanding the country had.

And while we think we are over that, maybe we are, and yet it still persists in that we are willing to accept a level of noninformation too often about foreign policy that we just plain wouldn't accept about the Jackie Gleason Golf Tournament.

*

If you think after reading this verbatim report that Ron Nessen must have been a nice person who somehow got locked in by something or other, think again. Most of the previous press secretaries could have shrugged off any criticism by saying, that's the price of the game. For example, Bill Moyers, who was the press secretary for Lyndon Johnson, used to tell involved, funny stories about how he outwitted the correspondents. Fifteen years ago, many of the correspondents laughed at Moyers's wily ways. Not any more. Because the correspondents now sense that they are the Other Government, they were enraged by Nessen—just as they were enraged by Jody Powell.

If Cannon had been talking about Nessen when Nessen was absent, it would probably come out about the way Dennis Farney of the *Wall Street Journal* said it in 1975: "Last Friday's briefing found angry reporters calling Nessen a liar, accusing him of a coverup, and after about fifty-five minutes of unproductive questioning, telling him that they didn't want to listen to him any more that day."

7

Investigative Reporting

*B*rit Hume, a reporter who once worked for Washington columnist Jack Anderson, had an experience early in 1972 that illustrates the central problem of the news correspondent in Washington. Hume had acquired a two-page memorandum that he described as "the single most incriminating piece of paper I had ever seen." The memo, dated 25 June 1971, had been written by Dita Beard, a Capitol lobbyist for the International Telephone and Telegraph Company (ITT), and was addressed to W. R. Merriam, head of the Washington office of ITT. In the memo, Beard urged Merriam to use more discretion in discussing the company's pledge of $400,000 to underwrite the 1972 Republican National Convention, which was then scheduled for San Diego. The memo also made it quite clear that the pledge was helping ITT, already one of the largest conglomerates in the world, to negotiate new mergers that had previously been opposed by the federal government.

The Antitrust Division of the U.S. Department of Justice had brought three landmark suits against ITT to prevent the mergers. All three suits were settled in July 1971, a few weeks after Beard's memo. In line with the settlement, ITT was permitted the largest merger in corporate history. Soon thereafter, Richard McLaren, chief of the Antitrust Division, was given a federal judgeship in Chicago. The coincidences certainly seemed suspect, and the Beard memo implicated both President Nixon and Attorney General John Mitchell.

When Brit Hume confronted Mrs. Beard, she admitted writing the memo and even confessed that she herself had worked with

Attorney General Mitchell in drafting the agreement by which ITT got most of what it wanted. But she denied the main point of her own memo: that the ITT pledge to underwrite the Republican convention helped the company win a favorable settlement from the Nixon administration. All the principals in the case, government officials as well as company executives, also denied that point. But as Hume and other reporters broadened their questioning to an ever-widening circle of government officials and ITT executives, the contradictory statements became rampant and incriminating.

As an example of such contradictions, we might consider the role of Richard Kleindienst, the assistant attorney general, who became embroiled in the controversy when he was nominated to succeed Mitchell as attorney general. When the chairman of the Democratic National Committee became suspicious about the settlement of the ITT case in 1971 and inquired at the Department of Justice about it, Kleindienst wrote him a letter saying that the settlement was "handled and negotiated exclusively" by Richard McLaren and his Antitrust Division staff. But when Brit Hume had called Felix Rohatyn, a director of ITT, to ask about Dita Beard's memo, Rohatyn said that he had met with Kleindienst half a dozen times to handle "some of the negotiations and presentations" for the ITT settlement. Jack Anderson's column cited Hume's investigation in accusing Kleindienst of an "outright lie."

Hume and Anderson published column after column reporting their findings and accusing ITT and the Republican administration of striking a mutually beneficial deal. Testifying before the Senate Judiciary Committee, Kleindienst admitted meeting with Rohatyn but denied that he had "influenced the settlement of government antitrust litigation for partisan political reasons." For his part, Rohatyn told the Senate that he had not actually negotiated anything in his meetings with Kleindienst, that he was merely making an economic case for the mergers.

The Senate finally confirmed Kleindienst as attorney general by a vote of 64 to 19. President Richard Nixon eventually resigned in the midst of an even messier web of stalls and lies and obfuscations. But these historic events are less important to our thesis here than the basic questions that haunt anyone who investigates controversy: What and whom should I believe? How should I evaluate the facts?

For example: There is no doubt that a memo from Dita Beard exists, but was the memo accurate in saying that the ITT pledge of money was helping with the company's antitrust merger cases? Or was this memo no more than an instance of self-aggrandizement by Mrs. Beard in an effort to show that her work for the company was effective? Lobbyists often claim to do more than they have done. Was Beard being truthful in her subsequent denial of a connection between the pledge and the settlement?

There is no doubt that Kleindienst wrote a letter saying that he took no part in the ITT negotiations. But was Felix Rohatyn accurate in stating that he had handled "some of the negotiations" with Kleindienst, or did he misstate the nature of those meetings to persuade Brit Hume that *his* work for ITT was effective and that Beard's memo was inaccurate? Did Rohatyn's quite different testimony to the Senate committee accurately describe the meeting with Kleindienst?

Such questions can be multiplied, but even a hundred questions would not show how complicated the central problem really is. The true complexity is suggested by asking whether any reader should believe the account of the ITT case sketched in these pages. Some of the principals would surely argue that it is not accurate, or at least that it misleads, and that the account should have included other bits of evidence.

And what would be the effect on the reader if, instead of describing Anderson as "Washington columnist Jack Anderson," I had described him as "muckraking Washington columnist Jack Anderson"? What if this account had cast doubt on Anderson's credibility by pointing up one of his grievous errors, as when, in 1972, he erroneously reported that Senator Thomas Eagleton, who was then the Democratic nominee for vice president, had been arrested for drunken driving? Introducing such a fact would certainly cause at least a few readers to evaluate this case quite differently.

To evaluate all the relevant facts in the ITT case, one would first weigh the probable truth in the oral and written testimony of the principals, the government officials, and ITT executives and lobbyists; then the probable truth in the accounts of that testimony published by Brit Hume and Jack Anderson; then the probable truth in the account published here; and finally, and not least, the degree to which one's judgments of "probable truth" were themselves affected by one's *own* whims, idiosyncrasies, leanings, biases, and prejudices. Even if one has no political leanings or beliefs because one considers politics a dirty business, that attitude would certainly be pivotal in one's judgments about the principals. If one considers politics a bore—not even worth one's attention—then the opinions expressed by a person one respects are likely to shape one's judgments. In short, evaluation of such issues is bound to be somewhat personal and subjective.

Nonetheless, Kleindienst was guilty. He was allowed to resign on 30 April 1973 during the Watergate mess. The next year, however, Kleindienst pleaded guilty to a misdemeanor charge that he had refused to testify "accurately and fully" before a congressional committee on the ITT antitrust settlement in the Federal District Court in Washington, D.C. He received a suspended sentence on 7 June 1974 on the ITT case.

Investigative reporting sounds dramatic, exciting. It can be. But it also requires persistence, stubbornness, and even a special type of personality; it is difficult, time-consuming work.

The investigative story is a giant step away from the straight news story of the past. And in this area, newspaper correspondents are leagues ahead of their colleagues in television (and probably always will be). Because the television correspondent must be on the air daily, or nearly so, he or she cannot devote the days, weeks, or even months to investigation that a print-media reporter can. Tom Pettit of NBC said that he goes ahead on a story only after he knows that he has the facts, "and that the facts can be filmed." His beginning probes, like those of almost all TV broadcasters, have to include the question of visuals: Is the story the kind that can be translated into moving film? Can it be made understandable within the framework of the medium? For the broadcast reporter, these kinds of questions often mean that the complex, abstract story, such as stock manipulations or real estate frauds, is never pursued. The daily by-line is important to the newspaper correspondent as well, but good investigative reporting, on the other hand, can win prizes and high esteem.

Correspondents disagree about the definition of investigative reporting. For example, Max Frankel, who is now the editorial page editor of *The New York Times,* was the diplomatic correspondent on the *Times* Washington bureau staff headed by James "Scotty" Reston. They had different opinions about what kinds of news were worth digging for. At one point, Reston insisted that Frankel should invest sufficient time and energy to be able to report the identity of the new U.S. ambassador to Moscow three days before the appointment was to be announced officially. Frankel objected, arguing: "Scotty, I can find that out. It's easy. It's going to take me two days. In those two days I might learn something far more substantial, which we would never learn if I didn't invest the two days. But the ambassador to Moscow we will find out by the announcement." Reflecting later on that disagreement, Frankel said: "Is it important? Reston regarded me as insufficiently zealous for feeling that it isn't. Always want to be first, he argued, because vigilance resides in that instinct. He feels that if you get in the habit of waiting for government to tell you *when* it wants to tell you, you're going to lapse on more serious matters."

The eager-adversary approach that Reston promotes should guide journalists in their daily work. Maintaining the sharp edge of vigilance is pivotal to a good reporter and a reputable newspaper. But is a story that unearths the name of the ambassador to Moscow investigative?

Perhaps, depending upon what editor or reporter you ask. One editor proclaims, "All of our reporters are investigative reporters." This is facile, of course, and misleading. Leonard Sellers, professor of journalism at San Francisco University, writes: "The investigative reporter is the one who goes after information that is deliberately hidden because it involves a legal or ethical wrong." Some investigative reporters who have been lost in the semantic swamp of defining their work have responded to this definition with, "That's it! That's it."

By Sellers's definition, investigative reporting is the practice of opening closed doors and closed mouths. Like analysis, investigative reporting focuses on problems, issues, and controversies. In most cases, however, an analytical reporter has little trouble, because he is usually explaining public events and can find many sources who are happy to help him. In fact, one of the chief dangers of most political reporting is that too many sources want to provide too much information that will serve their own interests. In contrast, the investigative reporter tends to walk into a lot of brick walls.

Are the brick walls new? Hardly. Even before the beginning of the United States, one publisher created an adversary role for himself with the government. In 1690, Benjamin Harris produced the first, and only, issue of *Publick Occurrences, Both Forreign and Domestick*. Because some of the "occurrences" were seen as criticism of colonial policy, and because he was not printing "by authority"—that is, he was not licensed by the General Court of Massachusetts—the newspaper was banned. The lesson was not lost on future publishers, and it was not until 1721, with James Franklin's establishment of the *New England Courant,* that a newspaper dared oppose government policy. Franklin, Benjamin's older brother, was the first to indulge in "crusade" journalism, and refused to print "by authority." Unfortunately his crusade was against smallpox inoculation—in retrospect, the wrong side of the issue—but the cause became a rallying point for those fighting the local Puritan leaders. James Franklin ultimately spent some time in jail (not unlike some modern journalists), but in the meantime he had made the singular contribution to American journalism of establishing the principle of printing "without authority."

Clashes with authority have continued throughout the history of journalism, but an organized focus on wrongdoing did not truly begin until the opening of the 20th century; the first decade of the 1900s was the golden age of muckraking.

Muckrakers were a salient force in American journalism from about 1902 to 1912—though there were strong examples of such reporting both before and after that period. The era began with the *McClure's* magazine trio of Lincoln Steffens, Ida M. Tarbell, and Ray Stannard Baker, who started the pattern of what historian Judson Grenier calls the "systematic uncovery of socio-political corruption." Steffens's *Shame of the Cities* and Tarbell's *History of the Standard Oil Company* set the tone for a new literature of exposure. "Early in the century muckrakers had recognized that a sense of uneasiness about the malfunctioning political, economic, and social institutions which had begun to become evident several decades earlier was troubling increasing numbers of Americans," according to journalism researchers John Harrison and Harry Stein. "They found the medium for the message—more precisely, perhaps, the medium found them—in the popular magazines that represented one current manifestation of the communications revolution that had begun at least half a century earlier. An audience was there, and the means of reaching it was at hand. The muckrakers availed themselves of that fortuitous combination."

The label "muckrakers" wasn't pinned on that small group of writers until 1906, when President Theodore Roosevelt, angered at David Graham Phillips's series *The Treason of the Senate,* borrowed the term from *Pilgrim's Progress* and castigated "the writers who raked the muck of society and never looked up." At first upset by the obviously pejorative term, the writers soon took it as a badge of approbation, something to wear proudly. Their conversion of the term has been so complete that Webster now defines the verb "muckrake" as "to seek for, expose, or charge corruption, real or alleged, on the part of public men and corporations."

Carey McWilliams, now-retired editor of *The Nation*, claims there is a cyclical pattern to reform journalism that began in the late 19th century and continues through today. "Ongoing, it seems to disappear at certain times only to surface later," he wrote in 1970, adding that new communications technology and a mood of social concern usually herald an upsurge.

To emphasize McWilliams's point about reform journalism as a cyclical pattern, an episode that involves the women who were covering Eleanor Roosevelt, the wife of President Franklin D. Roosevelt, was *not* an incident of investigative (or reform) journalism. During the Roosevelt administrations, the children of all the members of the Washington press corps were always invited to play with the president's grandchildren at the White House. Moreover, all the women who covered Mrs. Roosevelt's press conferences received flowers from the White House greenhouse when they stayed home with sniffles.

One of the women, Dorothy Roe Lewis, gave this information about the women's warm relationships with Mrs. Roosevelt—which, she said, was matched by the correspondents' friendship with President Roosevelt.

> On March 3, 1933, the day before the inauguration of FDR, I was expecting Mrs. Roosevelt to drive to Washington from New York in her little sports car. That night, at 2 A.M., I was asleep when my telephone rang. Answering the phone, I heard a high-pitched voice saying, "This is Mrs. Roosevelt. Franklin says I can't do that. I have to go with the official procession. I thought you girls would want to know right away." The women and I who would cover her joined the long procession of cars the next day to go to Washington. Mrs. Roosevelt rushed into the hotel room just before joining her husband for the new President's traditional call upon the outgoing President.
>
> "Now girls," she said, "if you'll just wait here, I'll come back and tell you what happened."
>
> She rushed back after an hour, bubbling with excitement, and said: "Oh, girls, I have a wonderful story for you! When we

arrived at the White House, Mr. and Mrs. Hoover were waiting
for us, and Mrs. Hoover poured tea, and we exchanged polite
small talk. But right away Mr. Hoover said to Mr. Roosevelt:
'Will you come into the study with me? I want to have a private
talk.' So they went into the next room, but they forgot to close
the door, and I could hear everything they said!

"Well, Mr. Hoover said to Mr. Roosevelt: 'Will you join me
in signing a joint proclamation tonight, closing all banks?' And
Mr. Roosevelt said to Mr. Hoover: 'Like hell I will! If you
haven't got the guts to do it yourself, I'll wait until I'm President
to do it!' Now, girls, I know you want to get your bulletins out at
once, so I won't keep you."

Mrs. Roosevelt smiled triumphantly, but none of the women
moved. "Why, what's the matter?" she cried out. "I thought
you'd be pleased!"

One of the women responded: "Mrs. Roosevelt, you don't
really want us to print that, do you? Don't you realize what
would happen if that story went out tonight? The New York
Stock Exchange would close. The London Stock Exchange
would close. The country would go off the gold standard. There
would be a worldwide panic. Besides, it's all hearsay. We
couldn't quote either President directly."

She stood there, very near tears, and said: "Oh-h-h! I didn't
think about all that! What are we going to do?"

The women looked at each other, then said: "It's all right,
Mrs. Roosevelt. If you will promise not to tell anyone else about
this, we will promise not to write it."

There they were, representing the most powerful news organizations
in the world: Associated Press, United Press, and International
News Service. None of the women ever wrote the story, or even told
their editors. A few days later, President Roosevelt issued the
proclamation. If Nancy Reagan had acted as Eleanor Roosevelt did,
the woman correspondent who paused would have been knocked
down and wounded by the high heels of the other women reporters
as they rushed to the telephone.

Thinking about what the modern investigative reporters do, what
makes an investigative reporter? What is it that directs an individual
into this abrasive, frustrating, and often drudgery-filled aspect of
journalism?

According to Howard Simons, managing editor of the *Washington
Post,* there is such a thing as an investigative reporter, and the
creature isn't quite normal: "I don't think everyone can be an

investigative reporter. Those dozen or so successful investigative reporters I have known share some common traits, traits unshared by other competent reporters. The singular most important trait is the uncanny knack of linking A to Z to F to Y all by reading Yiddish footnotes or eye movements. Investigative reporters, too, all begin to mimic the persons they are investigating. That is, in my experience, they begin whispering, view the world (even their editors) conspiratorially, and write in turbid fashion."

Simons, whose tongue may or may not have been in his cheek, was at least accurate on one point: not all journalists can or want to be investigative reporters. When Lloyd Lewis of the *Norfolk Ledger-Star* was asked if he was an investigative reporter, he responded, "Wrong pew. I don't mind swatting demagogues, but I'm too soft-hearted to enjoy it. If the fellow isn't downright dangerous to mankind, I'm inclined to be more amused than incensed at his perfidy." Other reporters have acknowledged that they have no desire to become involved in investigations, most claiming that they don't have an "aggressive personality."

The "personality" required for investigative reporting goes beyond aggressiveness. The basic requirement is what William Lambert called "a low threshold of indignation," an ability to get angry. Though it might seem to be a strong term, most investigative reporters suffer from a sense of moral outrage; they do become incensed at perfidy.

When Brit Hume was asked why he had picked investigative reporting as a field, he began his answer with a calm explanation of the public's need to know in a democracy. "The most important thing in journalism is giving the public the information the government least wants it to know," he said. "But to get down a bit from the theoretical, I have always believed that there was more corruption and deception than most people thought. And certainly more than most reporters seem to think.

"That really alarmed me," Hume said, his voice rising. "And I *hate* it. I just hate that kind of thing. Deception and corruption, it just makes me sick. It's depressing. . . . I find it depressing, I find it deeply troubling. I look on it as a decay, a kind of rot that is not simply unattractive, or part of the price we pay for democracy, or anything like that. I regard it as downright *dangerous*." Hume paused for a moment and drew a calming breath. "The rot has to be dug out," he said quietly. "It's a matter of self-interest."

This small band of reporters, those who belong to what Les Whitten called the "spoiled priesthood," usually lives with an odd mixture of aggressiveness and uncertainty. Committed to personal and social standards of morality, they need affirmation of those standards, if not from the public, at least from their editors. "An investigative reporter with editors who will stand behind him," wrote Nicholas Gage of *The New York Times*, "is a happy man."

What satisfactions does the job offer? Are there rewards other than alleviating anger? Keith McKnight listed those he found:

> I have been a general assignment reporter, a beat reporter, copy editor, rewrite man, layout supervisor, telegraph editor, city editor, and managing editor. I'm not interested in being any of those things again. In each one, there seemed to be so many built-in routines or procedures that there was little time left to something creative or worthwhile that wasn't ordinary.
>
> As an investigative reporter, I am free to explore what I please, with (at least in theory) no daily deadlines to worry me. When I report something I can write with authority and not with the fear that my ignorance of the subject will misinform the public and make a fool of me.
>
> There are fewer rewards, of course, because when you have to know what you're talking about you speak less often. But when you do, and you do it well, I suppose investigative reporting isn't much different than other professions in that the reward is the self-satisfaction you get, though others may never recognize it.

Bruce Locklin emphasized the challenge involved: "I'm still doing it because it's the hardest thing I've ever been asked to do. I don't take pleasure from hurting people. I have to force myself to ask hard questions."

The asking of questions may seem to be an easy thing, but in the domain of the investigative reporter it can become a subtle and ingenious tool. The most basic questioning is not to treat the question as a question. That is, the information being sought should be treated as a known fact. The reporter, instead of asking "Did you go to New Orleans last month?" will ask, "Why did you go to New Orleans last month?" As simple as it may sound, it is a productive technique. Instead of giving the subject the option of denying, he is put in the position of explaining. If no such trip was made, the reporter, of course, will quickly be told, but if the point of the question is to get confirmation, it can be easier if the subject is off balance.

In a somewhat more sophisticated version of this technique, the reporter hides what he considers the crucial part of the question at the beginning of the sentence, burying it under a more damaging accusation: "Is it true that when you went to New Orleans last month you spent the weekend on the Sneaky Oil Company yacht?" It is possible that the subject, busy denying or explaining the last part of the question, will unconsciously confirm the first.

An even more elaborate version, one designed to set up the entire interview, is explained by Brit Hume: "It is a common enough technique—you persuade the person you are questioning that you have been told a truly lurid story. In eagerness to disabuse you of it, the person will frequently tell you the truth." One reporter elaborated on why the technique works.

> A good tactic is to accuse the principal figure of something you know he can't possibly be involved in. Usually, in denying your outrageous charge, he will concede the truth. Collection agencies use this angle all the time. If they have trouble getting someone to pay a bill for $100, they'll send him a letter stating he owes $681, which must be paid immediately to avoid court action. This brings (sometimes) the debtor running in to protest that there has been a mistake, that he actually owes $100. Often he's anxious to pay on the spot. Police use similar tactics, accusing a man of deliberate murder when they know it's only manslaughter. Most people would rather tell the truth in such cases than take a chance on facing more serious charges. The same tactic works for me.

Another technique involves the sequence of questions. Jack Anderson has said that he always begins by asking a question to which he already knows the answer. "As the guy begins talking I say, 'Now wait a minute. Court testimony indicates. . . .' That throws him off stride." It often does more than that. It can make the subject uncertain as to how much the reporter does or does not know. If the reporter leads with a series of questions to which he knows the answers, it is sometimes possible to convince the subject that the reporter knows nearly everything, and the subject may become conditioned to giving only accurate answers. Ideally, at this point the reporter begins asking questions to which he *does not* know the answers. And if the reporter is truly Pavlovian, he saves a couple of unnecessary questions to use as reinforcers, making sure the subject is still responding truthfully.

Such interviewing tools are not so elaborate as they might sound, and some reporters use them as easily as raising an eyebrow. Indeed, even raising an eyebrow can help. As Ray Brennan said, "If you indicate you know something and ask a direct question, a man will always answer you, if only briefly. Often if you look expectant after he has finished his answer, he will keep on talking."

Even a single word can make a difference in whether a question successfully elicits information. Alex Dobish of the Milwaukee *Journal* managed to make a deliberate error work for him when, in attempting to get a city clerk to admit he had been involved in a land scheme, he referred to the buyer as the Root River Land Corporation. "He took the bait and announced that it wasn't a corporation but a company—then suddenly knew he had stuck his foot in it."

Unfortunately, the game can be played both ways. When UPI reporter Dan Gilmore was interviewing CIA Director William Colby, his final question concerned a rumor he and other reporters had been looking into. "Was the CIA involved," he said, "in some kind of salvage operation with Howard Hughes in the Atlantic Ocean?"

"That is just not so," Colby said.

Shortly thereafter it was revealed, by other news organizations, that the CIA had been involved in a $350-million effort with the Hughes company to raise a Soviet submarine in the *Pacific Ocean*. There is no way of knowing what Colby's reply would have been had the reporter managed to place the rumor in the right ocean, but Colby is said to have told an aide after the reporter left: "I'm glad he didn't pursue that last question."

Some veteran reporters don't rely so much on questioning as on bluffing—on misleading or on frightening a subject with a bold front. And it is also a handy tool in the reporter's kit bag of techniques. When the investigative reporter runs a bluff, it is usually as a last resort, when the standard digging methods have failed. In its simplest form, the reporter pretends to know something that he does not. But without proper preparation, it can be dangerous. The reporter who exposes his own ignorance has hamstrung himself. Some reporters refuse to use the bluff, while others use it extensively.

"Every reporter bluffs now and then, but it's not a good policy," said Herby Marynell of the *Evansville Press*. "If you are forced to bluff then you must have failed to do enough leg work, if not for documented evidence then for statements from people who know individual parts of the story."

But Peter Benjaminson of the *Detroit Free Press* disagrees. "Bluffing is a must," he said. "Quite often a diligent investigator can discover all but the final link in some train of criminal acts. That last provable link eludes him. At that point, going to the subject and accusing him of performing all the acts, while gliding over the absence of proof that he is connected with the crucial act, will often work. The subject, in his fear and trembling, may not remember how many traces he left and may assume you have all the proof you need and will admit all.

"Quite often, the subjects of an investigation don't want to admit that what they've done is wrong. Bluffing works easily in these cases since after a point the subject is less interested in hiding his actions than in appearing to have disclosed them himself, so that he can argue that he never did anything he thought to be wrong."

There may be an additional reason subjects will talk if they think the reporter already has what he needs. Jack Anderson, in giving advice to one of his staff about dealing with senators, said, "Pretend you know all about whatever they're doing, even if you don't. A lot of those guys don't have any news judgment and they don't know what's a story and what's not."

Anderson himself is a master of that type of manipulation. He explained how he trapped California Senator George Murphy:

> I had learned from a source that Murphy was collecting money from the right-wing millionaire Patrick Frawley, through Frawley's corporation, Technicolor, Inc. I learned this because Murphy had become concerned that he might be in violation of the new Senate code of ethics, so he called on the chairman of the committee, John Stennis, and described the situation in confidence. Secondhand, I got the information. I knew from past experience that Stennis wouldn't tell us anything, so I called Murphy and said, "Senator, I have evidence that you're collecting $20,000 a year from Technicolor, that all or part of your apartment is being paid for by Technicolor and that you use a credit card belonging to Technicolor. I called you as a matter of courtesy to hear your side of the story." Senator Murphy said, "You're wrong. You have been misinformed." I said, "Senator, I like you. I like your personality. I used to

enjoy your movies. Because I like you, I'm going to give you another chance to answer that question. I don't think you want to go on the record with the answer you just gave. So let's do it again." "Yes," he said, "damn it, I am." Of course, I couldn't have printed it without Murphy's confession..

There are, however, different degrees of "confessing," as people who regularly deal with the press are aware. Reporters who are working with uninitiated sources should make clear the standard ground rules for confidentiality and anonymity. They are fairly simple:

On the record: All statements are directly quotable and attributable, by name and by title, to the person who is making the statement. Unless otherwise agreed, all comments are assumed to be on the record.

On background: All statements are directly quotable, but they cannot be attributed by name or by specific title to the person commenting. The type of attribution to be used should be spelled out in advance: a White House official, an administration spokesperson, a government lawyer, or whatever. The kind of attribution to be used has some importance, since sources often worry about how traceable a leak might be.

On deep background: Anything that is said is usable, but not in direct quotation and not for any type of attribution. The reporter is to use the information on his own, without saying it comes from any government department or official. (Reporters normally dislike this type of attribution, since officials often use it to plant stories or to float trial balloons without having to take responsibility.)

Off the record: Information given off the record is for the reporter only and is not to be printed or made public in any way. The information is also not to be taken to another source in hopes of getting it put on the record. It is generally understood that any off-the-record arrangement must be agreed to by the reporter beforehand. (The danger in agreeing to off-the-record information is that the reporter is locked into not using it—even if it is received in another manner from another source—until someone else prints it. Most reporters automatically refuse to accept off-the-record information.)

Even supposedly sophisticated political figures who know the rules well sometimes slip up, and have to be reminded. After Jeb Stuart

Magruder admitted to Bob Woodward that the FBI had questioned him about a secret campaign fund, he added, "That's on background." Woodward told him that he should know better than to try to put something on background after saying it.

"But you've got to help me," Magruder pleaded. "I'll get in trouble if I'm quoted."

Woodward told him he might put *that* statement in the paper, too.

Once contact with a source has been made and the ground rules have been established, a reporter can find it increasingly easy to get information. A worried Hume, fretting about a source, was told by his boss, Jack Anderson, "I've been through this before. Sometimes when someone opens up to you the way she did, a sort of confessor relationship develops and the person will continue to talk to you."

Even the subjects who will talk are not enough; the need for documentation can be crucial, which is the main reason that Bob Walters of the defunct *Washington Star* thinks that the growth in investigative reporting is directly attributable to a machine.

> The single most important development that reporters have taken advantage of has nothing to do with this profession— that's the invention of the Xerox machine. It has done wonders for investigative reporting.
>
> Back in the old days a guy could come to you and say "I know there's a document that says this-and-this." You, as a reporter, knew that it was classified, or administratively confidential, or whatever, and you could never see it.
>
> You always had a terrible time, saying to yourself, "Gee, can I believe this guy? Is it really there?" Maybe, if you were really lucky, somebody would flash the document at you and you could copy off a couple of phrases. And that was it.
>
> Now it's a whole new ball game. We now have available to us great masses of documentation, which for an investigative story is crucial. It's not Party X charging so-and-so, and Party Y saying it's not true and he's innocent. It's on paper and you wave it in Party Y's face and you say "What do you mean? This is your memo and you signed it."
>
> The Xerox has done wonders for us. Any reporter will tell you that one piece of documentation is worth five allegations. And that's my great Xerox theory.

But if the information is the type that cannot be photocopied— eyewitness accounts, for example—the reporter has another protection: affidavits. Affidavits are written statements made under oath, sworn to before a notary public. And anyone making a false affidavit can be punished for perjury. Jack Nelson, the Washington bureau chief of the *Los Angeles Times,* strongly believes in the use of affidavits as a reporting tool.

> I've drawn up hundreds over the years, and they're very important. First, your source can't later say he was misquoted. You really have a legal document, and in all my experience with affidavits no one has ever said "That wasn't what I meant." Second, it strengthens the story. I'll give you an example: When I was with the *Atlanta Constitution* I had an affidavit from an operating room technician who said he had seen a nurse perform major surgery.
>
> Our libel lawyer said it wasn't quite enough to go with, and asked if I could get a member of the medical staff to say, under oath, that he knew the technician and would believe him. I got an affidavit from a doctor to that effect, and we went ahead with the story.
>
> I drew up so many damn affidavits in Atlanta while doing an investigation of state government that people would actually call up and volunteer, saying, "I'll be willing to sign an affidavit." The paper would come out with a story saying, "So-and-so, according to affidavits from five state employees . . ."

Although few of the Washington correspondents use affidavits, many other reporters need identification as members of the press that will open doors closed to the average citizen. When those doors are supposed to be open to anyone in the first place (access to documents that by law are public), denial itself is often a news story. On the other hand, some people, particularly among high levels of government officials, have an instinctive negative reaction to reporters. Identifying oneself as a newsperson can cause some doors to close automatically. Some reporters, then, are allowed by their employers to pose as private citizens, but often only with the stipulation that, if asked, the reporter will reveal who and what he is.

Such rules, of course, have been both bent and broken. One reporter for the *Washington Post,* which requires that its reporters identify themselves, has admitted to fudging a bit. "When necessary," he said, "I go use the telephone in the press room at the State Department. That way I can begin the call with 'Hello, I'm calling from the State Department. . . .'"

Violating an organization rule, however, is not light business. More than one reporter has lost a job that way. Broadcast networks, for example, have rather stringent policies regarding their reporters staging events for film. ABC fired one correspondent after he staged a trash-can fire—since all the real ones had burned out—while covering the troubles at the 1968 Democratic Convention in Chicago. Again in 1968, an NBC unit left a live microphone in a Democratic caucus room and reported the information picked up by it. The network officially apologized to a congressional committee, and the NBC employee responsible soon left the network.

Gene Patterson, editor of the St. Petersburg *Times,* laid out rules for investigative reporters:

> Number one, no bugging. I've never wired a reporter, I never will. I've never planted a microphone; if I can't get it by other means I just won't get it. No burglary. I fired a reporter for taking a document off the desk of a politician. No burglary whatsoever. No pay to a source. I've never paid a nickel to an informer. I wouldn't trust the information. Any guy wants to come in and tell me something about the public good, even if acting out of self-interest, I'll accept the information. But if he wants money for it, to me that's unsavory. That's like a cop buying evidence. And finally, impersonation. Very, very slow on that. If it's a consumer reporter going into the supermarket like any other citizen to comparison shop, I do that. But never send a reporter out and say "Now don't declare yourself, but just hang around, you know, pick this up under false colors." My instructions to a reporter are, if you can't get it as a reporter, it's no fair.

Patterson would not get along with the well-known Chicago reporter who quite literally has holes in his pockets from the half-dozen badges, some real and some phony, that he carries around. And he certainly would not have liked one of the legends of Chicago journalism, Harry (Romy) Romanoff. A master of telephone impersonations, Romanoff at various times in his fifty-year career played the president of the United States, the Chicago chief of police, a priest, a bishop, a railroad lawyer, and even a reporter for an opposition newspaper.

As *Time* magazine reported when Romanoff retired in 1969,

> On one occasion, a hospital got the impression Romy was Chief of Police Fitzmorris. It was twenty minutes before deadline when they inadvertently gave him an exclusive on the details of a gangland murder in the 1920s. Top officials and the Red Cross

of Texas City, Texas, thought they were talking to the White House as they poured out the story of the disastrous 1947 explosion and fire to Romy.

"All of us had an assortment of badges—police, fire, coroner's office," one Romy protege remembers, "and we would pull out the one that would help us the most." Another swears that he knew it was a big story when Romy would sweep his hands wide and say, "Carte blanche—you can be anyone you want to be."

Bob Greene, Suffolk county editor and head of a twice Pulitzer-honored investigative team for *Newsday,* has his own set of rules about posing. "We have utilized impersonation, but never in the context of somebody who has the power to compel information. Do we sometimes make believe that we are credit investigators? Yes, we do. Do we put somebody in a hospital as an orderly to look at possible mistreatment? Yes, we do. But we never pose as a policeman or a lawyer or anyone to whom people have to give information."

Paying out money for exclusive rights to information is not new, of course. Publishing rights for the "personal" stories of politicians, athletes, kidnap victims, and assassins have long brought a price from certain media. But while books and magazines may consider the purchase of "inside" accounts a normal part of business, straight news operations usually refuse to buy stories. The extent of the news media attitude can be judged by the highly negative reaction to the CBS payment of $25,000 to ex-White House Chief of Staff H. R. Haldeman for an interview. Criticism was quick, and the most biting comment came from Nicholas von Hoffman, who asked, "What has Haldeman got to say that could possibly be worth $25,000?" Former CBS News president Richard Salant later admitted to having made a "mistake."

Jack Nelson of the *Los Angeles Times* would limit what is paid for, though only once in thirty-five years of reporting has he ever agreed to paying. "I had a check drawn up to pay a source for documents," he said. "It's a difference in credibility. I can believe documents, but if I had to pay for what someone says, the whole thing becomes doubtful."

Free lance James Phelan has also paid for information. "Just once," he said. "I paid twenty dollars for it, and it wasn't any damn good."

Some news operations, like the *Washington Post,* have a simple stated policy against paying for information. When Benjamin Bradlee, the executive editor of the *Post,* was told that one of the people involved in Watergate was taking bids for inside information, Bradlee said, "I bid this . . ." and raised the middle finger of his right hand.

The networks and the broadcast stations labor under quite different laws than the print media. For example, Fred Friendly, former president of CBS News, still carries a card in his wallet that spells out "The Fairness Doctrine"—and most broadcasters know the doctrine by heart—because the requirement is a major issue in the industry, particularly to broadcast journalists. There were two thousand fairness doctrine complaints in one recent year. Any complaint filed against a broadcast station contains the possibility, no matter how small, that the station could lose its license and is almost guaranteed to make management nervous.

The doctrine influences investigative reporting in two ways. First, because management often interprets "a reasonable opportunity to the contrasting points" as a mandate for "balance" and "equal time," a demand is placed on reporters to present the other side— even when no "other side" exists. Second, investigative reporting in the form of documentaries and "specials" is expensive: not only do production costs run into the hundreds of thousands of dollars, but, because the viewer ratings are usually low, the networks and the local stations make far less in advertising revenue than they would in normal prime-time programming. When the fairness doctrine creates the possibility that *additional* free time may have to be provided on demand, it is likely that some stories will not be aired at all.

An example of the problems that can arise from the fairness doctrine is the case of "Pensions: The Broken Promise," an hour-long documentary by NBC. The program was quite critical of several pension plans, and concluded that "it is almost inconceivable that this enormous [system] has been allowed to grow up with so little understanding of it and with so little protection and such uneven results for those involved." Soon after the program was aired, many corporations and pension groups protested that the documentary was unfair and distorted.

An organization called Accuracy in Media filed a complaint with the FCC, asking that NBC be required to present the more positive side of pension plans. When the FCC agreed and asked the network to put together a second show, NBC decided to go to court.

NBC claimed that the FCC had looked at "Pensions" as if it were supposed to be a survey of the pros and cons on the subject. The network argued that the theme was the abuse of pension plans, and that the documentary had clearly pointed out that there were good pension plans as well. But the theme was the important thing—in fact, in 1974 Congress passed a pension reform law.

The court found that the FCC had failed to understand its own fairness doctrine: "The fairness doctrine will not insure perfect balance in debate and each station is not required to provide an equal opportunity for opposing views. Furthermore, since the fairness doctrine does not require balance in individual programs or series of programs, but only in a station's overall programming, there is no assurance that a listener who hears an initial presentation will also hear a rebuttal."

Journalists have long worked to develop formulas that will assure objective reports. Unlike most other professional writers, journalists generally strive to pursue unadorned facts and to report rather than to evaluate events. Also, unlike most other professionals, journalists will generally have no stake or interest in the events they report. Thus, it might seem that the journalism known as "straight" or "objective" reporting might indeed be reasonably objective. But the late Lester Markel, Sunday editor of *The New York Times,* pointed up the error in this too-comfortable assumption: "The reporter, the most objective reporter, collects fifty facts. Out of the fifty he selects twelve to include in his story (there is such a thing as space limitation). Thus, he discards thirty-eight. This is Judgment Number One. Then the reporter or editor decides which of the facts shall be the first paragraph of the story, thus emphasizing one fact above the other eleven. This is Judgment Number Two."

The problem for the contemporary reporter may be even more complex. If the reporter simply copies what a government official gives out, he or she faces only the question raised by Markel: What should I emphasize in my lead? But if the reporter also thinks of himself or herself as a member of the Other Government, the correspondent faces far more difficult, and more dangerous, questions: What is the truth? Where can I find it?

When Jerry Landauer of the *Wall Street Journal* died of a heart attack early in 1981 at age 49, he was one of the best investigative reporters anywhere—one who was described by another correspondent as a man who "knew when *not* to write a story, and that may be the hardest part of all." Landauer's concern for accuracy, and his insistence on documentary evidence, are almost legendary. At times, he would try to convince younger correspondents not to follow his example, to take more chances. Then, when another correspondent would show Landauer a story that the writer felt was completely nailed down, Landauer would rip it apart, shouting, "My God, this is the *Wall Street Journal!*" In person, Landauer was a genuine eccentric: explosive at one moment, sentimental the next.

Because Landauer was so insistent on having documentary evidence before submitting an investigative story, he investigated Vice President Agnew for almost six years. Well before Agnew was elected in 1968, Landauer went to Alan Otten, then the *Wall Street Journal* bureau chief, and told him that he had been hearing some odd things about payments to Agnew, first when he was county executive in Baltimore and then later when he was governor of Maryland. Otten and Landauer agreed that Landauer should begin checking the rumors, but go all out when and if Agnew was chosen as the Republican vice presidential candidate.

When Agnew was nominated by the Republicans, Landauer increased his investigation. His reports to Otten were much the same: Landauer was becoming more convinced that the rumors were correct, but he could not find anyone who was willing to be quoted, nor could he find any documentary evidence. As the campaign in 1968 ran closer to election day, Landauer was despondent at his failure to tie down the story. When Landauer began to hear that *The New York Times* and other newspapers were trying to track down the story about Agnew, he huddled with Otten. They decided that they would not let the competition push them into printing anything that they did not feel was complete.

After the 1968 election was over, Landauer continued going back to his sources and contacts and checking with new people year after year. Not until August 1973 did he manage to break through, publishing a long story headed "Spiro Agnew Is Target of a Criminal Inquiry; Extortion Is Alleged." Although the U.S. Department of Justice was conducting the investigation, U.S. Attorney George Beall, who became the prosecutor, said: "What can I say? It isn't in our interest to see any story printed."

Otten said of Jerry Landauer: "Jerry was not only a tremendously persevering and painstaking reporter, but also a very competitive one. Once he had finished reporting and writing a story—even one that he had spent months on—he almost always wanted it in the *Journal* instantly 'because the *Times (Post,* etc.) is on it now.' And if it sat around New York more than a day or so, he'd explode with his favorite comment: 'This isn't a daily paper—it's a goddamn monthly magazine!'"

As Landauer showed through his constant checking and rechecking of facts, many of the other investigative reporters go through much the same kinds of doubts. No matter how philosophical, or hard-hearted, or outraged the reporter tries to be, for many of them an uneasiness seeps through.

"One of the most agonizing times is just before we go to print," said Bob Greene. "My wife refers to it as 'The Time.' I am constantly flagellating myself with doubt. Because I do I keep falling out of bed. For the period of two or three weeks before that thing appears in print, I toss myself out of bed at night with a tremendous momentum, and hit the floor, or tables, or anything else around. I've broken two ribs. So now everything is removed from around the bed when the time comes, and I put pillows on the floor so I'll hit something soft. It's a family joke. And it's because I keep asking myself, 'Are we right? Are we right?' You carry that feeling. You have to carry that feeling."

It is difficult for any reporter to avoid becoming somewhat emotionally involved in certain stories, but the professional standard of objectivity—backed up by cold-eyed editors—is supposed to offset such involvement. It becomes particularly difficult for investigative reporters to keep a distance between themselves and some stories, however, if for no other reason than the sheer amount of time and energy committed.

In a *Wall Street Journal* story about Washington correspondents, a reporter wrote,

> The fact is that the influential Washington press corps' powers extend considerably beyond reporting and interpreting the news unfolding in the capital. Unknown to their readers, newsmen here, particularly investigative reporters, sometimes are the prime promoters or offstage prompters on the Congressional hearings, legislative battles and other events they are chronicling, theoretically with detachment. This practice of "not only getting it from the horse's mouth but being inside his mouth" is

"almost a way of life for many columnists and some reporters here," says an assistant managing editor of the *Washington Post.*

The investigating reporter in almost all cases needs publisher support. When a correspondent for *Time* magazine investigated Bert Lance, President Carter's director of the Office of Management and Budget, his investigation revealed almost as much about *Time* as it did about Lance. The correspondent was Phil Taubman, who now works in Washington for *The New York Times.* Although Taubman was covering labor and economic policy for *Time,* he did not have even a rudimentary knowledge of economics, learning while he was writing pieces about officials operating, making decisions, and coaxing Congress. But to Taubman's surprise, he soon learned that Lance knew as little about economic policy as he did.

"My initial contact with him was entertaining and informative," Taubman said, "and led to a complimentary story about his growing influence early in 1977. It was a lively story about a colorful guy. It was also a puff piece—not intentional, but as a personality piece, it didn't look beyond Lance's exterior."

While Taubman was writing his story, he was troubled by Lance's style and bits of gossip and information that appeared in the press. At the end of March, he drafted a memo (on page 137) to Hugh Sidey, then the *Time* bureau chief, and Ed Jackson, then the *Time* news editor.

The memo was accepted, and Taubman's goal was to find a detailed accounting of Lance's finances. The White House had released only a summary version, which listed Lance's debts as $650,000 or more. Taubman then discovered that the Senate Government Affairs Committee, chaired by Senator Abe Ribicoff, had held confirmation hearings for Lance. The committee had a full financial statement provided by Lance, which was available to the public. When Taubman studied that statement, he found that Lance's debts actually totaled $5.3 million. That immediately raised questions in Taubman's mind: How could Lance make the interest payments on the loan on a government salary? Also, what about the possibility of his being vulnerable to pressure from lenders?

Taubman then spent two weeks in Georgia, examining records and interviewing bankers and friends of Lance. He was the first reporter to probe Lance's finances, and most of his sources were not

March 30, 1977
To: Ed Jackson and Hugh Sidey
From:Phil Taubman

Re: Bert Lance

The stories and the hints of dubious activities in Bert Lance's past keep popping
up: a story in the Village Voice that his wife, LaBelle, overdrew her checking
account at her husband's bank by $100,000--without penalty; the White House
release of Lance's financial statement showing that he has outstanding debts
totalling a minimum of $650,000; most recently an AP story buried on page 14 of
The New York Times reporting that the Teamsters Central States Pension Fund,
presently under intense federal investigation for illegal practices, currently
has $23 million invested at the National Bank of Georgia. Lance was president
of the bank until he became director of OMB.

None of these reports prove Lance has done anything wrong. Ru Rauch
tells me that in checking around following Lance's appointment last November, the
Atlanta bureau turned up no leads about trouble in his past. Nonetheless, I
think his background would be worth investigating in greater depth. Lance is
a wheeler-dealer. In a very short time, he accumulated a large fortune in real
estate and banking. His substantial debt suggests that his finances may be a
house of cards--loans built upon more loans. The way he operates in Washington--
skimming through the bureaucracy like a greased pig, juggling phone calls to
senators and presidents of giant corporations, flying home every weekend on
the National Bank of Georgia jet (paying full charter rates, he says)--makes me
wonder whether he didn't stumble somewhere in his rush to make it big.

At a minimum, a closer look at Lance would produce a detailed story about
how one of Jimmy Carter's closest friends and most trusted aides made it to
the top. How he rose from bank teller to bank president. How he parlayed a
marriage to the boss's daughter into a powerhouse career. How he accumulated
$650,000 in debts.

The bigger payoff, of course, would be turning up something illegal. It
may well be that, like LBJ, Lance built his fortune on the edge of violating
the law. It seems to me it's worth finding out just who this guy is and how he
got to where he is.

If you feel the idea is worth pursuing, I'd propose spending a week or two
digging around in Georgia.

running for cover, because Lance had received almost no negative publicity. The people he interviewed were open and frank; bankers talked freely about the favorable terms they gave Lance. One man who had joined Lance to buy a large share of the National Bank of Georgia described Lance's predicament in having to sell his share by the end of 1977 at a price that was far below his original cost. The loss was expected to be more than $1 million. Taubman felt certain there was no way Lance could afford that.

Taubman also picked up strong indications that Lance and his family had benefited from many kinds of deals that Lance engineered when he was chairman of the family bank in Calhoun, Georgia. He then returned to Washington and interviewed Lance, who denied none of the facts Taubman had turned up. Instead, he argued that he could handle the problems and talked at length about his style of banking: gambling, taking risks.

On 23 May 1977 *Time* printed the story that appears here on pages 140-41.

At first, there was a strange silence after *Time*'s initial story. It could have been because the *Time* story was sandwiched in the middle of the Nation section, under the low-key, almost sleepy headline: "Budget Chief's Balance Sheet." Not until July did the *Washington Post* and *The New York Times* get into the act. From there, the story snowballed into the first major controversy of the Carter administration, culminating in Lance's resignation.

Taubman's efforts to push *Time*'s advantage were frustrated. He was unhappy with his first story because it was so brief and left out so much of the information he had developed. He offered another story a week after his first story was published. It was rejected in suggestion form; he did not write a second story. Taubman was told to go back to reporting economic policy. After the *Post* and the *Times* began with their stories, he returned to it, but by then he had lost his initial headstart.

Why was *Time* so hesitant about revealing more about Lance? The major reason may have been institutional: *Time* does not like to be out front, leading the way on controversial investigative stories. The executives prefer to begin reporting when the *Post* or the *Times* has made it safe. Also, *Time* operated from a disadvantage produced by the activities of its parent company, Time, Inc. While Taubman was working the Lance story, Time, Inc., executives were working on Lance in an effort to keep down postal rates. The potential for conflict between the news interests of *Time* and the corporate interests of Time, Inc., were immense. Only the executives of *Time* and Time, Inc., knew whether the magazine's lack of interest in Lance stories was an innocent mistake in editorial judgment or an intentional compromise with Time, Inc., management. *Time,* which had the lead on the biggest story of the year, let it go. Disillusioned, Taubman resigned in October 1977.

Most of the media are growing larger day by day. Some, for example, are being accumulated by a liquor distributor, which also has a book company, a hosiery firm, and several other wildly different corporations. Most of today's Washington correspondents should think this way: "Will I be happy as an investigative reporter on a great magazine or newspaper—which may be controlled by a tire manufacturer?"

Fortunately, most of the columnists have only one boss: themselves. How does Jack Anderson defend himself before opposing attorneys when he is found publishing transcripts of federal grand jury sessions? When Anderson was advised by his lawyers that publishing the grand jury transcripts was against the law, he nonetheless refused to bow down before his attorney opponents.

"Look," Anderson's lawyers had told him, "we are coming in as supplicants, not as aggressors."

Anderson replied, "Don't worry. You let me handle it."

The following was written by Brit Hume, Anderson's former assistant:

> Jack was playing boldly with a weak hand, but I have watched him intimidate other formidable people with that booming voice, ringing with certainty, and that stern expression of his. Harold Titus (the U.S. Attorney), however, is not a man easily cowed. He challenged Jack on his view that he was constitutionally entitled to protect his sources.
>
> "Not only would it be a violation of my professional ethics," said Jack, "for me to divulge my source, it would be a violation of my religion. The Mormon faith holds that the Constitution of the United States is divinely inspired. So I could never consent to identifying a confidential source, no matter what."
>
> Jack had earlier expressed his respect for Judge Sirica, so Titus asked:
>
> "Would you reveal your source if Judge Sirica ordered you to?"
>
> "No."

The Budget Chief's Balance Sheet

Bert Lance, the amiable Georgia banker and longtime friend of Jimmy Carter who is director of the White House's Office of Management and Budget, has become one of the new Administration's strongest advocates for conservative fiscal policies. But Lance's own financial position is far from conservative; he is, in fact, hip deep in debt. Says Dan Pattillo, one of Lance's banking and personal friends in Georgia: "I couldn't sleep nights if I had to service debts like Bert's."

Before Lance was confirmed as OMB chief by the Senate in January, he filed a statement with a Senate committee listing his "direct liabilities" as $5,343,-797. He valued his assets at $7,968,354 and thus his net worth at $2,624,557. That looked like a comfortable cushion. But the value of some of Lance's holdings has suffered a sharp decline. At the same time, his income has been cut drastically since he took his Washington job. How he can meet the estimated $370,000 in interest payments on his various loans this year and maintain his lavish living style mystifies his friends. It may turn out, says Pattillo, that "Bert just can't afford to stay in Washington."

The most serious problem facing Lance, report TIME Correspondents Rudolph Rauch and Philip Taubman, is his commitment under the Administration's conflict-of-interest guidelines to divest himself of the 190,000 shares he holds in the National Bank of Georgia, of which he was president before going to OMB. He had borrowed heavily to buy 164,228 shares of that stock in June 1975. He had paid $17.74 per share, or $2.9 million, as part of a move with two partners—Pattillo, a construction company president, and John Stembler, a

Georgia movie-theater chain owner—to gain majority control of the bank. Lance's entrepreneurial acumen helped to almost double the bank's assets. However, the prospect of his large block of stock going on sale, plus his own departure and the bank's falling profits, have caused the stock's market value to drop to $14 a share. If at year's end Lance is forced to sell his stock at its present price, he will lose about $614,000 on the 164,228 shares and more than $60,000 on the other 26,639 shares that he bought last September at $16.87 a share. This would mean that Lance would have to find nearly $700,000 from some other source to pay off the loans he used to buy the stocks.

At the same time, Lance's other assets apparently are also shrinking, mainly because of the general market decline since January. Back then, he listed his stock holdings (including shares in the Georgia bank and 135 other companies) as being worth $5,649,000. That figure is certainly less today, given the state of the market. And he is not making what he was a year ago. Where he had drawn $150,000 in salary and severance pay from his bank and picked up another $20,000 in consulting fees, he now earns $57,500 as OMB director. He may continue to get about $150,000 in dividend income and perhaps another $125,000 in capital gains, which would bring his income to an estimated $335,000. But that is at least $35,000 short of his 1977 interest obligations alone.

Blind Trust. Lance, of course, has more financial responsibilities than merely paying interest on loans. His rent is at least $12,000 a year for his house in Georgetown. He owns a 40-room mansion in Atlanta, a $100,000 house in Calhoun, Ga., and a vacation home on Georgia's exclusive Sea Island.

Where will the money come from? As required by Carter of all his Cabinet-level appointees, Lance's stock and other holdings have been put in a blind trust—an arrangement under which a person's holdings are managed for his benefit by a trustee, but without his knowledge. Lance's trustee, Thomas Mitchell, a Dalton, Ga., businessman, offers one answer: "I'll either have to increase the debt or liquidate assets."

Borrowing has never been a problem for Lance. Charles Presley, chairman of the Georgia Railroad Bank and Trust Co. and a longtime friend, admits that he loaned Lance $651,000 in 1976 in a deal that was "somewhat casual." As in some other Lance loans, there was no maturity date set; as long as he met interest payments there was no need to repay the principal. And being a banker, Lance got favorable interest rates on his loans; probably about 7%.

Lance brings an expert banker's dexterity to refinancing his personal debts. One example: a loan of $3,425,000 from the First National Bank of Chicago, originally a $2.7 million loan drawn in 1975 from New York's Manufacturers Hanover Trust Co. to buy his 21% interest in National Bank of Georgia. The Chicago bank took over Lance's loan from Manufacturers Hanover in December. The additional $700,000 in the loan, explains Lance, covered "accumulated interest and debts."

Taking Risks. Other Lance debts include: the $651,000 Georgia Railroad Bank & Trust Co. loan used to buy shares in another Georgia bank; $443,-466 from the United American Bank of Knoxville, used to buy 26,000 shares in his bank; $240,000 from Roswell Bank of Georgia, used for Lance's unsuccess-

ful campaign for Governor of Georgia in 1974; $185,000 from C & S National Bank in Atlanta, used to buy real estate. He also owes $340,000 on a mortgage on his Atlanta house and 8½ acres of land, which he valued at $500,000.

Lance stoutly defends his aggressive method of handling his financial affairs. "The only way you can build an estate is by borrowing money and working at it," he says. "A lot of people would say they weren't willing to take those risks, and a conservative fellow wouldn't take that sort of risk. I was willing."

Lance scoffs at the idea that he is overextended. "I'm not vulnerable as long as I've got assets that can be used to pay those debts off," he says, "and I do happen to have assets that can be used in that regard." He contends "it's sheer speculation" that his bank stock will be worth far less than he paid for it by year's end. But if it is, he says, "I wouldn't hesitate to ask the President for some relief" —meaning a waiver of his pledge to sell the stock. Lance's trustee, Thomas Mitchell, says flatly: "I am not going to dispose of that stock at current market value come Dec. 31 or any other time. I'm not going to drop Bert a million dollars for going to Washington. He'll have to get another trustee to do that."

If Lance asks Carter for a waiver, it would pose a problem for the President. It is Lance's contention that as long as all his debts and assets are fully disclosed, there is no possible conflict of interest at issue.

At the least, Lance's financial position contrasts sharply with the balanced-budget goals Carter has set for his Administration. Says Lance's Georgia friend Presley: "There were some smiles down here when Bert was selected to run OMB. That's not the Bert we know. He'll have to change his philosophy."

"What about the U.S. Court of Appeals?"
"No."
"The Supreme Court?"
"No."
"Now, how are we to reconcile your view that the Constitution is divinely inspired with the idea that you would not obey the order of the court specifically established to determine what the Constitution holds?"

Jack was in a box, but he never batted an eyelash.

"If the Supreme Court were to order me to reveal my source, I would only have to conclude that the Supreme Court was in error," he said.

Anderson has successfully resolved such confrontations many times, but many other investigative reporters have other problems. Peer pressure, for example, is one of the largest problems of Nicholas Gage of *The New York Times:*

> There have been reporters who have protested to my editors, written long memos, who have attacked me behind my back, and all that kind of stuff. I think a lot of that comes out of resentment, and the fact that you have a lot of very capable people at the *Times,* all of them very competitive. I remember at a meeting an editor asked if anyone wanted to do investigative reporting, and none of them wanted to do it. But they do resent seeing someone take six weeks on a story, and have ninety-five percent of that story on the front page, and to see someone get three or four columns when they have to struggle to get eight inches."

Is investigative reporting worth it? Given the long list of problems the individual reporter encounters attempting to dig out and to make public certain kinds of information, do the results justify the effort? There are a number of journalists who think not. One of them is John Hess, a reporter for *The New York Times,* who wrote that "An old Tammany Hall statesman once said, 'Reform is a morning glory.' This goes for muckraking too. We rake a little muck, and move on; the money boys stay."

Some reporters think investigations have little impact because they quickly become old news, which when coupled with the fact that the public seemingly has a short memory blunts the sword of reform. Robert Sherrill, in a story for the *Washington Post* News Service, surveyed a series of national scandals and their outcome. In case after case—from sordid side stories of the collapse of the Penn Central railroad to exposés of crooked congressmen to accounts of illegal bombing raids in North Vietnam—Sherrill pointed out that little was changed.

But Ron Ostrow of the *Los Angeles Times* has said, "Investigative reporting is going on all the time, and it has its impact. It's definitely worth it; the longer one spends in Washington the less doubt there is." And Ron Nessen, the ABC newsman who became President Ford's press secretary, added, "I can tell you from being inside the government that investigative news reports do affect the conduct of the government's affairs for the better."

There are also aspects of investigative reporting that cannot be measured. The mere existence of this kind of journalism may serve as a deterrent to malfeasance. It is, as Anderson once said, not so much catching the one as frightening the other seventeen. But such abstractions do not often satisfy the individual reporter. The investigative journalist, often a moralist by nature, wants to see the correction of mis-, mal- and nonfeasance. "The history of reform is always identical," Ralph Waldo Emerson once wrote. "It is the comparison of the ideal with the fact." Exposing the discrepancy between the "fact" and the "ideal" is the job of the journalist, and it is in the attempt to close the gap between the two that the investigative reporter encounters both frustration and glory.

Frustration and glory are also leading to a heightened sensitivity, and both the purpose and the methods of investigative reporting are coming under increased scrutiny. As mentioned earlier, it is true that investigative reporters are sometimes thought of as hunters, stalking corruption and evil, and that for some this image has a derogatory flavor. But before anyone judges investigative reporting by even that simplistic stereotype, it would do to remember the response of a turn-of-the-century journalist, Ray Stannard Baker: "We 'muckraked' not because we hated our world, but because we loved it."

8

The Many Kinds of News Bureaus

*B*y far the largest contingent of the Washington press corps is made up of correspondents for the nation's newspapers, but it is wildly heterogeneous. At the top are those lesser correspondents called "the Brahmans"—bureau chiefs and syndicated columnists who are so powerful that public officials are eager to have them "to tea or a weekend under sail." Next come the correspondents for *The New York Times* or the *Los Angeles Times* and the other large bureaus, less sumptuous, maintained by more than a score of metropolitan dailies and chain papers. The larger bureaus report major events almost as though there were no wire services covering Washington. Others specialize in depth reporting. The *St. Louis Post-Dispatch*, and the *Louisville Courier-Journal*, and a few other papers maintain crack, small bureaus that seldom find it difficult to surpass wire-service reports, some of which are superficial and many of which are bland denominators that will appeal to a diverse clientele. Writing for a news service, one UPI man complained, "is like having a thousand mothers-in-law."

Some of the small bureaus consist of one correspondent serving one paper or several papers. More than one hundred "stringers" supply stories to a number of unrelated papers (a small-circulation daily can get part-time service for little money and boast about its "Washington correspondent"). Instead of duplicating wire-service coverage, the small-bureau reporters and the stringers search the crannies between major news items for stories of special interest to Eugene, Oregon, or Augusta, Georgia. Most of the Brahmans are sniffy about the "localizers" and delightedly pass on an apocryphal tale of one who was so intent on finding local angles for readers in Fort Wayne or South Bend that he rushed out to cover a Washington traffic accident on Indiana Avenue. Ben Bagdikian, who was a one-man bureau in Washington and now is a respected author, points out that the localizers "serve the crucial function of telling the local citizen what the federal government is doing for and to him, and keep his distant representatives in Congress under a more or less steady spotlight."

An army of newspeople has long been as familiar a sight in Washington as the ubiquitous bureaucrats; and "army" is not a bad word to describe this all-seeing, but unseen, government. There's something *military* about a big newsroom, particularly a huge, old newsroom like the Washington bureau of United Press International.

How to describe the UPI bureau? Put yourself into a gymnasium, and then lower the ceiling to about eight feet. Cover the floor with asphalt and the ceiling with acoustical tiles. Cram the place full of desks, and then every few yards plop down a noisy, old teletype machine. Add video terminals to each desk, but destroy their air of plastic efficiency by surrounding the terminals with a chaotic array of notes and clips and other printed matter.

But the low ceiling is what finally does it. The room is like a bunker, a command post for some behemoth tactical maneuver. Every person has a role and fulfills it as if encapsulated in an invisible private environment, shouting into telephones, pecking at typewriters, and dashing from desk to desk with handfuls of notes. Something big is going on here. You can feel it. The wire services constitute the Other Government's Pentagon.

The man who runs the United Press International headquarters in Washington is Grant Dillman, a veteran correspondent up from one of the editorial desks. He has thinning black hair and the gruff appearance of a military professional—or of a big-city newspaper editor. But behind the lenses of his horn rims, his eyes seem sympathetic, almost serene. One can hardly envision this man playing out the stereotyped part of the tyrant editor, swearing and whining and threatening and firing to produce the daily complement of news. The fact is that Dillman does not fit such a part. He is the new breed of editor, elevated from the ranks because of his even-handedness, his managerial skills with both men and machines, and his corporate affability.

He is also a great interview. Ask Dillman a single question, and he is off: There are 105 people working for UPI in Washington, one of the largest operations in the capital. In terms of sheer newsgathering, UPI and AP are the biggest. Most of the people trade in information of the verbal kind. The television people are also a big crowd, but most of them are tied up with technical jobs.

Sixty of Dillman's people are on the general news side. These are the people who report and edit for newspapers. There are fifteen people in the UPI/Newspictures operation. The UPI audio operation—which services several hundred radio stations around the country—has only six people. Another ten or so regional editors also work out of Washington, D.C., headquarters, processing and routing information from the Virginia, Maryland, Delaware, and local District of Columbia beats.

UPI has computerized its operations over the last several years. Dillman says they have started calling his bureau a "newscenter" because of its expanded role in editing and routing information. He also claims that the UPI computer system is usually effective because UPI's reporters were allowed to help design it. Still, the mechanics of computer-information networking are sometimes convoluted. For example, reporters in the regional bureaus of Maryland, Delaware, Virginia, and the District of Columbia must file their copy with New York City's computer. Capsule summaries of the copy are then made available to the ten regional editors at the Washington bureau. They call up the copy they want, edit it, and send it out on the regional wire for distribution in the same general area in which it originated.

Dillman also bestows general praise on a favorite UPI service—what is generally called the Washington Capital News Service (WCNS). Journalists call it simply the "city wire." This is a specialized news service with about four hundred subscribers in the Washington area. Dillman says news bureaus, government agencies, public relations firms, lobbyists, and members of Congress make up most of the subscribers. The wire carries a heavy amount of Washington news centered on the workings of the government and the organizations that work with government. There is also a periodic cross section of national and international news.

The most important thing about the city wire, though, is its advisory service. The wire continuously carries notices of news conferences, briefings, committee hearings, and other "official" events. On Friday, the city wire also looks a week ahead and foretells what is going to be news. At last count, every major news office in Washington had the city wire, save one: *Newsweek*. The *Newsweek* editors are quick to admit that their AP service does not furnish nearly the nourishment available from the UPI machines.

Dillman has an assistant at the top of the organizational chart, but neither of them spends a lot of time in his office. Mostly they hover around the news slot, in which the cycle editor assigns stories and routes them through the rewrite people and into the wire system. There are three cycle editors: the night editor for morning papers, the overnight editor for early-afternoon editions, and the day editor for regular afternoon editions.

In a normal situation, the cycle editor is the key person in the editorial chair. He or she comes in early enough to review what was carried in the previous cycle, to review the other news media, and to talk to the reporters to get an idea of what is in the works. The assignments go out based on the cycle editor's judgments, usually without any kind of conference or consulting opinion. Dillman and his assistant are watching, but they intervene only when big stories are breaking.

The *least* experienced cycle editor has been with UPI for fifteen years; therefore, the cycle editors are well steeped in the mysteries of UPI's news judgments. What is news to UPI? That is sometimes hard to define; but after fifteen years with the company, one gets an intuitive feel for it. Much the same is true for the wire service's Washington reporters. With the exception of a very few star reporters, one does not get to Washington UPI unless one has come up through the ranks. The normal career pattern, Dillman says, is for a reporter to begin in a smaller bureau, to graduate to a larger one, and, eventually, through a combination of luck and skill, to come to Washington. Once a wire service reporter is working in Washington, he or she has earned the right to cover the news as he or she sees fit.

"As a matter of fact, we hold reporters responsible for knowing what's going on in their areas," Dillman emphasizes. The assignment desk's job comes into play only when a conflict arises or when a reporter needs help. If a beat reporter has two things to cover at once—say, simultaneous hearings at the Federal Trade Commission (FTC) and the Food and Drug Administration (FDA)—the reporter usually gets the pick of the stories; the cycle editor takes care of assigning the leftovers to whoever is "relatively free." That's a term Dillman used several times—relatively free.

Mike Conlon, the agency beat reporter, is an example. He covers agencies like the FTC, the FDA, the White House consumer office, and the industries and interest groups most concerned with those agencies. "Conlon's all over town, every day," Dillman says. "If he can do it, he does it all by himself. He may go to the FDA and file a 400- or 500-word story and then race over to the FTC and dictate another. . . . Then he may have to get reaction from consumer groups or trade groups about what the FTC has done. Or maybe they will get in touch with him as soon as they see it on WCNS. If Conlon is not available, they'll give the reaction to the desk, which will insert it into his story either as it is filed or later as an insert to it."

Rarely do UPI reporters get into squabbles over who covers what story. They are so overworked as it is, Dillman says, that they are usually very glad to get any kind of help on anything. Although Dillman has been pointing the bureau toward more specialization, all of the reporters have also been able to function as generalists. If they are "relatively free" when a breaking story demands a reporter, any one of them can be sent into the story cold.

The biggest group of UPI reporters is on Capitol Hill; ten correspondents are supposedly arranged five to the House, five to the Senate. But Dillman says that distinction is breaking down as the style of coverage changes. In the past, a reporter would cover a bill as it coursed through the House and then turn it over to someone in the Senate office. Today, that same reporter follows the bill all the way through Congress. "We're moving toward more and more mobility," Dillman stresses. "I don't know why we ever did it that way [handing off stories], but we did it for years and years."

Three UPI reporters are assigned to the White House, two to the Supreme Court, and one each to the major agencies. Two economic specialists work out of the Treasury Department, and the bureau chief has also created several new beats as part of his modernization effort. There is, however, a hiring freeze because of UPI's troubled finances, so Dillman has carved out the new beats by rearranging, not by enlarging. Now, for example, there are correspondents covering consumer, energy, and environmental issues; religious and social issues; and "people in Washington" feature stories. Dillman is particularly proud of that last category. He has one reporter who does nothing but profile the greats and the not-greats who make Washington run or not run.

There is also a political editor, though Dillman is quick to note that everything about Washington reporting has a deep political dimension. And UPI has named a "special projects reporter" for "in-depth, more subjective" stories. Dillman says he would have called the man an "investigative reporter" a few years back, but he believes the term has become overused; that it now means simply a "scandal" reporter. The special projects are written at least once a week, sometimes twice, in advance of their publication dates. "Let's face it," Dillman states emphatically, "the emphasis at UPI is on spot, breaking news, but at least 25% of our effort now goes into in-depth, magazine-type stories."

Dillman stresses that the media have not done enough surveillance of the federal bureaucracy. His projects man will spend four or five weeks looking at an agency or function, eventually writing, "what I must admit is a very subjective story, which is an area the wires once wouldn't touch." Dillman considers this approach necessary because Washington news stories have themselves become more complicated. "You don't have the wire space to run the stories in the detail that would enable the reader to make up his or her own mind; and the papers don't have the space to print them. So somebody has to pull it together."

Does Dillman like the change? "Oh yes. I love it, and the reporters like it, too." But he adds, "If we were to cover the bureaucracy properly, we would have enough reporters to let them run up and down the corridors of various buildings and peek in the doors and form acquaintances with people—with whistle-blowers. But we don't have that many people, and nobody does." UPI's subscribers, he says, simply won't pay for that kind of operation. "There's an economic lid on what we can do."

Of the sixty correspondents assigned to general news at UPI, fifteen work on the desk inside the bureau. Dillman is apologetic. He would clearly rather have them in the field reporting. But the changing character of Washington news, he feels, demands that a dozen or so people be kept indoors at the keyboards. In fact, much of the news writing actually takes place at the desk, because the stories are too complicated for one reporter to provide an adequate perspective. A small amount of the work of the fifteen desk people involves covering their colleagues' posteriors when one of the reporters slips up or doesn't get a reaction from every essential angle. But most of their work, according to Dillman, entails "pulling together very complicated stories."

Dillman cited the example of a news story in which the initial lead may be that Congress has passed an energy bill. UPI will then routinely get reactions from the White House, from the executive departments involved, from consumer and industry groups, and perhaps from the state government offices that have sprung up in Washington. "There's no way a single reporter who's covering that bill can pull all of this together," Dillman says, so the wire service uses the talented writers on the desk to do what they call the "big wrap." They also supply a series of sidebars on major stories, but the emphasis is on producing a single, comprehensive story. "Basically, somebody has to pull it together for the moderate or small newspaper that can use only one story."

Three of the fifteen desk people work the overnight cycle, five the day side, and seven the evening schedule. The night-desk editor's job—which Dillman once held—is "the best job in the bureau." It has the immediacy of breaking news, but there is also time to do some additional background and reaction research, "to put it into perspective and do a good, polished writing job."

The timing is so tight on the day cycle, Dillman says, that the service "lives or dies with the reporter on the beat." Part of the nexus of this problem (the other being deadlines) is the pace of Washington's business. As far as the reporters are concerned, life begins at 10 A.M. in Washington. "That's when the PR guys have had their coffee and are finding out what's going on in their own shops. That's also when they're ready to talk."

Thus, the first copy is flowing by 11 A.M. But because most Eastern dailies go down at about half past noon—some "a hell of a lot earlier," as Dillman put it—getting out a substantial amount of news is a difficult proposition. Because the desk cannot do much more than straight rewriting of leads in this amount of time, what the reporters write is just about what goes out on the wire.

The tight deadlines and the ever-increasing complexity of Washington news have also meant the wires are covering less of what Dillman calls the "tricky track." "It used to be," he explained, "that any member of Congress could make a speech on a major subject—it need not have been a major speech—and he would have been certain to have four or five hundred words on the A wire, probably under a by-line. Now the speaker has to be a senator to make the A wire, and the senator's speech must also plow *new* ground. Because most congressional speeches are self-serving and cover things already said, the UPI doesn't even bother to cover many of their speeches any longer."

Dillman has a sense that the press has become its own news in some respects, but he did not express it as anything more than a "sense." He thinks people, at least some people, expect too much of the press: "Part of it is our own fault. For years and years and years we did pass ourselves off as being omnipotent. It used to be that we were reluctant to correct our mistakes. A reporter usually knows when he's wrong, and depending on the magnitude, you can correct a mistake or let it stand. Now we make a bigger effort to correct every mistake."

If "Lou Grant" went to Washington for an episode, the producers of the series would probably choose the former *Los Angeles Times* Washington bureau as the set. The *Times* newsroom office, located in an upper story of a high-rise on Pennsylvania Avenue, features two mostly glass walls with one of the best views of Washington. Immediately across the street, at eye level, is the fantastic ornamentation of the Old Executive Office Building. Beyond are the Washington Monument grounds and the Potomac. The other two walls are covered with bulletin boards; and where there is no bulletin board, clippings have been taped up anyway. A Bill Mauldin cartoon portrays President Carter imagining the Statue of Liberty as a nude.

In this spacious but nevertheless crowded room-with-a-view, there are desks and equipment for twenty reporters and photographers, three editors, and several support personnel. The three editorial desks are grouped beside the entrance. A little sliding door opens through the wall into the wire room, allowing copy from the machines to be handed directly back and forth from wire room to editorial desk. On the sliding door is a sign saying, "One is born with chic. It cannot be taught. Elegance is another matter."

Dick Cooper, the *Times*'s chief Washington editor, has been away for a week's backpacking in New Hampshire's White Mountains. This morning he finds his usually neat desk in a terrific jumble.

Notes to him are scrawled on shreds of flimsy copy paper and scattered among a more vintage pile of clippings, news stories, phone slips, and various writing utensils. Cooper rather hopelessly exclaims, "I can tell Ostrow's been here at work." Ron Ostrow has filled in on some editorial chores during Cooper's absence, and, like many reporters, Ostrow has his own special filing system, which responds with great sensitivity to the confluence of fate and chance.

Typical of a lot of Washington reporters, Cooper observes that he is "atypical." He began as a "country editor" of a newspaper in Illinois that was partly owned by his family. "After a few years of that, I realized I was becoming a printer instead of a writer. William Allen White wasn't on the horizon, so I moved on." First, to the *Chicago Sun-Times*; then to the midwestern bureau of the *Los Angeles Times* for four years; then to Washington, following the 1972 presidential election. He had covered George McGovern during the election, and that helped bring him to Washington as a reporter. He was promoted to chief editor of the *Los Angeles Times'* Washington bureau in the spring of 1978.

Part of Cooper's job—and that of his two assistant editors—is to see that the reporters are kept working. Part of it is also fortune-telling—having reporters at the right place at the right time, not missing things the *Los Angeles Times* should cover. For the editors, the workday really begins the previous afternoon. Using their own leads, official notices, and the UPI's daybook, Cooper and his assistants "run over in our heads what stories are in play and what is likely, what needs to be covered. We make sure the evening before that our people will be covering things that need to be covered."

Cooper adds that "a typical day" might see *Times* reporters at a White House briefing, the daily State Department briefing, "two or three other briefing stories," a hearing or two, and maybe a decision at the Supreme Court. He says they also try to run several articles on single topics over a period of time to chart the evolution of a Washington story. He cited the natural gas deregulation legislation and the impending postal strike as examples of that kind of story.

The *Times*'s beat system is centered on subject matter rather than on government organization. Cooper says, "We try to avoid getting people tied down covering a place because, by and large, the news flows on issue lines." He contrasts this approach with UPI's organization, which places the reporters with various arms of the government on a more or less permanent basis: Whereas, in the old

UPI-style organization, a single story may pass from reporter to reporter several times, the *Times*'s approach allows a single reporter to stay on a story from start to some kind of finish.

By 11:30 every morning, Cooper and the other day editor, Mercer Cross, have produced a daily news budget. Around noon, one of the Los Angeles national affairs editors puts a call through to the Washington bureau, and the budget is reviewed. "If there's a story that seems of marginal interest to them," Cooper explains, "the *Times* editor in L.A. may raise a flag, at which point we can explain, yes, we need to run this because of something, or we can say, if you're not interested, we'll be glad to pass on it." Cooper says reporters rarely write something that's not printed: "If we write it, it's going in. All the mediating with Los Angeles goes on before that."

Cooper also notes that he fights the spot-news tendency of Washington reporters—the tendency to believe that events within Washington's federal structure are of importance to the readers in the rest of the country. In the *Times* bureau, reporters are encouraged to take a broader view of events:

> We try to stay in tune with the perspective on things, and they [the Los Angeles editors] try to have a sophisticated, in the sense of informed, understanding of the importance of what is happening here. That's something that requires constant effort on our part and on their part, and a lot of what goes on in our very extensive back and forth telephone conversations is that kind of sharing of perspectives and adjusting.
>
> Mercer Cross and I talk back and forth with the reporters here. Then we talk back and forth with the editors out there [in California] about what our coverage ought to consist of. Natural gas is on my mind at the moment.

The news had come in that morning that President Carter was cutting short his vacation in Idaho. Cooper suggests that a *Times* staffer should produce a story describing and analyzing the legislative battles that Carter faces with Congress—not spot events, he cautions, but a piece that focuses "on a bigger slice of time."

Analysis, says Cooper, is "the most important aspect of our coverage"; the *Times* has moved away from merely reporting events and assuming that they will be important to the reader and informative "in and of themselves."

> Even presidential press conferences are no longer in that
> category for us. There are lots of press conferences where there
> is not much news, and we don't write very much about them.
> What is the justification for asking the reader to give up part of
> his life to read this story? Most people are not interested in
> receiving one piece of a jigsaw puzzle in the mail every day for
> six months and being expected to put it together themselves.
> What's the long-term game? What are the players trying to
> accomplish?

This attitude is fairly new to the larger journalistic community, but
Cooper claims that he has felt this way since he began working as a
newsman. He thinks the newspaper industry has finally realized that
it had been taking its readers for granted. He also thinks that
television news is now undergoing the same reportage-to-analysis
change that swept the newspaper industry several years ago.
According to Cooper, the traditional view of television as spot-news
informer and newspapers as follow-up interpreter is not proving to
be entirely valid. "There's a great deal of significant spot news that's
just not covered by television." As a result, the *Times* still does spot
news, but it tries to write such stories with a slightly modified
structure: "The story has to contain within it the justification for its
place in the paper," Cooper says.

Cooper administers the office and is responsible for long-term
writing projects, while Mercer Cross takes care of daily spot-news
assignments. By 4 or 5 P.M. each day, the *Times* reporters have
begun to return to the bureau after spending the day gathering
information. Not every reporter hands in a story every day, but
those who do tend to wait until the afternoon to do their work. The
reporters give the editorial staff short summaries—"schedules,"
Cooper calls them—that furnish outlines of stories and estimates of
length. These go directly to Los Angeles on Telex or Rapidfax or
Telefax, informing the national desk there of what will be forthcom-
ing. The writing is finished around 8 P.M., and most of the copy is
on the way to Los Angeles by 8:30 or 9 P.M. Then, says Cooper, "I
do a fair amount of work-related socializing. It's a way of keeping
track of what they're [other newspapers] up to. . . . It's a real club, I
guess. Most Washington reporters pride themselves on that aspect of
their job, and they try to keep it that way."

The bureau desks are equipped both with video terminals wired
into the Los Angeles computer system and with a slick new

recording system to take incoming telephone information. On the whole, however, Cooper is not impressed by the impact of technology on journalism. "The changes in technology haven't had a great deal of effect on me. The bigger changes have been in the areas of attitude toward the news and the perception of what is news. It's not a uniform or coherent development. It's not even consistent within any one paper or reporter. There's a general movement in this direction of being more thoughtful about what the news is and a little more skeptical about government."

By "skeptical," Cooper hastily explains, he means something well short of the blind belief that all politicians are incurably corrupt: "If that was our attitude, then we would never delve much into the substance of anything. A hard-nosed cynicism can be an easy way out, which prevents a reporter from seeking a more complex interpretation for events."

Cooper thinks the media have "substantial power," but like many of his colleagues he has a bit of trouble putting his finger on the precise nature of that power:

> As with most other exercises of human power, the people who have it don't really have it under full control. In other words, we cannot always achieve what we set out to do, and we very often achieve things we didn't set out to do. There are so many factors that determine the play of a story and the attention span and attitude of the public. The same story could sink like a stone if it appears at certain times or in certain places, and in other times and places it could become a national preoccupation for months to come.
>
> The media have a great deal of power in shaping people's perceptions, the things people notice. Out of all the billions of things there are on earth to look at or to think about, the major newspapers and television stations decide there are six or seven that you ought to know about. You may ignore them, but you're going to have a lot of trouble picking six or seven entirely different things of your own to worry about.

Somewhere, Cooper sighs, the media are wrong in telling people what is important. As an example he cites the furor over the destruction of ozone in the upper atmosphere by fluorocarbons in spray deodorants.

> The media, for reasons we could spend a whole day talking about, decided to focus on this issue. A good deal of money was

spent—the issue got grabbed up. The public decided primarily on the basis of the news-media presentation that this was a serious thing. Congress and government got busy, and a lot of money has been spent on substitutes for the old sprays. This has consumed investment capital and slowed the economy. And now we know most of the fluorocarbons come from old refrigerators, so the problem may not even be solved.

Asked whether this selection power puts editors in the key position of the news-flow process. Cooper nods, then adds, "Yes, but bear in mind that we don't feel we have anything like complete independence. The news system is a complex series of checks and balances that work in unpredictable ways."

Cooper's reaction to press criticism is similarly ambivalent. On the one hand, he thinks that it is good to be criticized. On the other hand, he clearly believes a lot of press criticism has been characterized by what he calls "easy cynicism": "Most reporters deal with the inherent limitations of their craft on a daily basis, and having an academic critic point them out is not all that helpful. Mostly those abstract absolutes aren't even very relevant," he adds. "And the critics should know that perfection is not a common thing among human endeavors. You can destroy an institution pretty easily, but you cannot replace it so easily."

It would distort the feel of Washington to think of its press corps exclusively in terms of editors, rooms, establishments. Individual reporters form the backbone of the Other Government. To correct this distortion, we must visit a variety of personalities on their rounds and in their lairs—beginning with one man in a two-man bureau and then two members of the *Newsweek* operation in Washington.

Many sizeable newspapers send only one or two reporters to Washington. Generally, these papers also subscribe to one or more wire services, which give them an additional source of Washington copy, but they still expect a great deal from their reporters in the nation's capital. If UPI admits it is not adequately able to cover the federal government, what chance does a lone reporter have of doing an adequate job? How does the small bureau tackle Washington?

To put it glibly, the small bureau does so routinely. Arthur Wiese, chief Washington correspondent for the *Houston Post,* covered the capital by himself for six years. He also had a bureau secretary to help with filing clips and stories, but not until 1978 did he finally receive help from home—in the form of one more reporter.

Like many of the small news bureaus, the *Houston Post*'s offices are in the venerable National Press Building. This old structure, near the White House and fourteen blocks from the Capitol, has since 1908 been the focal point for many Washington news operations. The Press Building is showing its age; its dank corridors could have come from a set for *The Front Page*. But the building is undergoing a $45-million renovation. In the *Houston Post*'s office is a bright, modern, electronic news operation.

The bureau consists of four offices to accommodate a four-person-plus-secretary staff rather than the previous staff of Arthur Wiese, Jim Craig, and the secretary. Wiese's office has his desk at one end, a handsome couch and coffee table at the other. Behind him are bookshelves loaded with political science texts, almanacs, *Congressional Quarterly* weekly reports, and the like.

Wiese is a tall blond whose hair is straight and flyaway, often falling across his alert gray eyes. Like most of the working press in Washington, Wiese looks as if his suit had been slept in. Dapper attire is clearly not on his mind.

Wiese grew up in Huntsville, Texas—"where the state prison is," he volunteers. He graduated from Southern Illinois University in 1968, with a master's degree in journalism. One of his former teachers, who had joined the *Houston Post*, hired him, and Wiese returned to his native Texas.

After working special assignments for the *Post*, including a trip to Vietnam and Laos, Wiese transferred to Austin in 1970 and joined the *Post*'s state capital reporting staff. Finally, after three years in Austin, he was chosen to replace the *Post*'s lone man in Washington, who had made it well known that he did not like the scene there and wanted to return to Austin to report Texas politics.

Wiese doesn't wait for questions to begin talking about the problems of covering the federal government with a small staff. "Government has gotten so big that we can't even do a good job at scratching the surface," he says.

Wiese says he covers fewer "press releases, bill cosponsorships, and grant announcements" as he tries to be more analytic and informative to his readers. He relies heavily on his bulging file of news clips, which lie in horizontal cabinets in the outer room of the bureau. "When you get a story thirty minutes before deadline, the clipping file saves you," he says. Thus, the first thing Wiese does each morning is to clip the *Washington Post* and *The New York Times*. He spends about an hour and a half a day reading the *Post*, the *Times*, the *Wall Street Journal*, and the *Christian Science Monitor*. He reads the papers and clips for "story leads, for background, and to keep a feel of what might become news." Clearly, he means news *for him*—it's already news for somebody if it is in print. It is another aspect of the constant recycling of ideas and story topics in the news business. Stories are interexchanged so often and so unpredictably that it is impossible to describe the process quantitatively.

"The most important quality for the reporter in a small bureau is the ability to be a juggler," Wiese says, "to do a lot of things simultaneously, to know when it's worth messing with a press release and when it's not." Wiese says his editors give him a free rein most of the time. "Like all papers, they'd like to have twice as many stories half as long. But I get maybe five story requests a year. And then it's usually something the *Chronicle* has covered and we need." (The *Chronicle* is the afternoon paper in Houston. Its bureau in Washington has six reporters, sometimes more.)

In the outer office, Jim Craig, a former assistant city editor for the *Post,* is grumbling about bureaucratic ineptitude. The Department of Education has awarded a substantial grant to Prairie View University near Houston, an all-black college in the *Post*'s readership area. The people at the Department of Education know they have given money to Prairie View, Craig says, but nobody seems to know how much or for what. "You have to call the recipients to find what the grant is for. Nobody in the bureaucracy knows anything."

At 10 A.M., after a little more than an hour in the office, Craig is on the telephone to Prairie View, trying to find out what he should have found out from the Department of Education. Wiese sits down to do a story on the House-passed national parks legislation, because he has been "meaning to get to it for a couple of days." But before he starts writing, Wiese takes a few minutes to fill in a section of the weekly congressional voting chart that is published in the Sunday *Post.*

Wiese works and talks at the same time. He says that with his new assistant, he will now have the time to concentrate more on the members of Congress from Texas and to do more political analysis.

Craig will keep an eye on the executive agencies. One major goal for both reporters is to get rid of the "xenophobic attitude" still common among Texans. Wiese hopes to get across the idea that the national economy is more than a bunch of easterners coming south to plunder Houston, and that state governments are not as relevant to daily life as they once were: "They're a conduit for federal money and regulations. The local governments are the implementing arms, but the federal government initiates most of the meaningful laws and programs."

Wiese calls the office of Senator Lloyd Bentsen of Texas for a comment on the story he is pursuing about the national parks bill. He begins the conversation with a reference to a *Dallas Times Herald* story suggesting that the new wife of his colleague, Senator John Tower, is playing havoc with Tower's politics and with his Washington staff. Rumor has it that Tower's wife, who calls him "my John," complained to Tower's advertising consultant that he "had never really shown the people of Texas my John."

"Yes, that's true," the ad consultant replied. "That's why your husband has been reelected for 16 years." Tower now has a new advertising firm, largely the result of his new wife's influence, Wiese says. The story is typical of a lot of shop-talk among journalists and politicians in Washington. Rumors and backroom stories are the grist that eventually gets milled into news.

At 10:41 A.M., Wiese sits down again, after getting a packet of files from the next room. He types with two fingers, slowly at first. He pauses, then leans back in his chair and studies the acoustical tile of the office as if something—a lead or a nice quote—is inscribed there. He returns to the typewriter, churning out words, gradually speeding up his two-fingered pecking.

Craig interrupts: "Do we not have a file on the deepwater port authority?"

Wiese, not even looking up, answers: "It's under 'superports.'"

He mutters aloud the last few words he has typed, and then resumes typing at a steady clip. Talking now and then while he writes, Wiese finishes the national parks piece five minutes before noon. "This thing is long—outrageously long," he says. "I'll have to take time to cut it."

While Wiese goes over the copy, Craig ambles in from the outer office. He has been listening to Wiese talk about his work. "Art can write six stories, three of them in depth, while I'm looking in the telephone book." Wiese's story, finished at 12:04, is about 700 words long in finished form. He files it to be transmitted to Houston later in the afternoon.

Wiese turns now to the UPI wire and rips off a long piece of copy. It takes only a few seconds for him to determine that there has been no breaking story during the last hour. This is a pattern one can see everywhere in the news bureaus. No matter how large the operation, there is the wire, usually the UPI wire, with someone bird-dogging it to make sure that the bureau will be in the first pack to arrive after a news flash. The UPI wire is the salad bar of Washington journalism.

Shortly after noon, Wiese heads for Capitol Hill. He joins a group of several other journalists and technicians waiting for cabs in front of the press building. One of the men, mustachioed and of a distinguished mien, might have been a diplomat from the neck up. But his rumpled suit and scuffed shoes clearly mark him as another writer.

A cluster of cabs arrives very shortly; the hacks know that reporters spend a good portion of their time crawling in and out of Washington cabs, and they hover around the press building like bees. The first of the taxis is commandeered by a harried-looking woman clutching a bag of videotapes marked "Urgent."

The day is hot, miserable, polluted, utterly disgusting in every respect. It is summertime in Washington. The Blue Ridge Mountains to the west have blocked the breezes, and the humidity from Chesapeake Bay has crawled up the Potomac and commingled with the industrial pollution and auto exhaust of Washington's choked byways. On days like this, one cannot say for sure whether the sun is shining—the view skyward is a garish white light diffused by a wash of browns and grays. After 4 P.M., one can look directly at the setting sun without a squint. The radio in the cab declares the air quality index "very unsatisfactory."

The cab drops Wiese on Independence Avenue in front of the old Longworth House of Representatives Office Building. Wiese moves with familiarity through the maze of marbled hallways, finally ducking down a dark and private side hall, which provides a shortcut to the offices of Representative Bill Archer of Houston. Archer is one of Wiese's regular contacts on the Hill, along with both Texas senators, the other congressmen from districts within the *Post*'s readership area, certain staff members of key congressional committees, and, most important, a long list of haphazardly made Washington contacts with whom Wiese has cemented an enduring relationship over many years and through many quid pro quos.

Representative Archer's outer office is typically congressional: pictures of the Texas delegation, pictures of Archer with other politicians, the Texas and congressional seals, a mag-card typewriter, a selection of Selectric typewriters, whole walls of paper and card files, and, in honored corners, the coffee and Xerox machines— all of the stuff of which congressional offices are made. Wiese is taken through the outer office into the plush, wood-paneled personal office of the representative. Archer's new administrative assistant, Phil Mosley, is waiting, and small talk seems the order of the day. The sword tips touch before the match begins.

Mosley is concerned about tracing the Cajun name of his predecessor, who has just returned to Texas. The fellow began as a disc jockey on a Cajun radio station in Louisiana, and nobody remembers what he called himself then. "You reporters are supposed to be able to track things down," Mosley says. "Track this one down for me." While he's on the topic, Mosley also notes that Wiese's recent *Post* story about the changes in Archer's office "jumped the gun." "You sort of popped one on us there, didn't you? We were going to have a formal announcement of that."

Wiese, perhaps smarting at the tone of the conversation, excuses himself rather quickly. On his way out of the Longworth building, he passes several more Texas offices and notes that they are normally on his regular beat. Today, however, he is headed directly for the Senate press gallery. But after visiting the gallery and determining that there is a dearth of Texas-oriented news, Wiese decides to take the new Metro subway back to his office in the National Press Building downtown. Fifty feet underground and accessible by escalators so steep that they steal the breath away, the Metro tubes seem as polluted as the streets above. Fumes and smog have settled into the biggest stations, and the sleek silver train's headlights highlight the eerie glare of the filthy air.

By 4:45 P.M., Wiese is back in his office. The secretary is seated at the Dataspeed-40 unit, transmitting copy to Houston. Jim Craig has been at Senator John Tower's regular press conference and is scanning his notes for a suitable lead.

Wiese looks through his mail and sets aside several items that could be useful in the future. He takes a look at tomorrow's news budget and decides not to try a complex analytical story today. He will save it for the Sunday edition. Before he leaves the office that evening, he will make sure that all of the stories for Houston are properly filed and that nothing earthshaking has been recorded on the UPI ticker. For a Washington correspondent, there is no such thing as a normal day. But, as Wiese remarks, there are things that have to be done routinely if the news is going to get to Houston on time.

Wiese says that the key to staying informed, to being a good Washington reporter, is continuity, keeping on top of stories that are hovering near the top of the news-agenda heap: "It's who knows the most and who has the best contacts which makes the difference. . . . There's an office routine. Being a Washington correspondent is essentially being a generalist. If you're in a small bureau, which I think is anything under five people, the one thing you do best is usually juggle balls. Keep a number of them in the air simultaneously. If you can master that, you'll be a success here."

Mel Elfin, the bureau chief of *Newsweek* in Washington, blinks owlishly behind the lenses of his old-fashioned rimless glasses, then he throws his legs over his desk and begins his description of the office routine. The bottom of his left shoe reveals a gaping hole. "I get here about 9:30 and greet the early starters. There usually aren't that many. Washington reporters are notoriously late starters, and most of the time the hours of the newsmagazines give us much looser hours." His first action on arrival is to check his in-box, where there will be copy from reporters who worked late the previous night. Usually, there are also queries from New York editors and writers who have called for some Washington-based information.

At 10, or shortly afterward, Elfin and his editors gather for the regular "squawker" session by speakerphone with New York. During this meeting, the bureau editors review what is happening in Washington, while the New York editors explain what is coming up for the next edition. Elfin explains: "The first thing I do [to prepare for the squawker session] is think up a couple of jokes. That starts things off on a light note. I also talk to my reporters on the key beats to find out their situations."

Elfin is interrupted when his telephone rings. It is someone from the Washington bureau of *The New York Times*. A strike against the *Times* is threatened, and reporters are running for cover. "No. No, not for a week or two at least," Elfin answers. "You think it's going to go longer than a month? Holy Christ. We may just eventually do our bit by our colleagues." He hangs up.

"Somebody from the *Times* is looking for work," he says. "We will probably end up giving some of them part-time work if the strike goes on long enough." The same thing was going on at the *Los Angeles Times* and at bureaus throughout the city. In times of trouble, reporters look out for their own.

"Anyway," Elfin continued, "I talk to my reporters. I've already read the *Post* and *Times* at home and glanced at the Baltimore *Sun,* which is always a good checkpoint. I'll also read the *Wall Street Journal* and the *Christian Science Monitor,* and I'll look at the AP log for the day when I get to the office. With that I can fairly well answer whatever questions New York is gonna ask." Elfin adds that he would like to have the UPI city wire as well, but because the *Newsweek* corporation does not subscribe in New York, corporate protocol prevents the Washington office from having the wire. The lack of UPI service is usually "no big problem," Elfin says, because of the broader deadline of the newsmagazine.

Elfin continues: "The squawker usually takes about ten minutes, depending on what kind of laugh my jokes get." Immediately after the session with New York, Elfin translates the editorial decisions into verbal orders for the members of his staff. Later in the day, his decisions will be confirmed when New York sends down written queries, but Elfin says he saves time by getting the word out immediately. Then, with the major decisions made for the workday, Elfin settles down at his desk to read the mail—or not to read it.

"I go through all my mail personally. Here, I'm going through my wastebasket to show you." Elfin hoists his trash basket onto the desk and starts reviewing that morning's batch. "Just picking at random now . . ." Elfin picks out three envelopes, all of them unopened. "I know all these people," he says, tossing them aside. He picks out another, also unopened. Then he picks out an opened envelope full of National Theater information. "I was intrigued by what the schedule might be."

By now, it is 10:30 or 11 A.M. in Elfin's work day. Usually, he will call up the appropriate New York subeditors and talk over the news stories at some length. "Then I really don't know what I do with my time. It just goes as I handle things that come up. I feel more tired now than I did in the days when I was reporting or writing or doing something physical like makeup in New York."

Elfin is close to the bureau's reporters, whom he recruits himself—though they have "to go to New York to pass muster." He says he likes a good mix of "inside" and "outside" people. Washington, he says, is *Newsweek*'s pinnacle bureau, and he takes special pride in the effectiveness and the open organization of his bureau. "My secretary and I communicate by buzzer. She's way up in the front office. That's by design. My door is usually wide open, and anybody can come in here and talk to me. My deputy is the same way. There's no news editor in this bureau. We don't let a news editor come between the reporter and the person responsible for that reporter. It's difficult, but it works. The reporters are more comfortable. And besides, that's my style."

The afternoons are occupied with telephone calls and questions from reporters. Elfin has been answering those questions so long, he says, that it is seldom necessary anymore for him to give them much thought: "Reporters come in and pose questions, and without even thinking about it, I say, do it this way or another way." Elfin also rules on story ideas. "I'll say, 'That sounds good. Why don't you put it into a formal story suggestion?' or I'll say, 'Someone did that five years ago, and there's no new angle on it.'"

He spends quite a bit of time resolving jurisdictional questions among his reporters, who often find the lines of their beats blurring. The National Security Council, which has been claimed by both the State Department and the White House reporters, is an apt example. In addition to reportorial squabbles, which are more or less constant, according to Elfin, there are also occasional territorial skirmishes between bureaus. The scandal over former Senator Edward Brooke's ill-starred divorce was fresh in Elfin's mind. Both the Boston and the Washington *Newsweek* bureaus were concerned with the story, and a lot of negotiating went into the budgeting of the news coverage. "I'm a broker in many ways . . . between demands made on the reporters by New York—which sometimes are out of touch with the realities of the situation—and what is really available in this city and what can really be done. Unrealistic demands from New York sometimes make reporters deal with unmitigated bastards who aren't willing to give them the time of day."

Elfin also sees himself as a defender of his reporters—both inside and outside Washington: "I feel perfectly at ease calling the secretary of so-and-so or anybody else in order to defend my people. It's my job to open the doors."

Elfin explains at length the differences between "group journalism" as practiced by *Time* and *Newsweek,* and the journalism of the wire services and the daily newspapers. In the newsmagazines, reporting and writing are two different jobs, and one doesn't necessarily have to be good at both—the way one would as, say, a desk editor at UPI. "You can't be a linebacker and a guard at the same time," Elfin says. "You're not expected to be William Faulkner as well as Ernie Pyle. We have the Pyles, and one hopes we have the Faulkners."

Elfin calls *In Cold Blood,* by Truman Capote, the best journalism he has ever seen, mainly because it uses fiction techniques to tell a true story. "If tomorrow morning three gunmen wearing ski masks robbed the bank downstairs with sawed-off shotguns, the *Washington Post* would have this story: 'Three masked gunmen with sawed-off shotguns robbed the Briggs National Bank yesterday, and after making 42 patrons lie flat on their stomachs for two hours, they got away with $50,000.'

"*Newsweek*'s lead would be: 'It was like a scene out of Bonnie and Clyde. "Don't you move, you s.o.b., or I'll blow your head to ribbons," a gunman said.'"

News writing like this is not unauthentic, Elfin says. "You're closing in like a movie . . . it's a visual thing . . . it's using the techniques of fiction to tell the nonfiction story." He is amused at the mention of objectivity. It is an old saw for a newsmagazine man, an outdated concept that only a social scientist would ask about. "If objectivity is the goal, and if names make news, then the Manhattan telephone directory is the most perfect journalism ever done," Elfin says with self-satisfaction. "We're in a tougher business . . . maybe the ultimate business . . , the search for truth." He makes a critical distinction between what he calls the interpretive and the "very dangerous business of editorializing": Interpreting, he says, can be subjective, but it must analyze the truth without any hint of the reporter's opinions, pro and con.

For *Newsweek*'s Washington staff, the week begins not on a Monday but on a Saturday afternoon, when Elfin or his deputy bureau chief, Jim Doyle, talks with the New York editors to plan the coming week: "What's gonna happen next week? If there isn't much news, what kind of features can we do? What long-term projects are coming due next week?" "We're looking for the violin," Elfin says.

"It's called the violin because you're unleashing the cosmic music. It started in the days of Luce, when every *Time* magazine always had that cosmic sense in the lead: 'A mood of torpor spread across the land last week.'"

The second story, Elfin says, is called "the cello," and there is a whole series of such jokes all the way down to "the piccolo." During this particular week, Elfin was watching for developments on President Carter's raft ride in Idaho, and he was also giving a lot of attention to the upcoming Camp David summit.

Elfin does not work on Monday. His assistant, Jim Doyle, is in charge that day and will have one or more conferences with New York to make sure that the week's story assignments remain those agreed to on Saturday. These assignments are often "fine-tuned" on Monday, and they are sometimes changed altogether.

Tuesday is the decision-making day of the week. At about 10 A.M., Elfin has his usual squawker call to New York; but then half an hour later there is a more comprehensive call, which includes most of the New York editors. All final space assignments are made for both pictures and copy for the coming issue. The decisions made in this meeting are formalized by Telex.

Elfin spends Wednesday morning on the telephone, talking about the overseas edition of *Newsweek* and making certain that the Washington-based information required by that edition is available to the editors. Assignments for the domestic edition are sometimes changed at this late date, but only when absolutely essential for accuracy or up-to-date coverage of a world-class news story. Wednesday afternoons are reserved for visitors, and these are most often people looking for work, Elfin says. Beginning late Wednesday afternoon, the copy begins to flow. Elfin usually leaves by 6:30 or 7 P.M., but his deputy often stays late enough to read over the new copy.

How do Elfin's reporters organize their massive reports? Is there a set way of compiling information for *Newsweek*'s New York writers? "Group like-things and tell a story with them," he says without hesitation. "I learned this in New York, writing a cover story on sex on the campus the week that Kennedy got killed. The article was postponed by the shooting, and then it was postponed again and then again. It was a month later when I finally did it. I took the stuff home and grouped it by subject in piles on my living room floor. Part of the reaction went in one pile, college clinics in another, and so forth. Then I listed all these piles by topic on my clipboard."

To put together the finished report, Elfin sorted through each item in each pile, selecting the best two or three sources in each and setting the rest aside. Then he fiddled with the order on the clipboard, finally deciding on the way the story would read best. The clipboard is Elfin's portable brain. He still uses it, keeping a week's worth of notes and memos on it. If he wants to get the latest status on an assignment or look at the last query from New York, he goes to his clipboard.

Elfin often suggests to his Washington reporters that they reorder their stories in one way or another, but he says that his changes are usually not major ones. He estimates that about ten words come out of Washington for every word that finds its way into *Newsweek*. In a recent week, he said, the Washington bureau filed between 75,000 and 100,000 words—"whereas the whole magazine ranges from 65,000 to 75,000 words." Still, Elfin believes that there is not much occupational frustration attached to the fact that the bureau reporters seldom get much of their writing into print. That is the newsmagazine game, he says, and the reporters are used to it: "We probably have it better than the TV people. They are always scrambling for another *fifteen seconds* of air time."

Thursday is the heaviest day for copy at the bureau. On the average, about 40,000 words will flow through the three Telex machines. On one recent Thursday, the bureau filed more than 70,000 words. The flow of copy is a continuing problem—and responsibility—for Elfin, who says he has to keep it "from getting piled up. Some reporters tend to sit on their copy. It's much better to file it in small takes so that we can keep the copy going to New York. I run up and down the hall encouraging, beating, cajoling, begging, threatening—the gamut of human emotions—to get the stuff out of people."

Some reporters are always late, Elfin says, staying up all night writing and meeting the "farmboy" reporters who come to work shortly after dawn. Each reporter has his or her own key to the bureau and can come and go at will.

On Friday, the New York office puts the magazine together, and by Saturday the computer people have it set in rough form. Sometimes the New York editors will decide a story has been inadequately developed, and they ask Washington for some more information: "Maybe 10% of what we write is subject to 're-queries,'" Elfin explains. "For example, after the defense-bill veto, New York wanted some congressional reaction on whether Carter is developing as a strong or weak president. So we had to send them two or three pages on that."

By Saturday, the preliminary versions of the magazine are coming in from New York, and the Washington reporters review the articles based on their reports to make certain that there are no important distortions or omissions. "Each reporter is responsible either for coming up and looking at it or having it read to him and then making changes," Elfin emphasizes. "From 85% to 90% of the changes we suggest are made"—although the Washington reporters and New York writers sometimes get into a squabble over what changes to make. Elfin usually comes to the aid of his reporter when that happens: "I'll get involved and deal with the senior editor in New York. If that doesn't work, I'll deal with the editor of the magazine."

Elfin cites the Watergate scandals as a period when there were many such squabbles. Television news programs were full of denials about impeachment from the House Judiciary Committee. But Elfin says his reporters knew better. Regardless of what was being said on television, the *Newsweek* reporters felt that the impeachment votes were there and that President Nixon was on his way out, one way or the other.

How did the *Newsweek* reporters know? "By being up there on the Hill constantly and sensing it in private conversations," Elfin says. "That is another difference between the newsmagazine reporters and the television reporters. The television people cover a lot more ground on their beats and are not always able to get close to their sources—and of course a congressman will say privately what he could not say in front of a network news camera. New York was uptight about our coverage of Watergate at that time, but our reporters were on top of the situation. I would have bet on their accuracy."

Does Elfin look forward to the day when *Newsweek*'s writers and reporters stop pecking at their typewriters and switch over to video terminals? His look was one of true dismay. "Thank God we don't write on them. I would find it very hard," he says, glancing at his venerable Remington 50. *Newsweek* and *Time* may be modern journalistically, but some of their people cling to the "Front Page" image of the journalist hunkered over his old clunker.

Newsweek correspondent Bill Cook is full of surprises. Though slimly built, he is not really small. He may seem smaller because of the slight typewriter droop of his shoulders, but his voice also reinforces the unobtrusive aspect: he speaks in a semi-whisper after the fashion of country singer Whispering Bill Anderson. His laugh is staccato and arid.

An impression of icy hauteur falls away when he chooses to let it. His bright eyes brighten under his loose, sandy hair as he swivels his head toward you: "I mean, what the fuck?" he asks you. The word itself means nothing, but somehow you just do not expect it from Cook. The truth is that thoughtful Bill Cook considers his phrases with an eye toward fun. At once ironic and softly human, he is one of the most complex personalities one can encounter in Washington.

He covers the energy and environment beat for Elfin's *Newsweek* bureau. A veteran of the organization, he came to Washington recently from a long stay in the San Francisco bureau. No long-time specialist, Cook has covered everything from offshore oil to Patty Hearst. He took up his current assignment after *Newsweek*'s energy reporter crossed the line to become a government public-information officer.

Cook is trying to make his office livable after the remodelers' comings and goings. Boxes of papers are piled everywhere, and pictures that should be hanging on the wall are propped up along the baseboard. But the typewriter is in place on its table, ready to roll; and the bulletin board features the weird trivialities that most Washington reporters seem to cover: a picture of himself bulleting down the sidewalk on a skateboard, a press pass from Evel Knievel's abortive attempt to jump the Snake River Canyon on a rocket-assisted motorcycle.

Bill Cook is a Monday-through-Friday reporter, keeping regular office hours. He gets his traveling orders on Tuesday:

> Generally on Tuesday and Wednesday I go like hell. Last week I worked on the history of the natural-gas situation. I saw the secretary of energy for a while on Tuesday. I also did a report on Boeing. Basically I was just checking to see that the writer's view was the correct one. You see I worked really closely with this writer in New York talking about the gas story. It was very complicated.
>
> That was a case where I sent them fifteen pages just to educate the writer. Later the editor of the national section called me up frantically. Basically he wanted me to explain once again what it was he was editing.

Cook wanted several changes made in the story, and every one of them was made. *"Newsweek* has this bad habit of putting adjectives in front of everything. What I succeeded in doing with that natural gas story was getting every one of those taken out." The final version of the article, which had a bright screen of orange superimposed on it in the magazine, was not the best one Cook could have visualized. "But they cut texture and kept substance, and that's what they're supposed to do."

Is it really impossible to handle a complicated political issue in a few words? Cook says yes, it is impossible. Then he rethinks it. No, no, he says, it is not impossible, just "damned hard. Those who do it well are the very best television correspondents—Roger Mudd or Tom Brokaw or somebody like that—you have to leave out an enormous amount, yet somehow you have to suggest what's there, a phrase or a graph or at least a list—that's hard."

Cook says writers in New York do not do as much research as they should, and his problem sometimes comes down to educating the person who will actually write a piece:

> They never do as much as one would hope, but their problems are altogether different. I've always been critical of writers for doing less than they should.
>
> Group journalism is a large compromise. You trade readers for control. It's a product of several people, but in exchange for that you get one hell of a lot of people reading it. A lot of people don't like the newsmagazine reporters, and a lot of reporters think of us as somehow being highly suspicious. It's a matter of . . . I don't have any particular pride in my prose. One word follows another, and that's not particularly interesting to me. I'm interested in the information I gather.

Cook graduated from the University of Oregon in 1958 and spent three years in the Air Force working with radar—no writing. After working for a year or so for the *Salem Capital Journal,* he went to Stanford for his master's degree, landed a *Newsweek* internship, and went to work for the magazine in 1963. From there, Cook went to Atlanta, where he covered the civil rights strife. Then he went to Vietnam—"Like all the civil rights reporters, we all ended up in Vietnam together."

He returned to San Francisco near the end of 1966 and spent the next eleven years in the Bay area. "They tried to move me to Chicago earlier, and I refused rather angrily," Cook recalls. "But then I was asked indirectly whether I'd be interested in coming to Washington and I said, 'Yes, I'd consider it.'"

Cook thinks reporting is "different" in Washington. First, he covers a more structured beat in the District of Columbia, and the longer he is on that beat, the better he gets at it: "Every week I add to my ability and information," he says. "You get more sophisticated as time passes." The second difference has to do with Washington's deferential treatment of the biggest news media. "It's very important to them what *Newsweek* says," Cook observes. "It gives you access to the public figures in the news."

Is the Washington office really a crazy place? Are people always standing out in the hall screaming? "Yes. That is a weekly confrontation. You sit down the hall outside Mel Elfin's office, and you listen to him screaming at them. This happens several times a day sometimes. My principal fear of coming to Washington was the reputation of the place as being crazy. This job, being nutty, running up and down the hall screaming. It turns out Mel does run up and down the hall screaming, but that's just Mel running up and down the hall screaming. I doubt he'll get an ulcer."

9

ABC-TV

*T*hirty years ago, when D.W. Brogan wrote his classic *Politics in America,* he did not consider it necessary even to mention the role of the media in the American political process. Today, after Vietnam and particularly after Watergate, a political analyst, such as Paul Weaver, will insist (in *Fortune* magazine) that the reliance of television news on the "single omniscient observer, and its commitment to the notion of a unified thematic depiction of events—all make TV an extraordinarily powerful mobilizer of public attention and public opinion. . . . Television news . . . is perhaps the most powerful centralizing machine ever let loose in American society."

Richard Reeves, one of the most influential members of the Other Government, agrees:

> It is about time television grew up and admitted what it was, and that the rest of us begin to view the tube realistically: TV is more than a medium; it's our environment. Television is both a political force and our political arena. Everything we see—from "The Nightly News" to "The Gong Show"—shapes our cultural and social values and our political ideas. If millions of people watch a docudrama on Robert Kennedy—and one is being prepared for 1981—that has more effect on Edward Kennedy's political future than his record as chairman of the Senate Judiciary Committee.

The effects of television on national politics are not necessarily salutary in the opinion of most media critics. For example, in *The Unseeing Eye,* a study of the 1972 presidential campaign, Syracuse University Professors Thomas Patterson and Robert McClure claim:

172

"The nightly network newscasts of ABC, CBS, and NBC present a particularly unauthentic picture of politics. The networks ignore major election issues. They ignore the candidate's personal qualifications for the presidency. In place of these serious matters, ABC, CBS, and NBC substitute the trivia of political campaigning that makes for flashy pictures. Hecklers, crowds, motorcades, balloons, rallies, and gossip—these are the regular subjects of network campaign stories." Although television executives, stung by such criticism, have succeeded in bringing somewhat more depth to their network news coverage, the medium itself necessarily limits the intellectual acuity and even the objectivity of the material to be presented on the small screen. While newspapers or magazines can provide precise information on a wide variety of subjects, so that the reader can choose what to read and what to make of it, television news is composed of pictures—very expensive pictures—that must and inevitably do emphasize spectacle over complex information and analysis. Russell Baker was right when he wrote that "People do not listen to television. They *look* at television. I had to cover the first Nixon-Kennedy TV debate in 1960 and so didn't have time to look at it. I had to listen to it. If you listened to it, Nixon won. Not by much, but he had the edge. Most Americans watched it on television. The didn't listen. They looked. And Nixon lost by a knockout."

Anyone who watched NBC during the primary battles in 1976 would have understood what a knockout means. Tom Pettit of NBC had decided, in advance of the primary, that then-President Ford would defeat Ronald Reagan in the North Carolina primary, and that Jimmy Carter would defeat George Wallace for the Democratic nomination. Pettit had cleared with the NBC news executives the story theme that Reagan and Wallace would lose. He and the camera crews of three and four men worked eighteen-hour days for a week before the primary. Pettit wanted to picture Ford triumphant and Wallace scowling.

Pettit believed that Wallace's crippled condition would be a problem for the Alabama governor, so he told his camera crew to take pictures of Wallace in a wheelchair. Unfortunately, many of the angry Wallace assistants ordered the NBC crew out of a television studio because a local station was filming Wallace in his wheelchair.

Meanwhile, Ray Farkas, a field producer, and Jay Fine, a tape editor, were reviewing the videotapes of pictures in Charlotte, North Carolina, for more than fifteen hours. On the one hand, they were looking for film clips of Reagan demanding a firmer defense policy. On the other hand—and much more significantly—they also wanted pictures showing that he was likely a loser, as Pettit was predicting in the story. Farkas decided that some of the best pictures showed President Ford confident with a "double whammy"—exultantly lifting both arms in a victory pose. By 5 P.M., an hour and a half before the program aired at 6:30, Farkas and Fine were still looking for pictures of Ford at his optimistic best. A tape of President Ford climbing the steps to Air Force One came into view, and Farkas and Fine moaned as the president turned: "You turned the wrong way." Then the television men cheered as the president turned again to wave to the crowd, giving a double whammy capped with an over-the-shoulder handclasp. They chose that clip to illustrate the story.

Fine also summoned pictures of Carter looking optimistic. He ran a second-long sequence of Jimmy Carter back and forth through the editing machine, until he was able to clip it at the exact time when Carter's mouth was tastefully closed instead of hanging open. That, too, conformed to Pettit's story, and was chosen.

At the end of all that tedious work for Pettit, Farkas, Fine, and the camera crews—and untold hours for many others—Pettit appeared on the air for three minutes and twenty-five seconds. Pettit was right about Carter. He was wrong about Ford, who lost in the North Carolina primary to Reagan.

Fortunately, the correspondents for ABC and CBS did not decide that they, too, would picture Reagan and Wallace as losers. The impact might have been stunning had the same pictures appeared on the same night. We do not know that such ideas as Pettit's might have swayed the voters, but Pettit himself said: "You can't let the viewer wonder what he's looking at, and you can't confuse him by talking about something different from what he's seeing." Thus, whatever the pictures show, they must drive the narrative. Quite literally, *tons* of information during any presidential race were junked because they did not conform to the pictures the networks wanted to show.

The power of television, both to inform and to deceive, is certain. And yet, paradoxically, nowhere is this dual power more obscure and less convincing than in the operation of a television news bureau. A visit to the former ABC network Washington bureau demonstrated that television news decisions are the work of confused, anxious, highly competitive men and women, and that one minute of television news time may represent hundreds of hours of behind-the-scenes effort by hundreds of diverse souls. The notion of political danger or even of political bias from this powerful medium seems an absurdity from the chaotic corridors of ABC-TV, Washington.

The facade of ABC News's Washington bureau, perfectly flat and marble white, seemed modest, stark, orderly among the sumptuous hotels and office buildings along Connecticut Avenue. But beyond the tiny foyer and the skillfully camouflaged door, leading back into the core of the building, the suggestions of simplicity and order are shattered. Everywhere there are chattering people and buzzing, flashing electronic gadgetry squeezed into little rooms that mushroom from the side of winding halls. Piles of wires and relay racks clutter in the less-used walkways. The morning's *Washington Post* carries a story about ABC's decision to build a new headquarters for itself. It is only rumored—nothing factual yet—but one look inside the "old" headquarters leaves little doubt that it is true. "We've got to walk down this hall and cross the alley into another building," says the secretary to the bureau chief. "It'll sure be good to get into one big building one of these days."

Down the hall, across the alley, and up on the second floor of another crowded building, a security guard chooses not to challenge anyone to sign the guest registers. We stroll self-consciously past him and proceed into a very large, very noisy L-shaped room—the producton facility of the bureau. Perhaps one hundred feet long and half as wide, the room is an absolute jumble of humanity and machinery. At one end—the one nearest the door—are the desks of secretaries to the news executives. Behind them, in the slot, are the assignment editors and crew coordinators. Their desks are arranged like two giant U's, with the closed, base ends bumped up against one another. In one U sit the assignment editors who are responsible for keeping track of what is happening and for deciding which reporters should be where and what needs attention first. Across from each editor is a camera crew coordinator who must arrange for the electronic news-gathering (ENG) equipment that will be used by the reporters. If a reporter has a hot story on Capitol Hill, the assignment editor can make the arrangements with the crew coordinator without either of them leaving his or her desk.

Around the uprights of the U's are the assistant editors, each with a typewriter and at least one ringing telephone; and beyond the editors, under the big clocks that show the time in New York, in

California, in Moscow, all over the world, are another group of desks for the producers and news writers. Behind these desks is an open area dominated by two big color television cameras and a profusion of hanging lights. The walls are heavily laden with ABC logos, big tricolored maps, and art-deco stripings. This is where the Washington segment of "World News Tonight" is produced.

It is still early morning, so there is not much activity in the studio area. Most of the commotion centers on the editors' desk and on a small, glassed-in room adjoining the studio. Behind the glass, twenty of the new thermal-printing wire-service machines sputter quietly, making unfamiliar little hissing sounds as the matrix printer races back and forth across the wire paper roll. There are the usual AP and UPI wires—several of which cover the local, state, and national scenes—and there are the specialized services: Agence France Presse (AFP), Reuters, *The New York Times,* and the *Los Angeles Times-Washington Post.* Now and then, an editor slides back the glass, and the refined hiss of the machines swells over the room.

The outer walls of the big news room open into reporters' and executive offices. At one end, near the entry corridor, are the executive offices and a big conference room where everyone gathers each morning to decide on the news for the day. At the other end are the reporters' offices, some private, some shared, all cramped and modest at best.

By contrast, the offices of the executives—the vice president in charge of operations, the producer, and the chief news editor—are spacious and elegant, with big plush sofas, fine bookshelves, three television receivers, and walls peppered with pictures of former presidents and other celebrities.

It is nearly ten o'clock now, and some of the news room personnel are beginning to converge on the conference room near the executive offices. It is a daily ritual: Precisely at ten every morning, the corporate headquarters in New York telephones its bureaus and affiliates to plan the news agenda for the day. As the meeting time grows closer, the bureau executives rush into the room, and the chief editors and correspondents reluctantly seat themselves around a long table with fifteen or twenty chairs.

In the center of the long table is a telephone and the little attachment that makes it possible to hear and be heard without having to bother with a receiver. One can hear the control switchboard setting up the conference call. This morning it involves

Washington, New York, Dallas, Atlanta, Los Angeles, Chicago, and a special line to Camp David, where ABC has taken over a big part of the Cozy Motel in Thurmont, Maryland. The fidelity of the call is horrible. Screeching and rumbling erupt from the speakerphone: "Dallas on the line . . . SQUAWK, SCRRRRRRR, BLPPPP. . . ."

A secretary comes in and distributes a seven-page Xerox of the daily "troop movements." It tells where the ABC reporters are today, where they can be contacted, and what they are up to. There are five pages of stories that may qualify for "World News Tonight." Some of them are complete and "in the can," others are expected to be completed today, and still others are in the work-up stages, coming in in a day or so.

On the speakerphone, the New Yorkers are beginning to mutter among themselves. "I wonder what they *do* up there that takes them fifteen minutes to get going every morning?" someone in Washington says softly, turning his head away from the speakerphone. Finally, one of the New Yorkers starts calling the roll. As each city is called, the answer comes back "Here." The people gathered at the table in Washington now settle into a resigned state of attention.

New York begins by turning the speakerphone over to each of the bureaus, allowing them to report what they have to offer for the day's news budget. Camp David is first. Someone there advises that there will be a press briefing by Presidential Press Secretary Jody Powell at 1 P.M., with another one possible at 4 P.M. The network's heavies—Frank Reynolds, Sam Donaldson, and Barbara Walters— have been sent to Camp David, but apparently there has not been much for them to do except take the press handouts and sniff the air for rumors. "We don't expect much before the weekend, but we'll see what breaks," the producer at Camp David concludes.

The Washington bureau gets its turn next. Bob Zelnick, the director of news coverage, outlines what Washington will offer. He leans out over the table, craning his neck toward the speakerphone: "Connally and his wife are testifying at the White House. Brit Hume and Vic Ratner are covering. William Miller is testifying before the Senate Finance Committee. Levinson is covering. We are covering with Levinson because we expect something on capital gains soon. New York already has a piece on this. Wordham will be monitoring the defense authorization veto. We think it's unlikely that there'll be a piece generated on this today. Dunsmore will cover the regular

State Department briefing. Bergman is working Claybrook at NHTSA [National Highway Traffic Safety Administration] for a future spot. Bell will cover the 3:45 press conference. Gregory is working on a missing cafeteria at GSA [General Services Administration]."

After a short pause—and without any acknowledgment of the day's plans from Washington—the voice from New York says, "The other two networks were at Congressman Flood's. Did we know he was going to be indicted?" Both CBS and NBC had camera crews at the Pennsylvania home of Congressman Daniel Flood, who had been indicted the previous day. ABC had scored a clean miss on this one, and the Washington bureau was being held responsible.

"No, sir," Zelnick says. His lips slam shut as if the word "sir" ended with a "p." "We had no information that he was going to be indicted yesterday."

"I thought we had some kind of word several days back on this," the squawking voice says.

"Well, I wasn't working. I'll check it out and find the slip," Zelnick responds, and the matter is ended—at least for the moment. The entire room has grown ever so slightly tense during the exchange. While Washington's role as a news-gathering center is surely uppermost, the shots are still called in New York. Washington missed one, and there is no hiding that from the people in New York.

The New York voice breaks the order of the round robin with another question for Camp David, which is coordinating its summit coverage with the Washington bureau. "Is there some way we can get information on where they're meeting? Anything we can get sketches from?"

"There'll be still pix of the inside, but that's all we can expect," says Camp David.

No answer from New York. Briskly, the voice in the box calls: "Chicago." Chicago reports it may have 330 people in jail in Marion, Ohio, where a teachers' strike is worsening. The Chicago editor suggests putting a crew on that story.

"Absolutely," says New York. Permission granted.

"And we'll get in some footage on the farmworkers. This is coming from our Columbus affiliate. They're a bit more reliable than Toledo."

Los Angeles now takes its turn. A researcher has discovered how to manufacture artificial insulin. The piece will be ready by 3 P.M., the California voice says. The time is important. The speaker meant 3 P.M. *Eastern* time—network news runs on Eastern time.

"Seattle integration will not happen today because our teachers are on strike," says Los Angeles. "We've also got an AP story on Howard Jarvis out of D.C. Three times before, he's raised cash for Senator Goldwater, Senator Hayakawa, and Right-to-Work, and every time the money was dispersed before it got where it was supposed to go."

New York asks about Seattle: If the integration story won't run, how about the teacher strike? "We'll have something by noon," replies Los Angeles.

Atlanta takes its turn with an odd assortment of offerings that arch eyebrows around the room. There is a small story on a runoff election, and there is a routine policy story out of Memphis. Jim Bouton is coming to Atlanta from the minors. "Lake Fontina has an excellent feature for Steven Geer and his crew. There's a square dance festival of the world. Sounds like a fun-type piece."

New York asks about a Castro news conference. Miami will cover, says Atlanta, but it is going to happen too late for today.

The Atlanta voice rises and falls in a smooth, rounded Southern way, laconic in its presentation of its stories. Nothing is said from New York except: "Dallas."

"Dresser Industries is all we have," Dallas says.

Atlanta is back on the line to finish its budget. It wants to talk about a "tree-house story" that is destined to make it onto the air that evening as one of those oddities of human activity. "The crew will advise us if it's possibly competitive for tonight's show," Atlanta says. Plunging on to talk about the restive situation in Nicaragua, Atlanta says that nothing seems to be happening there. "If it doesn't, we can think about pulling out of there if it isn't too premature."

The sexual metaphor from the drawling Georgia editor is too much for his many listeners. Everyone around the table in Washington finds this exceedingly funny. Laughter briefly punctuates the static chattering through the telephone lines from Los Angeles and New York.

Atlanta is still not finished. It wants to talk about the lobster war. "I had copies of the *Miami Herald* sent up overnight. It might be a good story and apparently hasn't gotten much play yet."

Suddenly, the telephone is overcome by bursts of clatter and an intermittent shrill tone. New York's turn has come, and it will not be put off. The editor shouts over the noise. The Russians are trying another dissident. There's another Indian flood. ABC is buying videotape of the disaster from UPI's television syndicate, and ABC will add its own announcer's audio at its London studios. Then there are the French and British air shows, which will make good frames for other stories if nothing else. Coverage of the Pope is being shipped to London from Rome.

New York pauses. Everybody pauses.

"Anybody else?" New York asks. The words do not seem to mean what they are meant to say. Everyone bolts, the line goes dead, and the meeting is at an end. ABC's news agenda for the day is set. Unless something really shattering happens, the news will be generated from these possible stories.

As the people file out of the conference room into the noisy chamber of the main news room, somebody from the "Good Morning America" crew hails one of the evening news producers. The "Good Morning America" people have secured footage on Congressman Flood. "Screwed up again, huh?" the crewman jeers. "Once again, the morning news saves the collective ass of 'World News Tonight.'"

Nobody laughs. New York's mere reference to the missed story was plenty of retribution for everyone. This is national television, where stars will rise and fall on mistakes like that one.

Today, the news room is preoccupied with coverage of the Egyptian-Israeli Camp David summit, which begins this evening. On big events like this one, the three networks pool their equipment and take turns providing the feeds. ABC and CBS have also pooled in a separate arrangement to hire a helicopter to send signals back to Washington from Camp David. One of the ABC editors is gleeful that CBS had trouble with its feed this morning. "They just kept getting all this static. I don't think they ever got a piece on the air."

One of the women seated around the editorial desk notes that "Roots" is going to be back on the air during the summit. "There's no way they're gonna put this thing on during 'Roots,'" she comments, then turns back to one of the four monitors hanging from the ceiling next to the world map. A telephone rings at the crew coordinator's desk. An ENG crew—broadcast language for the new vans full of electronic equipment that send signals directly to the bureau for rebroadcast on the network—is moving from wherever it is now over to the Senate where a hearing is scheduled. They want to know where to meet what reporter assigned to them. One of the producers barks an order from the television console on which he is trying to evaluate a newsman's audition. That is what he calls it, an "audition."

"He's pretty good," the producer says. "He has good delivery and presence. But I'm not sure about him. He's so disorganized. He had nothing worked out for us. He sat down and wrote out his copy in longhand. Just scribbled furiously, didn't even want to use the typewriter. I've got some reservations about that part of it."

It is nearly noon now in the ABC news room, and, despite a moderate amount of activity, very little seems to be happening. Most of the reporters' desks and offices are empty. Near the entrance hall the reporters' mailboxes are filling up as the second mail of the day arrives. Someone regularly leaves the editorial desk to check the big bank of wire machines. The assignment editors and crew coordinators speak frequently into their telephones as reporters and video technicians check in, get orders. Producers confer now and then with the desk. Is everything right? Any problems? Changes?

Though each of the reporters has at least a piece of an office here at the news room, most of them are where reporters spend a good deal of every day—getting information, making the rounds, getting ready to sprint back and produce a piece of reportage if what they are covering turns out to be relevant enough in the producer's judgment to make the evening news.

The bureau chief walks quietly to the editorial desk and asks about the preparations for the evening news. Everything seems to be in order, the editor says; nothing is out of control. But there is no news coming out of Camp David. That worries all of the bureau supervisors. A big chunk of the bureau has been moved to locations near the Camp David summit meeting. The morning situationer shows more than thirty-five people either in Thurmont or in Gettysburg, Maryland. This does not count the people down from New York—including Barbara Walters and her support crew. The D.C. bureau has also sent three of its three-person ENG crews to the summit. So many people and machines—yet there is no news.

Business hasn't stopped in Congress just because of the summit, and a fraction of the ABC news bureau is going through its daily routines of monitoring hearings, listening to press briefings, and checking contacts. The situationer shows four events as "possibles" for today's news programs. The biggest in the minds of editors is clearly the Kennedy assassination hearings in the House of Representatives. They decided in yesterday's 5 P.M. story conference to assign two ENG crews to the event. Reporters Brit Hume and Vic Ratner will be there monitoring the proceedings. Federal Reserve Chairman William Miller will testify before the Senate Finance Committee on how deeply taxes should be cut. Levinson is covering this along with two ABC film crews. Bill Wordham and one ENG crew are monitoring debates about the defense authorization veto in the House Armed Services Committee. At noon there is a scheduled briefing at the State Department. Correspondent Barrie Dunsmore is there with a film crew.

No reporter assigned to events on the Hill has reported in to the bureau today. Like Washington reporters in the other media, the ABC reporters focus their work on the story of the day while covering all their regular contacts. On the one hand, the reporters are covering something specific, a hearing or a controversy, a press conference or a junket. On the other hand, they are looking ahead for the future issues in their areas of expertise. At the simplest level, this means taking an early morning glance at the United Press International's "daybook," which relays notices of the important scheduled events in Washington and New York. But virtually every other Washington reporter has developed a personal system as well for keeping on top of a beat. They will return to the bureau when the reporting is done for the day, but there's literally no need for them to check in to the office before their work is done.

For Capitol Hill reporters, "the beat" revolves around the press galleries. Government staffers sort and post the constant stream of committee notices, news releases, and statement transcripts that flow from publicity-seeking government officials. At least once a day—and usually more often if time permits—the reporters will gather to survey the day's news offering.

Oddly, the press facilities for television news—generally acknowledged to be the most influential news medium in the nation—seem little more than an afterthought to the spacious galleries assigned to the newspaper reporters. There are no television studios. The reason viewers see most television journalists standing on a Capitol lawn in the rain is that there is nowhere else for them to go. Sometimes, they retire to the committee rooms or to the foyers of the great office buildings, but often these rooms are themselves cramped for space. Besides, the reporters and editors rationalize, a story centered on the Capitol demands a Capitol in the background. Still, few reporters are happy that their press room is an artifact of simpler technical times.

Today, ABC reporter Stephanie Levinson is covering the Senate committee hearing. Levinson will check with people she knows on the staff of the committee. She will chat with the administrative assistants of key senators, and she will probably have a conversation with someone on William Miller's staff. She will also observe and perhaps discuss the story done by her competitors—the reporters of the other two networks.

While the reporters work, they keep in close touch with the bureau's editorial desk. If the hearing turns out to be a turkey, they call the desk and tell them it looks like a poor story. If something big is happening, they will tell the desk to clear the way. Most often, it is simply a case of monitoring and confirming news events already on the network budget. The networks are extremely good at being there for news that can be scheduled—news they know will make for a visual report that can be processed by air time.

By 2 P.M., the reporters begin to write their copy and rough out the camera shots that will accompany it. They offer their pieces to the producers back at the bureau, who decide what they will propose for the evening news program. Then the editors get together with New York and begin to set the schedule for the evening's broadcast. This is not a cut-and-dried process. Beginning in the early afternoon, the schedule for the night's news grows firmer and firmer as stories are produced and evaluated, but the final schedule is not set until very soon before the actual broadcast. And when there is a big story like the Camp David summit, the final order of the broadcast is barely set at all, with adjustments in timing and content occurring even after the first portion is on the air.

Back in the ABC bureau, activity increases as the noon hour passes and the evening news air time approaches. The assignment editor and the operations coordinator chat often, exchanging schedule items. The editor is on the phone more frequently as the day passes. He is getting reports from correspondents on what stories will be available. He receives calls from reporters and other acquaintances about events he may want to schedule for future news. He works with the operations coordinator to make sure a film or ENG crew is available to a reporter who needs one.

The editor—youngish, tan, face covered by a big, bushy beard—talks briskly into his telephone. "No there won't be a verdict today," he says. "The guy got into a fight with the judge."

The operations coordinator—older, balding, thin as a rail, and beak-nosed—has bought himself a headset so he will not have to hold the telephone receiver. "I just got tired of having to juggle the receiver while I was trying to do other things with my hands," he says. "So I got this thing." He speaks to an ENG crew chief about tomorrow's news. "You are in the White House at 7 A.M. tomorrow morning," he tells someone. He turns to his typewriter and fills out the work order. Everything is logged.

Shortly before noon, the bureau chief walks to the slot desks and asks about the coverage of Vice President Walter Mondale's departure and his arrival back in Washington, but no one seems sure who the "pool" is. One network will "pool" the event, providing pictures for the other two. The bureau chief and the operations coordinator think CBS is the "pool," but a reporter at the White House is nervous. The equipment does not seem to be in place.

It cannot be resolved, so the editors decide to see what develops. The bureau chief shrugs. Everyone else shrugs. He goes back into his office, and the editors turn back to their typewriters and telephones. There is a fatalistic attitude about it all. They have seen so many tight ones that one more or less doesn't excite them. Something will work out. The news will be on the air on time.

Fifteen minutes later, the bureau chief comes back to the desk. Now they will have to shoot Mondale landing at the reflecting pool. One of the assistant editors wonders whether they are getting too involved in filming everything that happens. "Are we going to shoot Mondale every time he comes and goes from the White House?" he asks. The question slides by everyone.

The news editor hangs up his telephone. "No picture exists of Mondale getting into the helicopter," he announces.

"I'm sure there are a lot of tourists up there who shot the picture," the operations coordinator says. There is laughter, but this is regarded as a serious matter.

There is a flurry of telephone calls between the bureau chief and executives at the other networks, between the editor and his field contacts. "I just talked to Linda at NBC, and they're very upset over there." They decide to go with coverage of Mondale landing and forget the problem at Camp David. It will work out.

An assistant editor brings a piece of wire copy to the desk. "Look at this," he says. "TASS [the Soviet news agency] says even the name 'Camp David' shows American bias toward Israel." Everyone laughs heartily at this, and the editor takes the wire copy from the assistant editor. Later, the story is relayed to Frank Reynolds in Camp David, and he includes it as a sidelight in his commentary on the summit.

At about 1 P.M., someone remarks, "The word is that Jody Powell will do something for the cameras."

"Do you want to buy the line?" asks an assistant editor.

"I'd go for it, I really would," the editor says.

This routine continues with growing intensity throughout the afternoon. By 4 P.M., the news room is a magnitude noisier than it was four hours earlier. Several reporters have returned to the bureau and filed their stories. Now they are back at the set of the "World News Tonight," trading stories.

As 5 P.M. nears, the cameras and studio monitors are turned on. Little red lights glow like eyes in the darkness. News assistants who were sitting at their desks chatting about auto repairs, are now running from one part of the news room to another, shoving bundles of copy into one box, picking up paper from another, and scurrying off again. Now and then, a particularly obnoxious telephone bellows a piercing tone—something you'd expect to hear in the president's bedroom just as World War III begins.

The research director slides across the floor with packets of information. She leaves one here, heads back into her office, and heads out with another envelope full of background on something. In the producer's office a meeting is under way to firm up the schedule for tonight's program. Everything seems firm but the Camp David stuff. There is a rough plan for that, too, but it will be firmed just at air time.

As the schedule for the evening show is shaped, the editors and reporters cooperate to synchronize the video with the audio scripts, which are written to a specified time—usually not more than a couple of minutes. The control and editing rooms are isolated from the main news room. As the editorial desk brings home the stories of the day and sends them on to the production people, the focus shifts from the news room to the production facilities, to editing and splicing and timing and writing transitions.

For the most part, all of this goes on in a different part of the two-building complex. To reach the editing and control facilities, one goes back down the elevator into the basement, winds through several corridors, and comes up into the hallway that gives access to the production facilities. Down one connecting hall are the film processing crew and facility. By this time of the day, they are well on the way toward finishing their work. The stories that have been filmed were completed early in the day, giving these people the time they need to produce a filmed spot for the evening.

Straight down the hall and through swinging doors are the editing facilities—little rooms crammed with electronic gear. Each editing setup consists of two videotape machines. One serves as the source for the video and the audio. The other is used to edit the source material to a particular time and order. Around each editor, in front of the rack, sit a writer and a production assistant. They talk among themselves, discussing what shots are most consistent with the copy that has been written. They bend over their work, furiously spending energy on a piece of work that will be seen by millions of television viewers in less than an hour. Their sophisticated machinery beeps and buzzes. They utter short remarks that hold much meaning. People and electronic gadgetry work together like some kind of specialized organism, half biological and half bionic.

Back in the news room, last-minute changes are still being made in the evening script. An intern checks the wire copy and finds something he thinks deserves to be put into the show. He shows it to one of the people sitting around the rim of the editorial slot. He does not like the reply. "But that's ten tons of marijuana," he says emphatically. "This is a good story."

The editor takes it. New York agrees. It is a good story, and it gets on the air as a short item. A DC-7 from Colombia has crashed in the Ozarks. It is loaded with marijuana.

It is now 4:58 P.M., almost time for ABC's direct electronic feed (DEF). Throughout the day, Washington's reporters have been filming and taping pieces they have offered the editors for the evening news. But not all those pieces get used on the national program, not by a long shot. To keep from wasting the materials, the producers try to see that as many as possible are used somewhere else. The DEF provides a service to ABC's affiliated stations. Everything that does not get onto the evening news and is considered newsworthy is offered as a separate piece to the affiliated stations. The engineers tape the half-hour feed, then the broadcasters select whatever stories they want from that half hour and insert them into their local broadcasts. Unfortunately, no one really knows how much of the DEF is used. The reporters, especially, regret that they have no idea what happens to their work.

At 5:15, someone shouts, "New York! New York!" People start scurrying for their telephones. The call is for one of the assistant editors. Everyone is on pinpricks until she is put on the line. When New York calls, Washington listens.

The noise rises again, swiftly now. Several telephones are ringing, including the one that emits the electronic scream. The wire room's sliding door is open, letting the clattering and sputtering spill out into the news room. The editors are discussing the final order of tonight's show, checking to make sure nothing is missed. The public relations assistant's voice drones on as she calls more journalists and reads a release to them. The thick acoustic tile on the ceiling mutes all this cacophony. There is great noise without echo.

By 5:30, the work is pretty much over in the news room, but nervous energy is so thick one could draw sparks off fingertips. Everyone is up, moving around, gossiping, drinking the next in an endless series of cups of coffee. One of the assistant editors comes out of the wire room and makes an enormous ball out of 10 or 15 feet of wire copy. He tosses the paper at the rest of the people sitting at the slot desk.

In the office, tomorrow's Washington schedule is already under discussion. Assignments are being made for tomorrow's news programs. There is discussion of today's show, which will be on the air in less than an hour. The din in the news room has begun to taper off gradually. The operations editor speaks into his headset to Camp David. "Have him bring back ENG Four because we're gonna need more equipment hauled up there in the morning."

Several of the monitors are hooked into the editing feeds. The introduction with Frank Reynolds and all of the Reynolds transitions between Camp David stories have already been videotaped and are being played back. Reynolds appears on the screen and welcomes the viewers to the evening news. A second later, he is saying, "Thank you, Barbara. Now here's another report on the summit." At 5:35 the control rooms are still quiet. In five minutes, people will start pouring in, and the scene will become true pandemonium.

The engineers and two of the production staff take their places at the desk in the interior control room. They begin running the Reynolds introduction and transitions. It is now twenty minutes until the first version of the evening news is on the air. They can do up to three versions—one at 6 P.M., one at 6:30, and another at 7 P.M, if necessary. On a slow night, and if there are no production foul-ups, the first take on the show can simply be replayed. On a night like tonight, though, when things are happening at a remote location, there are likely to be changes in all three versions.

The West Coast will see the latest version of the three. What is live in the Eastern and Central time zones is usually taped for the viewers on Pacific and Mountain time. Now and then one will see a live insert done in Los Angeles, but that is relatively rare.

"Stand by," says one engineer into his headset.

"Roll twenty-one," he says. "That's page 11."

The stories for the news are on numbered pages, but the pages are never used in order. The order is rearranged as the producers in New York, in consultation with the Washington crew, evaluate the late-breaking news. Conversation is terse, spare. Very few words mean a lot. These people are used to working together under pressure. A word, a gesture, a vibration is all that is needed when something requires attention.

Ten minutes before the first news show is aired, the word comes that Anwar Sadat has left Camp David. A motorcade has just left Camp David. The producer is in the room now. He sits on the ledge between the inner and the outer control rooms, where the sliding glass window has been pulled open.

"Do we have a live picture?" he asks. "Is that Reynolds live?"

Reynolds is standing in front of a sign saying "Camp David" on one of the monitors. He shifts his weight from one foot to another and talks to someone off-camera.

"That's a live shot," says one of the engineers.

"We'll need copy if we're going live," says the producer. "Are we going live at the top? What does New York say?"

Because Sadat has left Camp David, it is decided that the pre-taped introduction by Reynolds will be scrapped, and Reynolds will start the show with a live broadcast from Camp David. The control rooms are filled with noise and commotion as six o'clock approaches. Both rooms fill quickly. Six people enter the outer control room—most of them assistant editorial personnel from the news room—and begin talking to New York or to the other end of the building on the telephone.

"Sadat is already gone. Nobody knows why he's left or where he's going," says a woman sitting at a telephone.

Reynolds's voice is audible through a speaker in the inner control room. "Someone's screaming in my ear," he says, rubbing his little earphone wih the back of his hand. "I just had somebody yelling in my ear. I don't want to be able to hear anybody while I'm on."

The engineers are having trouble with a special effect that will be superimposed. A green line appears across the top of their feed monitor whenever the effect is added. Fiddling with knobs, an engineer turns the superimposed material first white, then yellow. The green band disappears. Next, the engineer "supers" a quote from the Pope's prayer for Camp David. It looks fine.

"Do we have it, or does New York?" asks the producer.

"New York," someone says.

It is now time for the show to begin. The monitors show Reynolds standing in front of the cameras. The helicopter is in the air, beaming the live feed to Washington and on to New York for distribution throughout the network. Reynolds stretches his mouth widely open and runs his tongue around his lips.

Air time. Reynolds takes thirty seconds, saying ABC will have much to broadcast from Camp David. He says Sadat is out of the site now for some unknown reason. At the end of the script for Reynolds's introduction, somebody in New York blows it. A commercial rather than the intro comes up on the feed monitor and swiftly disappears. The music and the introduction for the evening news appears as swiftly. That took perhaps five seconds.

"What was that?" someone in the inner control room asks. No reply.

In his beginning remarks, Reynolds referred to the road behind him that runs up to Camp David, but the camera stays tight on Reynolds. "Where's the road?" asks the producer to nobody in particular. "Where was the road in that shot?"

"The folks at Camp David said not to shoot the road in," someone says.

"But I saw it on NBC yesterday."

"Well, maybe that's when they decided we couldn't shoot it."

The broadcast now has still black-and-white shots of Carter, Begin, and Sadat on the air. Earlier in the day there was much concern about these pictures. The networks wanted visuals of today's activities, and they ended up with still black-and-whites.

"That's the first time we've ever seen the goddamn things," remarks the producer. "The stuff we've got on tape is better, but of course these are *today*'s pictures"—stressing the word "today" sarcastically. Immediacy over quality, evidently, is not always his judgment.

Thirteen minutes deep into the broadcast, the woman on the telephone to New York looks up with a stricken face.

"The helicopter's running out of gas; we've got to get Frank [Reynolds] on again soon if we're gonna get him at all."

"Get on the phone to Camp David," says the producer. "Find out what's happening."

"We've got to have priority on Frank," says somebody in the interior control room. "Donaldson's piece can stand. The copter's running out of gas."

The control rooms are thick with cigarette smoke. The producer and his chief assistant—the woman on the phone to Camp David—are chain smoking.

At 6:17, more still pictures come on the monitor.

"That really makes a picture, that series of stills," says the producer sarcastically.

"Sadat's coming back!" shouts the woman on the telephone. "New York says we're going live at the bottom!"

But before they can get to that, the picture from Camp David disappears entirely. Snow replaces the picture on the monitor for the Camp David feed. Then a picture, foggy and blurred. Then nothing. Then a clear picture for ten seconds. Then nothing.

Suddenly the screen clears, and in the picture is Sadat's motorcade, driving up the road into the Camp David enclave. Then nothing.

"Did we get that?" asks the producer urgently. "Did New York?"

"New York has it."

New York has twelve seconds of Sadat's limousine. It could be any limousine in any forest from the looks of the shot, but Sadat is in there. There is not time to put it into the first show, but it is edited into the second and third versions of the evening.

As the program ends with Reynolds's recitation of the Pope's prayer, the producer turns his attention to the pieces that will be redone. Sam Donaldson's report from Camp David needs work. The Brit Hume report on the assassination hearing has a minor flaw that can be fixed. Within two minutes the scenario begins again. New York is ready to begin the second take of "World News Tonight."

Reynolds appears again, this time on tape, and the program gets under way.

The previous half hour has been a ballet of nuance and swift decisions. One word, two, three at most, and an engineer makes the changes needed in a tape or a superimposition. Sadat leaves and returns, and the entire program is upended to try to include him. Reynolds goes live just in case. New York, Washington, Camp David, all feeding electronic signals among one another, all chattering continuously on the telephone as they coordinate the bits and pieces of information that go into the program.

Not all nights are this hectic, but when they have to, these people work together well and swiftly. The emphasis is on immediacy. So what if one can't tell the difference between this limousine and the limousine at the local funeral parlor? This is happening, *now*, and a crew and a helicopter are there to get it onto the air *now*. The significance of all this is not discussed. It has been decided that this will be the lead story, and whatever is there to be covered will be covered, whether it represents any news or not. Tonight it does not.

ABC News in Washington has a total of twenty-seven "working reporters," including anchorman Frank Reynolds. The support personnel total 225. In other words, there are ten people working in the bureau for every one you might see on the televison screen. In the mysterious and influential world of broadcast journalism, this is an important ratio to remember: All we viewers ever see is the tip of a massive iceberg.

10

The Media Stars

When Walter Cronkite made his occasional broadcasts from the Washington studios of CBS Television, the 20 million Americans who watched him might reasonably have assumed that Cronkite was manning the news desk singlehandedly—just Uncle Walter, the camera, the lights, and the Truth. In fact, Cronkite was invariably sitting in the midst of more than fifty other CBS correspondents and staffers, all of whom had contributed in some way to the scripted message that the anchorman delivered to the American public. Moreover, of the twenty-four minutes of the actual news time in a thirty-minute broadcast, Cronkite was generally the chief spokesman for only about six minutes of the program. "Cronkite tells" was marked in the nightly script remarkably infrequently, and yet it always seemed (and CBS did its best to *make it seem)* that Walter Cronkite was fully in control throughout the entire program.

There he sat, night after night, an undismayed solidity, his voice maintaining its characteristic resonance and omniscience whatever the news. Paul Weaver of *Fortune* said of Walter Cronkite:

> He is the exemplar—who is positively godlike: he summons forth men, events, and images at will; he speaks in tones of utter certainty; he is the person with whom things begin and end. But the omniscient pose is also adopted by reporters in the field. The "eyewitness" story format offers a particularly useful illustration: The reporter usually stands in front of the building or scene in question, his head and torso many times larger on the screen than the physical object and persons involved in the actual events being reported. Throughout the report, the actual

occurrences are like putty in Cronkite's masterful hands. He cuts from one shot to another; he stops the president in mid-sentence; he "voices over" images of kings, congresses, wars, and citizens. At every point he conveys the subterranean but nonetheless powerful suggestion that the reporter is larger than life, that he literally as well as figuratively towers over the mere mortals, whose doings and undoings he so easily grasps and unerringly grasps, and whose pretenses he sees through in an instant.

He never seemed to say less than he knew, nor did he ever indicate by silences or hesitations that there were things that he did not know. And, at the end, when he said, "And that's the way it is . . . ," most of America was content that the state of the nation and of the world had been fairly and accurately described. Cronkite was and is the master of television-news technique.

As I observed one such broadcast from the Washington bureau studios of CBS News, I found that even with the distractions of the studio background, I was caught up as usual with the confidence, the authority that Cronkite always projects effortlessly through the television camera. He seemed a mythic figure on the screen; and, indeed, even off-camera, among the news reporters who are characteristically so jocular and jaded, Cronkite was given all of the distance and respect of the cultural demigod he had become.

When the news program ended, for example, Cronkite got up from his studio desk, walked past Roger Mudd, and made some teasing remark that invited laughter from Mudd and other personnel within earshot. The invitation for laughter, however, apparently did not extend to a gathering of the staff around Cronkite for a bantering rehash of the night's program. Instead, Cronkite moved to a large desk well isolated from the many others surrounding the studio area. He sat with his feet on the desk and watched the next program, a presidential press conference, over his shoetops. *No one* went near him. As he sat quietly, the others in the room kibitzed and conversed. A reporter walked to the monitor, pulled a handkerchief from his pocket, and wiped the perspiring screen forehead of the president. The others laughed. Cronkite smiled. But no one approached him or referred to him. He has, even among his colleagues and peers, an eminent and mythic celebrity.

What is Cronkite's magic? Apparently, there is something about his mien and the timbre of his deep baritone voice that can suffuse the American spirit with faith and confidence. In addition, Cronkite is an intelligent, experienced, hard-working, and responsible news reporter with a fairly straightforward and sincere Middle Western persona. He projects trust because he is, probably above all else, a sincere and responsible and honest man. What is Cronkite's magic? Call it the combination of genetic blessing (the voice, the face, and the intelligence), a practiced broadcaster's charisma, and a worthy soul.

The validity of this assessment came to me later, when I watched Walter Cronkite present a rousing commencement address before two thousand largely cynical students at Stanford University. It was almost like a presidential address at the party convention. Key phrases were inevitably interrupted by huzzahs, and, at the end of the speech, the entire audience stood up, clapping and cheering, for almost two minutes. Still, with due thought, one was left with the question: What exactly did he say?

The next day I, in fact, asked many students who were there what Cronkite *had* said and why they had liked him. They answered that he was wonderful, and. . . , well, he just spoke wonderfully! I, too, had been moved by his deep baritone and drawn to his familiar figure and face, but his *words* had seemed to me no better or worse than those of many another commencement speaker. Indeed, much of the address sounded as if it had been exhumed from an old stock speech, brushed off, and updated a bit. Nearly all of the speech would have gone over equally well in 1956.

This is how Cronkite ended his address to the students—the climactic moment: "There isn't any doubt in my mind that I speak for most of us of the older generation when I say with all my heart that I envy you the glorious experiences that lie ahead of you; the bright future that is in your power to build. For, the more and the greater the challenges, the greater the heroism of thought, deed, and courage of those who surmount them—and for them, the more exciting the prospect of the combat and the sweeter the taste of victory. Good night and good luck."

If that speech had been read on the page rather than heard, the more critical members of Cronkite's audience would surely have become immediately skeptical and unenthusiastic about the ringing clichés of that paragraph. But Walter Cronkite's mythic personality and charisma somehow allowed him to transcend such banalities and to make them seem fresh and significant. For more than a generation, he performed the same sleights of hand for CBS News.

James Reston is a different genre of myth. He is not nearly so widely known as Cronkite. He is rarely seen by the public. Although Reston writes his news column for *The New York Times,* which has a weekday circulation of almost a million, and although his column can also be carried by more than three hundred newspapers that contract for *The New York Times* News Service, Reston gets nothing even approaching Cronkite's (and now Dan Rather's) daily audience or public adulation (not to mention salary). But Scotty Reston is as much the superstar among newspaper reporters as Cronkite is among his colleagues in the electronic media.

Within the press corps, Reston is a myth beyond question. There arc already "legendary" stories like this one:

James Thompson, writing of the time when he was a young newcomer to the State Department, recalls nervously joining ex-Secretary of State Dean Acheson for lunch at the exclusive Metropolitan Club in Washington. "As I was sitting there," Thompson says, "exhilarated by the presence of a score of notables among our fellow lunchers, a murmur of excitement filled the room, and two men made their way slowly, in single file, toward a table at the end. From all over came respectful calls of greeting—'Hello there, Scotty!' 'Hi, Scotty!' 'Good to see you, Scotty!'—to each of which the rather chunky man in front responded, queen-mother-like, with a nod, a gentle smile, and slight benediction of the hand. As conversations resumed, Acheson turned to his friend Paul Nitze [a former secretary of the Navy] at the next table and asked, 'Paul, *who* is that with Scotty Reston?' 'I don't know,' said Nitze. 'But I'll give you a call after lunch.'

"I should have known then and there where power really lay," Thompson writes.

Like that other superstar of the news world, Reston's honesty and professionalism are above reproach. *The New York Times* never doubts Reston's reporting, even when it proves wrong, as it did in December 1972. On 13 December, the *Times* ran a front-page story from Reston, who was in Paris covering Secretary of State Henry Kissinger and the Vietnam peace conference. Reston reported that the Vietnam peace talks were going well, and it was obvious that he had gotten his information from Kissinger. However, William Beecher, who was then the *Times*'s Pentagon reporter, learned in Washington that the talks in Paris were foundering and that the Nixon administration was considering immediate action to revive them, including resumption of the bombing of North Vietnam.

Beecher had filed what the *Times*'s editors recall as "quite a complete story" on the imminent resumption of the bombing, but the *Times* editors were reluctant to publish the story because it contradicted James Reston. One source from the *Times* said that the "instincts" of the *Times*'s editors "were that things were great and the Pentagon was leaking to Beecher to upset the negotiations." Beecher was asked, perhaps challenged, to go back for more confirmation, and later to "recast" the story to include the South Vietnamese role in the breakdown of the negotiations. On 16 December, a news conference statement by Kissinger about difficulties in the negotiations—which had been predicted in the Beecher story two days earlier—finally convinced the *Times*'s editors of the validity of Beecher's story.

One experienced reporter said, "Things like this happen from time to time. But it's not as rare as a comet." Reston certainly surmounted that mistake. His writing is as clear as a bell. Unlike the columnists of olden times, who once wrote who-where-what-when news stories with jerky transitions, Reston writes sentences and paragraphs that are so linked to one another that the reader has the distinct experience of following a connected line from the first word to the last.

Someone once said that there are so many things to be outraged about nowadays that it is difficult to rise to every occasion. Nicholas von Hoffman rises. As a syndicated columnist, von Hoffman is shocked, appalled, disgusted, and, in his lightest moods, disappointed.

One of his columns began:

> It happens every time they acknowledge a crime. "See," they shout, "the system works!" Doubtless we shall be hearing those words now that eight miserable Ohio National Guardsmen have been indicted for the Kent State killings.
>
> Even when they are acquitted, for surely no jury that can read a calendar is going to convict them, they will have been

punished. With the cost of lawyers today, indictment is punishment.
The way the system works is that the farther down you are
and the less responsible you are, the stiffer the punishment.
Therefore, it follows that the bigger losers in the crimes and
punishments of Watergate will be those pathetic Cuban bur-
glars.

Von Hoffman went on to lament that Maurice Stans and John
Mitchell were standing trial through some foul-up; that if convicted
they would get about as much punishment as was given the
businessmen who pleaded guilty to illegal campaign contributions;
and that, thanks to a fix, former Attorney General Richard
Kleindienst's plea bargaining was being held up "while all parties
scour the law books to find a misdemeanor minor enough for him to
plead guilty to." (They found one: testifying inaccurately.)

Eloquent outrage is apparent in the concluding sentence of von
Hoffman's column: "This is their system, wherein they ride in
limousines from place to place to explain the sacrifices of public
service, after which they name bridges, schools, dams, and highways
after themselves and aspire to have their likenesses cut into
mountainsides, while recordings of their voices instruct us that the
highest form of citizenship is to vote for them and refrain from
displaying hostile placards."

That is the voice of one who speaks for the outsiders. Von
Hoffman met them during eleven years of working on the south side
of Chicago for the Industrial Areas Foundation of the late community organizer Saul Alinsky. Hired by the *Chicago Daily News* in
1963, von Hoffman used and enhanced his contacts among blacks
and other minorities in Chicago, then went to Mississippi to cover
"Freedom Summer," a project to register black voters and to teach
basic educational skills. In a fairly typical report, von Hoffman
wrote: "Some whites have come to recognize the rebellion welling
up in the people they still refer to as 'our nigras.' They are galled by
it, though, like the vindictive Hattiesburg housewife who said,
'When I saw that little colored girl of mine waiting in front of the
courthouse with those common niggers, I could hardly believe it. I
would have let her go anyway. She was spending more time
eavesdropping than cooking.'"

The *Washington Post* hired him away from the *News* in 1966 and
soon sent him back to Mississippi, this time to cover James

Meredith's march across the state. Von Hoffman's reports were as vivid as ever, but Benjamin Bradlee, editor of the *Post,* who holds that von Hoffman "tilts at more cherished beliefs and more traditional institutions more effectively than anyone since H. L. Mencken," also said of him, "Nick von Hoffman can't write a news story to save his prematurely gray head." Bradlee spelled out what he meant in the preface to a collection of von Hoffman's writings titled *Left at the Post:* "if Meredith's name appeared in the copy, it was purely an accident; there would be no normal time frame, and Nick always did feel that exact geography was barely relevant. An editor always had to write a lead to the story, explaining to the reader that this was a piece about James Meredith, and that the events occurred yesterday."

Post editors were baffled about how to use such rough-hewn talent. Finally, as one said, "We decided on turning him loose in one corner of the paper. He could not fit into our news columns, and yet he is not a columnist really, either."

Hardly had von Hoffman gotten settled into his corner than he became a columnist, devoting many more "Posters" to armchair comment than to the kind of pointillist reporting that lured the *Post* into hiring him. The commentaries are both street-smart and readable, but some *Post* editors grumble that von Hoffman should get back out in the street and do more of those sharply focused descriptions that both report and comment.

If in "Poster" von Hoffman seemed to be the authentic Angry Man, some of his other writing and his television appearances suggest that he is more complicated. In an article in the magazine *New Times,* he protested, apparently seriously, that the righteous have gone too far in investigating Watergate and in pursuing its perpetrators. Speaking out for a little healthy corruption, from the background of a veteran of the Chicago streets who had done some corrupting himself, von Hoffman argued for "ordinary, necessary, socially useful illegality."

On the CBS television program "60 Minutes," where he once appeared as a regular commentator opposite conservative columnist James J. Kilpatrick, von Hoffman was even less predictable. His biases were as obvious as a vaudeville joke, and usually as laughingly overdrawn, as when he suggested that the best way to end the Nixon presidency was with a public hanging. Von Hoffman poses, declaims, once referred to himself as an "effete commie-pinko-radic-lib freak," and agreeably admitted, when he was charged with being an attacker, "I don't want people to think I'm an affable eccentric, so from time to time I get vicious."

Later, von Hoffman was fired by CBS. Still later, Ben Bradlee spoke of von Hoffman as though he hoped the newsman would also leave the *Post.* "How the hell do I know what he's doing? I haven't seen him in a year and a half. If I never see him, I can pay 75 bucks a week to a syndicate and have all the Nick von Hoffman I want." Almost as though von Hoffman heard those words from Bradlee, he switched to become a columnist for the King Features Syndicate.

Von Hoffman treats his profession, like most everything else, with a light derision. Asked about the most damaging of journalistic practices, von Hoffman responded, "Accuracy. We've got too much accuracy." Are the charges true that all journalists share the same political leanings? "No," he replied. "Actually what happens is that we meet once a year in a basement and draw lots for different viewpoints so we can service the entire market. Next year I've got to be a Southern racist."

> The Devil works at me. The Devil does not tire;
> He floats above me like the air, impalpable.
> I gulp him down, I feel him set my lungs on fire
> And fill me with desires, endless and culpable.

These lines show another Les Whitten, escaping his adversary chores as investigative reporter and former Jack Anderson partner by assuming one of his private roles: translator of Baudelaire for literary magazines. Whitten also follows the more traditional pursuits of teacher of creative writing and author of children's books, mysteries, biographies, and political novels. Since he was graduated *magna cum laude* from Lehigh in 1952, Whitten has done many kinds of reporting—for Radio Free Europe, United Press International, the *Washington Post,* the Hearst newspapers, and Jack Anderson—and has been tested in most of the reporter's crucibles: strikes, trials, floods, hurricanes, suicides, murders, and wars. "Used-car hoodlums and militant revolutionaries have threatened me physically, and I was gassed and pushed around by the Chicago cops at the 1968 Democratic National Convention," Whitten said. But Whitten's worst panic came when Navy ships put on a show for the press off the coast of Cuba: "One of their missiles got out of whack and was pointed at the ship I was on only a couple of hundred yards away."

Somewhere along his reporter's route, Whitten developed investigative techniques to match his instincts. He broke key elements in the Billie Sol Estes scandal, and his story on an insurance man's gift of a stereo set to Lyndon Johnson was one of the better stories in the Bobby Baker criminal case. Such work led Jack Anderson, who inherited Drew Pearson's column in 1969, to make Whitten his junior partner. When Anderson was away, Whitten broadcast Anderson's daily radio program and ran the Anderson team: three other reporters, two reporter-interns, and two secretaries.

Although Anderson often gave credit to his assistants, his column was sometimes such a mix of teamwork that readers could not always tell who dredged up what. In his eight years with Anderson, Whitten turned up hidden information in Laos, Cambodia, and Vietnam, and sometimes interviewed Viet Cong as they came from battle. He has reported from Israel and from Egypt, and he once searched the waters off uninhabited Florida Keys for treasure buried by the CIA.

In Washington, where Whitten spends most of his time, he has often contributed to Anderson's reports on the odd financing that entangles high officials. His exposés have caused several members of Congress to be defeated and others to retire. But Whitten thinks his best work was a story about Senator Everett Dirksen of Illinois, who died in office. Whitten showed that Dirksen had put one of his aides on the board of a bank with the help of Roy M. Cohn, a former aide to Senator Joseph McCarthy of Wisconsin, then had intervened in a court case to help Cohn. "I liked that story because I had time to do it right," Whitten said. "I conclusively nailed up Dirksen at a time he was slippery enough to be hard to nail up."

Whitten became nationally visible in his own right in 1973 as a result of a phone call from Hank Adams, a young Indian leader who had participated three months earlier in the occupation of the Bureau of Indian Affairs (BIA) building in Washington. The Indians had made off with tons of documents. Adams had stayed in Washington to smooth things over and, to show good faith, was giving some of the documents to the FBI and promising BIA officials that all would soon be returned. Adams called to tell Whitten, who had written several columns about the contents of the stolen papers, that he was giving three cartons of documents to the FBI that morning.

Disappointed, because Adams said the documents were not newsworthy, Whitten nonetheless offered to help Adams take them to the FBI office. Adams said that a friend had promised to provide transportation, but Whitten skipped breakfast and hurried to

Adams's apartment. The friend did not arrive, so Whitten and Adams prepared to load the cartons into Whitten's car. Suddenly FBI agents surrounded them—Adams's "friend" was an undercover policeman.

Whitten began taking notes, but an agent snatched away pen and paper and handcuffed him. Whitten's notes were returned at the FBI office, but he was fingerprinted and photographed. But Whitten had to ask the agents to photograph the cartons, which Adams had marked with the name of the agent who had received other documents and to whom Adams planned to give the cartons. Charges were made that Whitten "did unlawfully receive, conceal and detain three cardboard boxes of Government documents, books, and records with intent to convert the said property and records to his own use and gain."

Whitten could see no use or gain for himself in old legal opinions or land records or a volume of the U.S. Code. Neither could the grand jury, which refused to indict him. The Department of Justice dropped the charges at the same time.

Early in 1981, Whitten wrote for the *Washington Post* a long story that was entitled "The Mysteries of the Washington Column Revealed." Although he wrote that story with such subtitles as "Two-Byline-Double-Edged-Sword," "The Bearded Interview Two-Step," and the "Adjectival Gush," he was not having fun. He was telling the truth—and one of the Washington reporters said, "Whitten doesn't just reveal what the columnists do; much of that story is what we *reporters* do."

For example, "The Two-Byline-Double-Edged-Sword" is an honored method among the columnists who have partners. When a pair of columnists publishes an exposé of a high-level official, who is a good source for one of them, the official will call the seemingly friendly columnist to complain at length. The columnist may say, "If I'd been in town, I could have stopped it," or, "My partner is uncontrollable. If I'd blocked it, he'd have quit the column. You can't image the trouble I've had with him. . . . Now while I've got you on the phone, how about that confidential memo we were discussing last week. . . ."

Whitten also explains "The Bearded Interview Two-Step" by describing how a clever columnist *seems* to be at high-level meetings of the officials. Rowland Evans and Robert Novak began one of their columns this way: "Within hours of his confirmation as Secretary of State, Alexander Haig put final touches on a document for President Reagan's signature that would enthrone the State Department and its new boss as undisputed foreign policy makers in the Reagan Administration."

While many of the Evans-Novak readers envisioned the columnists at Haig's elbow, Whitten went on to write:

> Certainly there was rage in Haig's bunker over the leak. Surely there was trembling in the camp of White House National Security Adviser Richard V. Allen lest Reagan's inner circle or Haig think Allen leaked it.
>
> But what would the column *mean* beyond what it says?
>
> Well, one rival columnist would venture it meant that Haig was in trouble with Edwin Meese, the president's closest adviser. In fact, this rival columnist will eat the Evans and Novak column in the National Press Club's ballroom with only house dressing if someone very close to Meese didn't have something to do with it.
>
> Why Meese or one of his meeses?
>
> Scrutiny of the column shows mention of eight people and three agencies that might have known about Haig's memo. But only one, Ed Meese, was mentioned with any real approval.
>
> Then the intrepid Joseph Kraft shortly came up with details on Haig's would-be putsch, mentioning the Meese-Haig disagreement but with much information on Meese's allies and little on Haig's.
>
> A few days later, The Post's own Don Oberdorfer also wrote about the situation, going a step farther by putting us inside Reagan's inner circle (three men, one of them Meese) and quoting a "senior official" as saying Haig tried a "power grab."
>
> A solid case for Meese or one of his pals having leaked the story? So you might think. But hold on.
>
> In the Evans and Novak column, Allen looked the wimp. This is a time-tested red herring for putting irate officials off the track of the true leaker.
>
> A few days later, in a second Evans and Novak column, Allen was the *hero*. Reagan, report Evans and Novak, "authorized Allen to leak a story" in order to save the life of Korean dissident Kim Dae Jung. Could it be that Allen, not Meese . . . ?
>
> Where would that leave us? With one thing still certain: Al Haig will sure as hell be using everything short of the wiretapping he helped with in the Nixon days to find out who has the Wally Hickel Memorial Ax out for him at the White House.

Whitten went on to explain the shorthand method, which is called "Adjectival Gush Analysis." When a columnist terms anyone "effective," "brilliant," "conscientious," "dependable," or "enterprising," the reader can be certain that the subject has leaked or is on the verge of leaking a good story to that columnist. As for the lesser adjectives—"hard-working," "able," "capable," "earnest," "zealous," or the affability series: "affable," "amiable," "good-humored," "friendly," "good-hearted," and "kindly"—the same *may* be true.

Whitten finished his analysis of the adjectival gush by making up sentences that illustrate how columnists guard themselves from libel suits. He showed how a columnist can insert a favorable adjective in an unfavorable story: "*Affable* Ivan Repressovich hardly seems the type of federal judge who would molest children, but . . ." Or "One of the nation's most *hard-working* anti-Semites is Charlington Goering-Smythe."

One ruse that the readers of Whitten's story did not know was that he was talking about himself in explaining a variation on the nondenial-denial. He wrote about an official with secret transcripts to leak. Whitten and his 84-year-old mother drove by the official's building at 11:30 P.M. The official handed a manila envelope through the car window to the mother and later was able to testify that he had neither met Whitten nor given him anything.

Whitten so often reports, or is involved in, conflict and controversy that some of it inevitably turns up in his other life of poet, biographer, and novelist. In his readable novel *The Alchemist,* a flexible government attorney and a seductive woman official who schemes for the vice presidency are both crooked and surrounded by crooks. At one point, the attorney, who does not quite speak for Whitten, says that there are "splendid exceptions" among the crooks, cowards, and liars in politics, but . . .

"She belongs in jail," he said flatly.

"They all do," I said quietly.

"They all what?"

"They all belong in jail. All politicians."

In a recent *New Yorker* cartoon, a television viewer was pictured leaning forward, looking intently at the screen while urging his wife: "Quick, Edith! I need an outside opinion. Is Cronkite sneering?" For a great many critics of television news, that is the central question: When are newscasters sneering—and raising eyebrows and intoning skepticism? The suspicion that some do vexes officials, too, but officials who are deep in trouble have a more pertinent question: Do viewers *believe* what they are seeing and hearing?

Dan Rather never sneers, but he once reported from the White House with a force and a directness that made it seem that Truth itself was speaking, even when it was not. In 1971, Rather's somewhat abrasive approach caused a confrontation in the White House between Rather on one side and John Ehrlichman and H. R. Haldeman on the other. Ehrlichman charged that Rather was wrong in his reporting 90% of the time. Rather responded, "Then you have nothing to worry about; any reporter who's wrong 90% of the time can't last."

Haldeman complained: "What concerns me is that you are sometimes wrong, but your style is very positive. You sound like you know what you're talking about; people believe you."

Ehrlichman added, "Yeah, people believe you, and they shouldn't."

Rather responded: "I hope they do, and maybe now we are getting down to the root of it. You have trouble getting people to believe you."

Rather's style on camera seems so open and direct, and his voice is so nearly toneless, that the impressionists who deftly imitate Cronkite, David Brinkley, and other TV journalists give up on Rather. There seems to be no distinctive feature: just a cowboy-handsome Southwesterner, who has lost most of his Texas twang, saying it straight. His style in asking questions shifts slightly; his voice becomes tense, his body seems taut. Indeed, if he asked soft or pointless questions, Rather might seem self-important—like the smooth announcers who dominated television news when it began, nearly twenty-five years ago, as the bastard child of show business and journalism. But Rather is always a sharp interviewer.

That is not surprising. Rather grew up in journalism:

> In that time and in my home place, being a reporter meant being a newspaperman, so in my dream of dreams I always saw myself as a newspaper reporter. I threw papers, sold them on street corners, and hung around newspaper offices trying for and sometimes finding errand-boy and copy-boy jobs. In college, I was a journalism junkie, going around on what seemed now and then a continuous high: writing and reporting for the twice-weekly college paper and the local town weekly, stringing for AP, UP, and INS—including covering electrocutions— reporting and announcing sports for the town radio station.

After working for United Press International and the *Houston*

Chronicle, Rather began reporting for KHOU-TV in Houston, and in 1961 he covered Hurricane Carla so well that CBS hired him. He performed so competently in covering President Kennedy's assassination that the network assigned him to the White House. The questions he directed at another Texan, Lyndon Johnson, were sometimes as sharp as those he later asked Nixon and his aides, but the attention the Nixon administration focused on the media helped make Rather prominent.

When Spiro Agnew began his attacks on the media, Rather posed this reverse-twist question at Nixon's next press conference: "Mr. President, is there anything that the vice president has said about the media with which you do *not* agree?" The traditional question in such circumstances is so obvious—"Do you agree with the vice president's speech on the media?"—that the other reporters laughed in approval. Nixon, who had been responding smoothly to other questions, opened his mouth—and for a moment nothing would come out. He recovered, of course, and delivered an innocuous answer, but that question helped mark Rather.

He was more clearly marked later, in an hour-long television interview with Nixon, which CBS assigned to Rather over protests from the White House. Many of his questions challenged the president in a fashion approved by most political journalists:

RATHER: Public opinion polls—the Harris Poll was the last one, the Gallup Polls before—indicated that the American people, in overwhelming majority, give you high marks for decisiveness, for willingness to change. But in the case of the Harris Poll, about 50% said that you had failed to inspire confidence and faith and lacked personal warmth and compassion. Why do you suppose that is?

PRESIDENT NIXON: Well, it's because people tell the pollsters that, of course. So that's what the people must believe. But on the other hand, without trying to psychoanalyze myself, because that's your job, I would simply answer the question by saying that my strong point is not rhetoric, it isn't showmanship, it isn't big promises, those things that breed the glamor and excitement that people call charisma and warmth. My strong point, if I have a strong point, is performance. I always do more than I said. . . .

RATHER: But the same Harris Poll indicated that only a third of the people thought that you had kept your campaign promises. . . . So would you explain, obviously as briefly as possible but as fully as you think necessary, in 1968 you said, "I pledge to redress the present economic imbalance without increasing

unemployment"—direct quotation. Now, unemployment was, I believe, 3.6[%] when you came in; it's at or near 6% for the last several months.
PRESIDENT NIXON: Let's take that one first.
RATHER: Yes, please.
PRESIDENT NIXON: Unemployment was 3.6 when I came in, at a cost of 300 casualties a week in Vietnam. Since I've come in, we have got 400,000 people home from Vietnam: There's two million people who have been let out of defense plants and out of the armed services as a result of our winding up—winding *down*—the war in Vietnam, and if those people were still in the defense plants and still in Vietnam, unemployment would still be 3.6 That's too high a cost.
RATHER: But wasn't that foreseeable, Mr. President?
PRESIDENT NIXON: [Beginning to stumble] That was foreseeable, but my point is—my point is that that we were—what I was saying was . . .

Throughout the interview, Rather kept Nixon off balance:

RATHER: Mr. President, do you consider Governor George Wallace and what he stands for a threat to holding this society together?
PRESIDENT NIXON: Well, I noted at the moment that he has decided to enter the Democratic primaries, and I really think your—that question should be directed to the Democratic candidate when you have him on the equal time that I'm sure is going to be requested after this program.
RATHER: Well, I'd like very much to ask the Democratic candidate that, when it's decided who it will be, but the question was put directly to you.
PRESIDENT NIXON: That's really the problem—it's not the problem here of our party as far as Mr. Wallace is concerned. . . .

The questions that brought such stumbling responses outraged many Nixon supporters—and others who thought that whoever occupies that presidential office should be approached at least gingerly, if not obsequiously. CBS received hundreds of protesting telephone calls. But in Nixon's infrequent news conferences, Rather continued to question the president closely.

In an August 1973 conference, Rather began, "I want to state this question with due respect for your office. . . ." Nixon interrupted: "That would be unusual." Several months later, when Nixon was being questioned at a meeting of the National Association of

Broadcasters in Houston, Rather introduced a question with, "Dan Rather with CBS News, Mr. President," and was interrupted by applause and a few boos. Nixon asked, "Are you running for something?" Rather responded: "No sir, Mr. President, are you?"

Even some of those who admire Rather thought that was going too far. There are not even unwritten rules, but the usual practice is for a journalist to stop short of personal arguments with a president. In the Nixon era, however, others had been pushed into something like public bickering with the president, including Clark Mollenhoff, former Washington bureau chief of the Cowles newspapers, who had earlier taken a year off from reporting to work for Nixon in the White House.

Rather's straightforward reporting for "60 Minutes" and as CBS anchorman will in time submerge that acid little byplay for all but the most reverent Nixon nostalgics. The personal level of his relations with Nixon perturb Rather, who said that he wants a reputation as a tough questioner, not as an antagonist. But the incident with Nixon does not preoccupy Rather. He has said of his work: "The ecstasy of it has never stopped. I can truthfully say that I have never started on any assignment any day in this work that I wasn't eager to get there, and once there to stay on it!"

Ironically, the rebirth of columnist James J. Kilpatrick began when Nixon resigned. Three months earlier, he had become the exclusive interviewer of President Nixon, and Kilpatrick wrote a long report rather than an opinionated column. In essence, he reported that Nixon had said that he would not resign, and that Nixon sounded as though he were put upon and valiantly protecting those who were in error.

This reassurance was sorely needed by many Nixon supporters who were awaiting a sign from an honest conservative. Kilpatrick's reporting of the interview was printed in the three hundred papers that syndicated his column, in most of them, on the front page. For a time, letters poured in congratulating Kilpatrick on his brilliant reporting.

Then, in August, Kilpatrick wrote the most sorrowful column of his career. It said:

> I write on Tuesday morning, 12 hours after the bombshell disclosures of Monday night, and I am close to tears. Grown men ought not to weep. I have been covering politics and

politicians for more than 30 years and have seen enough of duplicity to be immune to shock. Nixon's duplicity is almost beyond bearing.
The thing is: I believed him. Millions of other Americans believed him also. When he said, over and over, looking us squarely in the eye, that he had known nothing of the Watergate coverup until March of 1973, we believed him. "Your President is not a crook," he once said. I believed him. It no longer greatly matters. My President is a liar. . . .

Kilpatrick remained staunchly conservative, but he also realized that millions of people were relying on *him* for his view of the truth. He proved himself a responsible and a courageous reporter.

Kilpatrick's journalistic beginnings were devoutly conservative. A native of Oklahoma City, he went to the University of Missouri, then got his first full-time job as a reporter with the *Richmond News Leader* in Virginia in 1941. "I have been covering politics since I was 20, and I was pretty naive at the time. I suppose I once believed that all politicians meant to fulfill all their promises. One matures."

In Richmond, in a time when civil rights were at issue, he learned the lessons of conservatism from the general manager, John Dana Wise, an aristocratic South Carolinian. When Kilpatrick asked him to publish a liberal columnist to balance Kilpatrick's conservatism, this formal colloquy ensued:

"Well," said Wise, "I am perfectly agreeable, Mr. Kilpatrick, perfectly willing to authorize the expenditure for this purpose if I could justify it. But do you believe you're propounding the truth as to, say, civil rights?"

"Yes, Mr. Wise."

"And the columnist you would propose to buy would take the opposite view, correct?"

"Yes," said Kilpatrick.

"Then you would be taking for our paper what you conceive to be in error?"

"Well, in a sense, Mr. Wise, I would say so."

"Well, then, how can you justify to me your wishing to carry in our editorial section what you honestly conceive to be error? Is this the function of your editorial section, to deliver error to your readers?"

"Well, er . . . ," Kilpatrick would begin.

Wise would then say, "Oh, but you certainly have been expressing yourself very sincerely in your editorial pages in these matters."

"Yes, Mr. Wise."
"You believe you are speaking truth, do you not?"
"Yes."
Kilpatrick later said, "We never hired a liberal columnist. I accepted that, as I had to be editor of the paper. To be truthful, I didn't argue very fiercely. He was persuasive."

In 1964, he continued as editor of the *News Leader* and began writing a column three times a week at the invitation of *Newsday.* He was one of the few right-wing columnists at that time, and he was joyously and fiercely conservative. The column was picked up by so many newspapers that, the following year, the *Washington Star* offered Kilpatrick a base in Washington. He took it. The number of papers that are publishing him have increased from three hundred to nearly four hundred. Significantly, some papers claim that they have begun to publish Kilpatrick because he has changed his tone slightly and has become less conservative.

In fact, his columns have many evidences of a centrist tendency. In a column headlined "Who's to Watch the Watch Dogs," he wrote of one whom he had supported strongly: "J. Edgar Hoover, for all his good qualities, was a man of obsessive prejudices. As FBI director, he had massive powers to pursue them. He dealt with a succession of presidents, attorneys general and congressional leaders who had weaknesses of their own. Hoover's skill was to understand these weaknesses and to capitalize on them."

At an earlier time he had congratulated the new U.S. Postal Service on moving into private enterprise. In 1976, he began a column: "More than four years have gone by since the old U.S. Post Office Department became the new U.S. Postal Service. The idea at the time—and it seemed such a good idea at the time—was to get the mail out of politics. A dismal conclusion has to be voiced: We had better get the mail back into politics again."

Kilpatrick is one of the best of the writers in Washington. His style is sprightly and compelling. John Leonard of *The New York Times* wrote, at the twentieth birthday celebration of the conservative *National Review:* "James Jackson Kilpatrick, the antebellum Oscar Levant who plays musical chairs with Shana Alexander on CBS's '60 Minutes,' was the master of ceremonies. He wore a kilt. He spoke entirely in heroic couplets. They rhymed, they scanned, and they were clever."

Kilpatrick's passion for language was particularly marked in a column he wrote about Governor Jerry Brown, who at the time was running for the Democratic presidential nomination. Kilpatrick said that "in the jaded world of the Washington press corps he is a bright-plumed bird of passage," then ended with: "What was that word again? In my dingo shorthand, the symbols for 'r' and 'l' look pretty much the same. I thought he had said 'placatory,' a nice $2.95 word, but I ran after him down the sidewalk to check. He had said, 'precatory,' a three-dollar word if there ever was one. That was when I started wagging catty-wampus. I'm skeptical of Brown; but I'm impressed."

How did these stars become so influential? Cronkite, Reston, von Hoffman, Whitten, Rather, and Kilpatrick had never been enrolled in an Ivy League university. Without the prestige of graduating from the Ivy League, they had to begin at the bottom. Had they gone to Harvard, Yale, Princeton, or another prestigious university, they would have been discouraged after a few years of reporting and would have quit. *All* of them have two things in common: intelligence and persistence. Because they are persistent, these stars are influential.

11

Conclusion

*A*lthough most Americans are content to rely upon the Other Government for the truth of what has happened in the world, few are aware of the vagarics of its presentation of the facts or what masquerades as the facts. Consider what occurs in the time span between a news event and the news report:

1. Something happens in government.
2. Government officials decide how to announce this occurrence. This may differ from (1).
3. Through a press secretary, the news reporters are presented with the government's announcement of the occurrence. This may differ from (1) and (2).
4. A reporter produces a story about the occurrence. This may differ from (1), (2), and (3).
5. A media organization processes the reporter's story for presentation to the public. This may differ from (1), (2), (3), and (4).
6. The public receives a report of the occurrence. This may differ from (1), (2), (3), (4), and (5).

Thus, from initiation to presentation, a news story must hurdle four crucial obstacles. Hurdle number one is set up by government officials and bureaucrats. The official responsible for creating or addressing the news-making occurrence will winnow an announcement from the efforts of many subordinates. The latter may be reluctant or displeased with the task and its results, but the official usually succeeds in having the announcement phrased and timed in a way that may please *him*.

Next, for hurdle number two, the official ordinarily relies on a press secretary (or one known as a public-information specialist), who may or may not think well of the newly winnowed bulletin. The press secretary submits the announcement to journalists and, at that point, has an unusual role; for he or she is there to answer questions. If questioned perceptively, the secretary has an opportunity to suggest that the journalist check with a higher official, or to answer the questions directly in the way he or she prefers, or even to guide the journalist to submit further questions to an unhappy subordinate. The choice of the press secretary is hurdle number three.

Hurdle number four is usually the journalist's editor. An editor will generally pass a bland story as it is written. That encourages journalists not to look beyond the obvious and to write or broadcast information exactly as it was given out by the government. Most correspondents today abhor such reporting and are strongly adversarial toward government-issued news. But the editor has final authority and is more likely than the reporter to take a cautious line.

These hurdles—indeed, the whole six-part process of "newsmaking"—can be vastly more labyrinthine, as, for example, when something happens and is kept secret, or when something that *should* happen does not happen. Either instance would be only step number one en route to a distortion; the responsible official's decision on how to announce the event or how to avoid announcing it would merely be step number two. There could be four more levels of obfuscation. Clearly, the surety for the citizenry at the end of this conveyor belt is too often just a matter of expert packaging. Yet we respond to that end product as if it were a pristine recreation of reality, mainly because we know so little about the process in between.

The news media are often termed the "mirror on the world." But the process is a double mirror, and it is selectively narrow. Indeed, even that mixed metaphor may be too simple an analogy. The news media may be better understood as a prism, which picks up rays of information from all directions and refracts them, bends them, before sending them out again. The image is sent to many diverse audiences for information—as well as back to the original politician or other newsmaker, who then responds to the media image of himself or herself.

Each facet of the media—television, radio, newspapers, magazines—has its own particular angle. Refracting according to structural limitations of time, space, film, and deadlines, each medium sends out its uniquely altered message. What the public hears on the five-minute radio news will not, of course, be the same as what it sees on television. And neither report is precisely the same version that one gets in the newspaper. *All* will differ from the account offered by magazines.

We should recognize that the information we receive about government or news events is not necessarily the same thing as the government or the event itself. Although we are not often deceived deliberately, as Soviet citizens are deceived by the no-news policy of the Soviet government, we must be wary of our tendency to respond merely to the image on the six o'clock news rather than to the reality. When we decide to support—or not to support—our government's policies, we must be concerned whether our decision was made on the basis of solid information carefully gathered and evaluated from several different sources, or whether we made up our minds mainly on the basis of a slickly biased article in a weekly newsmagazine.

The problem for the contemporary Washington correspondent may be even more complex. The news media have a power that shapes the leaders and the policies of the official government. The crushing power of the media is to select among the millions of words and the thousands of events occurring each day in Washington. Which words and events are to be projected on the wall of the cave for mankind to see? What is the truth? What is important? From the point of view of the politicians, the officials, and the other actors in the official government, there is also this crucial question: *What will the media people ignore?* In most cases, the words and events that fail to be selected might as well not have occurred.

What is the primary self-criticism by the Washington news media? By and large, it is that the members of the Other Government do not take themselves and their role seriously enough. Those who are serious have faced up to the fact that they project the shadows by which the society of the United States of America judges itself successful or faulty.

As for criticism of the press corps from outsiders, the most frequent charge is that there is a political consensus—usually liberal—among Washington's news correspondents. Do they, in fact, form a cohesive elite that, unconsciously or not, molds the political attitudes of the American public?

We might begin to address these questions by referring to my own research, in which a number of correspondents were asked to write the lead sentence of the story they would most like to write. The exercise pretty well proved that Washington correspondents don't even dream alike. Collected just after the resignation of President Nixon, the fantasy leads revealed that the avowed conservatives among the correspondents were defiantly hopeful that conservatism would survive the Watergate scandals:

• *Columnist James J. Kilpatrick's* lead: "Barry Goldwater, the big loser of 1964, counted himself the big winner today as late returns increased the margin of his victory over Edward Kennedy."
• *Columnist Kevin Phillips's lead sentence:* "Conservatives swept today's national elections, winning at all levels from the White House down."
• *Columnist Ralph de Toledano thought he might prefer to put the nation's political problems into more familiar hands:* "Standing solemnly before an equally solemn audience on the steps of the Capitol, Ralph de Toledano took the oath of office as president of the United States."

Several of the liberal journalists had other, more immediate political hopes:

• *Reporter James McCartney:* "Richard M. Nixon was convicted of high crimes and misdemeanors by the U.S. Senate today and ordered for trial before Judge John Sirica."
• *Reporter Duane Bradford:* "Former President Richard Nixon, arms raised to a small group who waited for hours to greet him, emerged from Lewisbury Federal Prison today, where he spent six months on a tax evasion conviction."

Other correspondents have decided that the really big story would have little to do with politics:

• *Alan Otten of the* Wall Street Journal: "The first visitors from outer space emerged from their space ship yesterday and declared that. . ."
• *Dick Zander of* Newsday: "God said yesterday . . ."
• *Richard Valeriani of NBC:* "I have just returned from death, and I can report to you that . . ."

• *Dan Rather of CBS:* "A way was found today that insures that people will be unfailingly kind to other people."

• *David Brinkley of NBC:* "The president, returning from the ceremony honoring the man who discovered the cures for cancer and heart disease, announced tonight the final step in carrying out the general, international disarmament agreement will be taken tomorrow morning, when the Army's last tank will be melted down and made into benches for public parks now crowded because they are free of crime."

Even investigator Les Whitten, Jack Anderson's former junior partner, found a way to combine hopes for a more tranquil future with his passion for an exclusive story: "Jesus Christ, whose second coming has been promised for almost two thousand years, landed at Washington National Airport secretly today and confided his plans exclusively to this reporter."

The only common tone among the correspondents seemed to bespeak a weariness of ineptitude, lying, suffering, and corruption in national political life. Nearly half the journalists composed variations on that theme, as though they wished for a time when they would have no news stories to cover. The balance of lightness and a general disgust with politics suggests the strange mixture of attitudes that characterize correspondents who now dominate Washington. Despite the stereotype of the national political reporter as Eastern-born and liberally bred at Ivy League schools, as were David Halberstam and the late Walter Lippmann (both of them born in New York City and shaped and colored by Harvard), the facts do not support such a generalization.

It rather tortures the facts, for example, to try to make an Eastern Ivy League liberal out of the extremely powerful columnist Jack Anderson, who was born the son of a postal clerk in Long Beach, California, and went to the University of Utah with other devout Mormons who did not go to Brigham Young. Or James Reston, who was born poor in Clydebank, Scotland, and got his degree from the University of Illinois (earning his only "A" in the journalism department in sportswriting). Another *New York Times* columnist, Tom Wicker, was born in Hamlet, North Carolina, went to the state university at Chapel Hill, and began his career in an unlikely job and place: as head of the chamber of commerce in another minuscule North Carolina town.

Broadcast journalists reflect the same sort of variety. John

Chancellor of NBC was born in Chicago, attended the University of Illinois for a few months, then rounded out his higher education in the U.S. Navy. Walter Cronkite of CBS left St. Joseph, Missouri, to get his polish at the University of Texas. He never finished. David Brinkley of NBC left Wilmington, North Carolina, to get his at the University of North Carolina. *He* never finished. Harry Reasoner of CBS, who is often charged with being the deftest of the eyebrow-raisers, may have developed his style in his home town, Dakota City, Iowa, or in his time at Stanford and the University of Minnesota, but he is a stranger to the Ivy League. His former partner on ABC News, Howard K. Smith, was born even farther from the effete East, in Ferriday, Louisiana, and went even farther south to college—to Tulane in New Orleans. Dan Rather, who inflames so many conservatives, was born in Wharton, Texas, and went to Sam Houston State Teachers' College.

Thus, a composite portrait of the typical political journalist in Washington, D.C., must include the East, but only a dash of it. Blend syndicated columnist Thomas Braden, who left Greene, Iowa, for Dartmouth, with Nicholas von Hoffman, another syndicated columnist, who grew up in Chicago and never went to college. The mix should also represent the relatively few women in political journalism such as Suzannah Lessard, a perceptive staff writer for *The New Yorker,* who was born on Long Island and educated at Columbia, and Marguerite Hoxie Sullivan, who was born in Palo Alto, California, and educated at Stanford. The mix should also have a bit of a Southern accent, which is fairly heavy in political journalism: Bill Moyers of Hugo, Oklahoma, a journalism graduate of the University of Texas, who also studied theology.

Many critics of the media believe that national journalists flock together and feed on one another, shaping their own liberal consensus in part by reading the same newspapers and magazines and watching the same television news programs. To test that belief, fifty newspaper correspondents were asked to name the newspapers, magazines, reporters, columnists, and broadcast commentators they relied on most often in their work.

Broadcast programs and broadcast commentators received the fewest mentions. This is probably because published stories are easier to use and are usually more comprehensive than broadcasts. It may also be because many print reporters manifest a disdain for broadcast news. "Zilch" was the most frequently cited broadcaster. The other results:

NEWSPAPERS
Washington Post   40
The New York Times   34
Wall Street Journal   29
Washington Star (now defunct)   15
Baltimore Sun   5
Boston Globe   4
Chicago Tribune   2

Nine others were mentioned once.

MAGAZINES
Newsweek   22
Time   16
The New Republic   11
The Nation   6
New York   6
Harper's   5
The Progressive   4
The Atlantic   3
Congressional Quarterly   3
The Economist (London)   3
Human Events   3
National Review   3
The New Yorker   3

Five others were mentioned twice; eighteen others were mentioned once.

REGULAR NETWORK BROADCASTS
CBS News   13
NBC News   9
ABC News   2
"60 Minutes"   4
"Meet the Press"   3
"Face the Nation"   3
"Issues and Answers"   2

REPORTERS
David Broder *(Washington Post)*   12 *
Dan Rather (CBS)   6
Seymour Hersh *(The New York Times)*   5
Morton Mintz *(Washington Post)*   4
Fred Graham (CBS)   3
I. F. Stone *(New York Review of Books)*   3
R. W. Apple *(The New York Times)*   2
Richard Harris *(The New Yorker)*   2
John Osborne *(The New Republic)*   2
Mike Wallace (CBS)   2
Carl Stern (NBC)   2

Twenty others were mentioned once.

COLUMNISTS
Rowland Evans & Robert Novak (syndicated)   6
Jack Anderson (syndicated)   4
Russell Baker *(The New York Times)*   4
Art Buchwald (syndicated)   4
Mary McGrory *(syndicated)*   4
James Reston *(The New York Times)*   4
Gary Wills (syndicated)   4
Anthony Lewis *(The New York Times)*   3
Tom Wicker *(The New York Times)*   3
George Will *(Washington Post)*   3
William F. Buckley, Jr. (syndicated)   2
James J. Kilpatrick (syndicated)   2
TRB (unsigned column by Richard Strout in
   The New Republic)   2

Nine others were mentioned once.

BROADCAST COMMENTATORS
David Brinkley (ABC)   3
John Chancellor (NBC)   2
Walter Cronkite (CBS)   2

---

* Five of the twelve mentioned Broder as a columnist. He is a columnist who is also a reporter.

Edwin Newman (NBC) 2
Roger Mudd (NBC) 1
Harry Reasoner (CBS) 1

With forty mentions of the *Washington Post* and thirty-four mentions of *The New York Times,* clearly most of the journalists rely heavily on liberal newspapers. Still, it is a mistake to focus only on the liberal bent of these two papers. The *Post* and the *Times* also seek the best journalists, pay them well, devote column after column to their reports and commentaries—and are quickly available after publication. Another, less liberal paper, the *Los Angeles Times,* makes a similar commitment to excellent journalism, but it is published 3,000 miles and three time zones away from Washington and New York.

Significantly, nearly all the self-professed conservative journalists who responded to this survey reported that they also rely upon the *Post* and *The New York Times.* They do so because they must; the conservative papers that are readily available on the Atlantic seaboard are less comprehensive. The conservative New York *Daily News,* for example, carries knowledgeable reporting and analysis, but its commitment to national and international affairs does not even approach that of the *Post* or the *Times.* The same is true of the Baltimore *Sun,* a once strong paper that has faded. Surely, if capital journalists had only a nagging thirst for liberal reportage, they could satisfy it best with *the* most liberal of metropolitan papers, the *New York Post.* No one does.

The liberal strain in the magazines the journalists rely on also seems strong—at least by the standards of Middle America. But the magazine list also needs analyzing. *Newsweek* and *Time* are the timeliest and provide the most news information. Printed over the weekend, they are available in New York and in Washington on Monday. The conservative *U.S. News & World Report* is so slow-moving, at least comparatively, that only one conservative journalist mentioned it. Although none of the next five magazines on the list— *The New Republic, The Nation, New York, Harper's,* and *The Progressive*—is mentioned by many respondents (only twenty-two of the fifty respondents mentioned any of them), all are liberal.

Liberalism is less evident in the other categories, which carry so many names that it is obvious that political journalists burn their candles at many shrines. The respondents avoid relying on feverishly liberal columnists, such as Nicholas von Hoffman, just as they avoid high-temperature conservatives, such as William Rusher and Victor Lasky. They prefer even-handed analysts who are close to the center, such as David Broder of the *Washington Post* (his opinions seem to put him just a bit to the left of center). They also favor columnists who work at *reporting*—the contemplative, nonreporting columnists are referred to as those whose methods are said to consist primarily of sucking the thumb of one hand while typing with the other. Broder is so much the reporter-columnist that the survey of his peers mentioned him more often as a reporter than as a columnist.

Why is Broder cited so often? I asked one of the reporters on the *Post,* Lou Cannon. Cannon answered definitively.

David is a great man—a wonderful colleague and a strong columnist—because he does the reporting. He is a kind of Renaissance man of political reporting. He has been very influential on the *Post.* The thing that he never really gets any credit for is that—unlike many reporters who are the political stars of a newspaper—Dave tries to get everybody in his area into the offense. On the *Post,* I've been able to do all kinds of important political stories that I know I wouldn't have been able to do on other newspapers. Dave is also particularly good with young reporters. He goes out of his way to make people who are part of a reporting team feel at home. He sees that they have an important role to play.

I asked Cannon: "It's a bit baffling that Broder is rated by correspondents on other newspapers and in broadcasting as the best political correspondent in the country. How can you explain that by Dave's reporting?" This was Cannon's response:

Dave's insights into the political process are superior to nearly all of his colleagues. He understands different types of political stories. He understands that, in a republic, almost every kind of story is political. Dave has something to say about a great many things, and he's thoughtful and fair-minded. I can't think of an issue on which he wouldn't be open to discourse. He values thoughtful people in the cross-ideological spectrum. These things that I'm saying are unusual things. Dave is also a good writer, but I think these things rate higher than the ability to formulate a phrase.

As to the charge that most political journalists share the same liberal political leanings and tend to explain political events and personalities in the same way, the responses were surprisingly varied:

• *Syndicated Columnist Marianne Means:* "Baloney! Put two political reporters in a room together—*any* two—and they wouldn't agree whether the sun was shining."
• *Martin Nolan of the* Boston Globe: "Horseshit! I'm so weary of conspiracy theories of the press. The press is a business, and most business people are Republicans. The American press is about 80% right-wing Republican. Nixon was endorsed by newspapers by a 30-to-1 margin over McGovern in 1972. The geographical anomalies of certain East Coast cities that have become havens for the civilized and the intellectually demanding have led to the counter-theory spouted by the Honorable Dr. Agnew et al. That was quite a feat, worthy of Goebbels."
• *David Brinkley of ABC:* "I have made no body counts of so-called liberals and conservatives, but I doubt it. I suspect the dominant view of American journalism generally is a mild conservatism. The biggest papers in New York, Chicago, and Los Angeles are fairly conservative, and so is the most widely circulated newspaper, the *Wall Street Journal,* and the biggest magazine, *Reader's Digest.* In my experience, a person holding strongly biased personal views resents reading or hearing *any* opinions, or even any facts, not supporting his own views. And in my experience, few of those making this charge have any real support for it beyond their own biases. No one ever thinks he, himself, is biased—only other people."

Other generally conservative journalists supported the charge:

• *Syndicated Columnist Ralph de Toledano:* "This applies primarily to the Washington press corps, which is, ideologically speaking, dangerously homogeneous. Perhaps not consciously, Washington correspondents tend to put their heads together to decide on the party line. I have seen this at the National Press Club, at national conventions, and on the campaign trail. The Washington press corps is about 85% liberal Democrat and vocally intolerant of those who are benighted enough not to share their point of view."
• *Syndicated Columnist James J. Kilpatrick:* "There's a good deal of truth in this, especially in Washington. Most of the leading columnists, reporters, and commentators are of a liberal persuasion. The

good ones keep their personal opinions scrupulously out of their copy, but most of them flock together so constantly that they tend to fly, flutter, feed, and twitter about the same way."

• *Syndicated Columnist Rowland Evans:* "The charges are substantially accurate. The New Deal produced a crop of young journalists sympathetic to its economic and political objectives, and that tendency to believe all problems are inherently solvable by government persists to this day. But it is weakening. More and more there are young reporters reexamining the thesis and disagreeing with their colleagues. Nevertheless, the instinct of the herd, both in reporting and in professed conviction, runs strong."

A few liberal journalists largely agree with the charges of left-leaning bias. Theodore White and Morton Mintz of the *Washington Post* have both criticized this bias. Fred Graham, who practiced law before becoming a reporter for *The New York Times* and then a Washington correspondent for CBS, said, "Generally, I agree. Journalists tend to have the same turn of mind—as do lawyers and preachers."

But most liberal reporters argued that the journalist's professional values counter their personal political orientations. Syndicated columnist Jules Witcover made a typical point: "It's true that most journalists in Washington have liberal leanings, but I'm a strong believer in the professional attitude and the ability of the professional to separate his leanings from his reporting. But one doubts that professionalism works so neatly in the rush of campaigns, in crises like Watergate, and in periods of naked antagonism between journalists and officials as in the Johnson and Nixon years."

Ben Bagdikian, a free-lance writer, provides a cogent analysis: "I'm not sure that political journalists have a common viewpoint in party or ideological values. But I do think that political reporting, like any other specialty, tends to develop a herd instinct, so that a consensus develops very quickly on issues, character of candidates, and villains-and-heroes. Some of this is useful in the sense of double-checking and collective knowledge and insight. But I would pass all this up for more loners who depend on their solitary reporting and conclusions."

In the end, the question is not whether political journalism has a liberal color; for it has—and more so in Washington, that insular city, than in New York. But the hue of this liberal bias is much lighter than the conspiracy theorists imagine. When a real radical, Hunter Thompson, showed up to report the presidential campaign for *Rolling Stone* (and to write his wild book, *Fear and Loathing on the Campaign Trail*), most of the liberal journalists were horrified by his standards—as he was by theirs. James Perry, a veteran correspondent, is probably right in arguing, "Most of us are centrists, with a slight tilt to the left. We are, that is to say, Democrats. But we are not at all radical, and a fair number of us are conservatives." Perry's analysis is borne out by those journalists who answered a question about their political preferences. Their affiliations were Democrat, 16; Democratic-Independent, 4; Independent, 9; Republican, 4; Whig, 1 (James J. Kilpatrick). Four respondents answered "None," two of them emphatically.

The central question is whether liberal journalism shapes—or perhaps distorts—the public's view of public affairs. If so, it has extraordinary and insidious power; for however liberal Washington correspondents may be, their reportage must make its way through an institutional ooze of Republicanism. More than 90% of the daily newspapers that endorse a presidential candidate favor the Republicans. And as Bagdikian has pointed out, of the more than two thousand accredited correspondents in Washington, no more than fourteen were working full-time on Watergate for any substantial period during the 1972 presidential campaign, which would seem incredible, if it were not for the status-quo attitude at the top.

It is also important to note that conservative political columns have recently begun to weigh far heavier in numbers and in the number of newspaper outlets than liberal columns. William F. Buckley, Jr., and James J. Kilpatrick are syndicated in more than three hundred newspapers, de Toledano and Kevin Phillips in more than one hundred. Both the *Washington Post* and *The New York Times* vied to hire one of Richard Nixon's speech writers, William Safire (the *Post* lost). Safire's column is now available to more than three hundred newspapers through *The New York Times* News Service. The *Post* and *Newsweek* then took on George F. Will, Washington editor of Buckley's *National Review,* and reportedly are happier with his sprightly, reasoned conservatism than is the *Times* with Safire's style, which has been termed "cute conservatism."

In broadcasting as in print, media executives are as likely to lean to the right as are most other business executives. They are able to tolerate the strain of liberalism among working reporters, but the agreement is not always bilateral. It is like an uneasy alliance between two nations, only one of which has nuclear capacity. On the other hand, most contemporary reporters are surprisingly free of "knee-jerk" liberal journalism, as well as of any blatant signs of self-congratulation.

Several Washington correspondents were asked: "What common practice, if any, is most damaging to good political journalism?" That "if any" provided an easy exit for those who think journalists have good reason to preen themselves. But only one took it. The others—liberals, conservatives, and undecideds—leaped at the chance to criticize themselves like so many Spiro Agnews.

• *Theodore White:* "We're all so vulnerable and so flawed—and so *used.* We're intermediaries who peddle immortality. We can develop dangerous friendships even with good men. Political journalists too often act as transmission belts for the compass men, those who orient others by what they're thinking."

• *Jack Nelson, Washington bureau chief for the* Los Angeles Times: "The acceptance of the 'official version.' Because the official version sometimes is an outright lie (as in Watergate), is often misleading, and is always self-serving."

• *Tom Littlewood, former Washington correspondent of the* Chicago Sun-Times: "The anchor to past procedures—those habitual standards for evaluating and presenting the news: the trite superficiality of most political reporting; the tendency to report politics as partly show biz and partly track meet. There are many, all equally depressing. There are or should be two prime goals for print reporters: First, to tell what is really happening, not what the polls would like us to think is happening, and this is nothing more than good reporting in depth. And the second objective is to make sense of what is going on, especially when it's complicated and confusing, as is often the case in the world of politics.

"Having been introduced to politics in Illinois, in Chicago and Springfield, I have few illusions. There are two levels to American politics: what is happening on the surface, the rallies and speeches and torchlight parades. And then there is the underside, which has to do with power and money—grantsmanship, contracts, the clash of economic interests, the bartering of influence, etc. This is something that is but dimly understood by most newspaper people and is seldom reported well, except when it is necessary to swoop down on scandal and become breathlessly indignant about some atrocity in public life.

"In fact, the basic elements of Watergate are *not* unique. Nixon, being Nixon, overdid it, to be sure. But enemy lists and political distribution of federal grants and surveillance of reporters—indeed, the whole concept of rewarding your friends and punishing your enemies—go back to the founding of the Republic. If the public were given some ongoing exposure to this side of political life, when it is functioning *normally,* not excessively, perhaps our political system would operate more efficiently. In no sense are the Watergate burglary and all the rest, especially the activity of the Plumbers, to be condoned. But shouldn't we do a better job of reporting the normal operation of that side of American politics?"

There are many ploys for dealing with Washington officialdom. Reporters like Jack Nelson, the tough, square-jawed bureau chief of the *Los Angeles Times,* resort to abrasive demands and intimidation if they think the story or the subjects warrant such methods. Seymour Hersh, formerly of *The New York Times,* the correspondent who exposed the My Lai massacre in Vietnam, is another one. His approach is never applesauce; instead Hersh attacks often, on the telephone. He is persistent, calling again and again those he considers sources. He badgers the strong ones and terrorizes the less confident. Some of them are cowed; others go into a rage when they hear Hersh exclaim sarcastically, "Ah, come on; *come ooon.*" After the initiation to Hersh, an official can be left speechless for a time. To the rest of the Washington press corps, he is the best investigative reporter anywhere. But the Nelson or Hersh approach is a tactic of last resort for most correspondents.

Sources are more often milked than muscled. More representative of most reporters is the technique of Arthur Wiese of the *Houston Post,* who regularly oils such valued sources as John White, who was chairman of the Democratic National Committee. Wiese's approach is masterly. He takes the elevator to the main floor of the national committee office and announces himself at an outer desk. Chairman White's assistant takes Wiese into his office, where the session starts with smalltalk, a touching of the tips. Wiese and White talk about jogging. Both jog, and Wiese has been trimming himself, reducing his weight and hardening himself physically. They get to business. Wiese grins—the grin of someone who knows when he is going through the motions.

"Well," he says to White, "let me ask you the *pro forma* questions about the election first." White leans forward in his chair. At least 6 feet are between Wiese and White's big desk. He returns Wiese's grin. "Okay, I'll be glad to give you the *pro forma* answers."

White defends President Carter's position in the public opinion polls, saying any rating of more than 40% approval is good for this time of the term. Wiese makes an allusion to President Kennedy's situation in 1962, but White declines to allow the comparison: "Politics in 1962 is ancient history. I don't think presidents are an issue in mid-term elections unless you did what Nixon did in 1974."

Wiese asks if the Republicans are locked into permanent minority status. "Naw," drawls White. "We'll mess up some way and bring 'em back to life."

Wiese presses White: "Who's going to make the mistakes?"

"Well, I'll go off the record with you," says White, proceeding to name names. This is background information, not to be published. It is to give Wiese a perspective, to let him develop the political picture as White wants it portrayed.

Such statements have to be made in confidence. *Confidence:* the word fits the situation perfectly. Wiese has developed a sense for keeping White's off-the-record comments to himself, and by now White has developed sufficient confidence in Wiese to be fairly blunt in his pronouncements.

White takes great care to orient some of his remarks to the media. He is simply thinking out loud on a topic he likes. The good political operatives are so stylistically consistent that one can never be quite sure whether they are giving it from the guts or whether their calculating political brains are clicking out leading questions.

Wiese then turns the conversation back to the polls. White maintains that the instant ratings furnished by the polls are not relevant to the long-term play of politics and opinion: "'Fair'" is really a positive rating. What the people are trying to say is that they don't want to get caught out on a limb for their judgments. I don't think most of the polling people really understand politics. You're forcing the people to make an answer on something they're not even thinking about."

As the conversation winds down, White says, "The Democrats want the . . . ," then his secretary comes in and tells White that he is late for the dentist. White works his jaw back and forth sideways.

"Tell him I'll be late," he directs her. "No—tell him to cancel; I'll go another day. I'm just finishing up here, and I've got other things to do."

The secretary leaves and returns a few minutes later: "The dentist says you'll have to pay whether you come or not."

"The hell I will," says White, allowing himself to be overcome with ire. "Let him sue me if he wants his money. I'm not going to be threatened by some chickenshit dentist."

With a few off-the-record comments by White, Wiese stops the interview. In a few minutes, he is down the elevator and back into the hot stew of the summer day. He mumbles, "I could have written that story without even making the visit."

Is he sorry he took the time?

"Oh, no, no," Wiese says emphatically. "You've got to maintain a working relationship with your primary sources. Later on, when I really need access to White, these low-key conversations will make it worth it." Such methods are necessary to any reporter who would do more than file straight-news stories.

The most famous of all investigative reporters, Carl Bernstein and Robert Woodward, came to reveal the dimensions of the Watergate case through unbelievable persistence and determination, a strong streak of courage, and the good fortune to have been neophyte reporters routinely assigned by the *Washington Post* editors to the Watergate break-in. They were the first to connect the burglary and the White House; the first to describe the "laundering" of campaign money in Mexico; the first to implicate Attorney General John Mitchell and Presidential Appointments Secretary Dwight Chapin; the first to explain how political espionage constituted an intrinsic part of the Nixon campaign; and the first to trace Watergate to Nixon's White House chief of staff. Had the *Post* assigned, say, a first-rate experienced reporter to the case, he would probably have gotten nowhere. As Ben Bradlee, the executive editor of the *Post,* put it, "A reporter who could call Henry Kissinger by his first name wasn't worth a damn on the Watergate story." Thanks to their tenacity, and probably to their inexperience, Bernstein and Woodward brought in the greatest story of the century.

Since Watergate, more and more correspondents are giving themselves diligently to investigative reporting—or to their own versions of it. Most of them seemed to have learned two of the three qualities that are basic: first, patience—an almost endless patience that soon turns off all but the few who are dedicated; and second, the skepticism and toughness of a Seymour Hersh or a Jack Nelson. The third quality seems to be undefinable. Robert Donovan, who is an associate editor of the *Los Angeles Times,* struggled to define an investigative reporter: "I'm not an investigator. People with a flair for investigation are hard to find. Sure, there are so many notes and documents lying around on the surface, but the incentive for digging . . ." He threw up his hands. "Somehow it's in the basic makeup of the reporter."

So many correspondents are now publishing investigative stories that, ironically, a backlash is in view. The respected Wes Gallagher, retired president of the Associated Press, chose his final annual meeting to sound an alarm: "The First Amendment is not a hunting license. Too many readers are beginning to look upon the press as a multi-voiced shrew, nitpicking through the debris of government decisions for scandals but not solutions. . . . It follows if we in the press try to use the First Amendment irresponsibly to overstep our privileges and powers, we will be hauled back."

No criticism the journalists make is as striking as the fact that there is so much acid self-criticism. Instead of feeling smug and self-righteous in this post-Watergate era, they voice a collective agony over their failure to carry out an important mission. Moreover, few political journalists react to the criticism of outsiders as they once did: like a herd of angry bulls, rumps together, horns out. They struck back at Spiro Agnew, but he was a high official and not exactly a disinterested critic. Their ridicule of Agnew was in sharp contrast to their treatment of critics who know what they are talking about and cite chapter and verse.

An example is Timothy Crouse of *Rolling Stone,* who got tired of writing about rock music ("the monotony of the subject was driving me mad") and went to Washington. Out on the campaign trail in 1972, he watched the political reporters at work and focused a penetrating light on them. When he published his devastating book *The Boys on the Bus,* the reaction from nearly all reporters (except a few who had suffered third-degree burns) was, "Yes, that's us; damn it."

Some of the self-flagellation has been in payment for the sin Crouse depicted most vividly: "pack journalism," also known as the "herd instinct." In its simplest form, pack journalism means dozens, even hundreds, of reporters covering a single event. Dave Schoumacher of ABC points out that the practice "defeats the obvious benefits that come from a multiplicity of sources of information and encourages false feelings of omnipotence by helping to confuse the journalists' view of the event with the event itself." If everybody's there, that's the place to be, and meanwhile, the rest of politics and government is spottily covered, if at all.

But there is more to pack journalism. Mel Elfin, Washington bureau chief of *Newsweek,* describes it as "the sheeplike tendency to follow the reportorial leaders as to story choice, story angle, and story play." The tendency is promoted, unwittingly in some instances, by editors who receive reports from the Associated Press, from United Press International, or from the big supplemental services, such as The New York Times Service and the Los Angeles Times-Washington Post Service. If an editor's correspondent on the campaign trail or in the White House fails to report the same story or to play up the same angle, the editor may get on the phone to find out why. In addition, as James Perry says, "We huddle together for warmth too often. We should be less afraid to go out in the cold all by ourselves."

On and on the criticism runs. "The most damaging practice is advocacy," said Dick Zander of *Newsday.* David Brinkley thinks it is "using material tending to defame or belittle a person without thoroughly checking its accuracy. And sketchiness and superficiality, because they cause informed readers and listeners to believe that we are ignoramuses." Such a torrent of self-criticism would have been unimaginable in the old days. It was called "nest-fouling" then, and journalists seldom did it, except in family gatherings at the press-club bar. Those who did foul the nest were cautious. When one reporter decided to expose journalistic sloth (and worse) in an article for *Harper's* magazine ("Washington's Armchair Correspondents"), the by-line was discreetly anonymous: "By One of Them."

Why has there been such a change? Theodore White, who has been reporting politics since the 1930s, said, "In the old days, most of those reporting politics were police reporters once removed. Now their talk is like one of your seminars at Stanford."

Another kind of self-criticism—that of people who think they should have been less trusting of officials—emerges from most responses to this question: "Has your attitude toward politics and politicians changed in recent years because of officials' reports on and explanations of the Vietnam War or Watergate or both?"

• *Fred Graham of CBS:* "Yes. There's almost a presumption now that they're lying."
• *Duane Bradford, political reporter:* "One new element figures more often now in my thinking than it did when I began reporting politics. I find that I am willing to believe that a political leader will

lie outright on more issues (some of which do not require a deception) rather than face the issue directly."

• *David Halberstam:* "The difference is not so much in attitude as in dimension, scope, and sophistication. What I have learned since I began reporting politics has confirmed my earlier attitudes. In the beginning, I was puzzled when officials lashed out at Sheehan and me. [Neil Sheehan, now of *The New York Times,* was a reporter in Vietnam for United Press International, when Halberstam won the Pulitzer Prize for his Vietnam reporting in the *Times.*] I'm not so puzzled any more.

"I always had that essential distrust of politics and politicians and believed very strongly in the adversary relationship. The last ten years or so has seen that sense deepen and has made me more conscious of the reasons that government officials behave the way they do and reporters behave the way they do. It now seems to me one of the major issues of the time."

• *Robert Sherrill, Washington correspondent of* The Nation: "I don't know that Vietnam and Watergate, and politicians' responses to them, can be especially blamed for it, but I find myself almost totally without sympathy for politicians of any kind and every ideology. I have got to the place that I just really don't like politicians at all. Not even when they mean well. Not even when they have good excuses. Not even when events have understandably overwhelmed them. I tend to think of them in scatological terms. When only 66% of the American people say they have no confidence in Congress, it only proves to me once again how basically kindhearted the public is."

• *Alan Otten of the* Wall Street Journal: "Officials' reports on and explanations of Watergate deepened my already substantial skepticism. This is not merely the result of Vietnam and Watergate, but of other instances of official fallibility. Yet Vietnam and Watergate are certainly the most dramatic instances."

• *Columnist Marianne Means:* "When I started reporting politics, I was very innocent. If a distinguished person told me something, I believed him. Experience has taught me to check everything. I am much more suspicious than I used to be, which is probably a good thing, but Vietnam and Watergate are not the only examples of persistent lying, just the most obvious."

• *Martin Nolan of the* Boston Globe: "I count myself fortunate in that I grew up in Massachusetts. I knew nothing but the most cunning of thieving rogues there. But at least they had some charm and a certain Shakespearean quality like villain's candor. Not so the button-down types I encounter here in Washington. I thought politicians lied only some of the time. Remember how shocked we all were when Arthur Sylvester [assistant secretary of defense for public affairs in the Kennedy administration] proclaimed the right to lie? Now I think the right to lie is part of the oath of office under mental reservation. After a while, you can tell which politicians lie and which don't. You become inured to it, too."

• *Columnist Louis Kohlmeier:* "When I began as a reporter, I didn't think city hall politics applied in national government. I still think that dirty politics and personal gain are not the hallmarks of the executive branch, despite contrary evidence in the White House of late. But, of course, my attitude changed because of the Vietnam War and Watergate—as much as Eisenhower and Kennedy differed from Johnson and Nixon—in the direction of less trust and expecting less personal honor. Maybe this is accidental: a facet of the personalities of our two most recent presidents. But then maybe it's not accidental."

• *Mike Wallace of CBS:* "I have become, with each passing year, more disenchanted with politicians. I see little to admire in them."

When so many seasoned journalists (more than 90% of the respondents) reflect on Vietnam and Watergate in such a way that they are obviously resolving to be more skeptical, and probably more abrasive in their reporting, the adversary relationship between journalists and politicians seems certain to become more intense. Does it follow that the credibility of political journalists, which is already weak among millions of readers, listeners, and viewers, will become weaker? Probably. For all politicians have followers who remember the slighting stories and forget the others.

On the other hand, the press has for two centuries been the American public's ear in the District of Columbia. In this time of vastly increasing federal authority, the public has become even more dependent on the Other Government, not only to be its ear in Washington, but to represent its first, third, fourth, fifth, and sixth senses as well. Like the muckraking journalism of another era, the new, more powerful, and adversarial journalism of our own time may one day be seen as a necessary response to changes in the reality of American government.

What is needed for the Other Government is not criticisms from officials, although the adversary relationship assures that they will be heard. The explicit need is for a citizenry that understands how the Other Government works and is prepared to criticize it, to challenge it, and to require that it live up to its best possibilities.

Index